The Image of Peter the Great
in Russian Fiction

Peter the Great. *Statue by Antokolsky, 1872.*

The Image of Peter the Great

in Russian Fiction

of Peter the Great

in Russian Fiction

Xenia Gasiorowska

The University of Wisconsin Press

Published 1979

The University of Wisconsin Press
114 North Murray Street
Madison, Wisconsin 53715

The University of Wisconsin Press, Ltd.
1 Gower Street
London WC1E 6HA England

First printing
Printed in the United States of America

For LC CIP information see the colophon

ISBN 0-299-07690-3

To Zygmunt, as always

Contents

Illustrations

Preface

This book is not another history of Peter the Great, nor a digest
of anecdotic materials about him, nor an evaluation of historical
novels set in the period of his reign. It is a study of the composite *image* of Russia's greatest and most controversial ruler
established in the popular mind primarily by historical novelists.
Though powerful, however, theirs was not the only medium to con-
tribute to that image: collected anecdotes on Peter's habits,
deeds, and pronouncements were widely read by the end of the
eighteenth century, as were the first Western histories of him,
which were largely based on these anecdotes. Parallel with the
development of serious historical scholarship in the mid-
nineteenth century came the vogue of semischolarly "historical
sketches" and the publication of documents, letters, annotated
editions of memoirs by Peter's courtiers, and the diaries of
foreign diplomats. Novelists of all periods of Russian literature
have freely and arbitrarily selected their historical materials
from all these sources. Hence the unconventional nature of this
study which had to cut across several scholarly disciplines and
literary genres, and to make use of heterogenous materials—fiction, documents, and hearsay reports alike. This unorthodox
method made it advisable to supplement the customary bibliographical information and Index with plot summaries of the sixty-
odd historical novels which, with very few exceptions, are not
available in English translations. Russian documentation is confined to the notes and the bibliography, but the Index provides
both English translations of titles as used in the text and trans-
literations of the original Russian titles. I use the transliteration systems of J. Thomas Shaw, *The Transliteration of
Modern Russian for English-Language Publications* (Madison, 1967).
System I, facilitating correct pronunciation by the reader un-
familiar with the Russian language, is used in the text and
Index; and System II, the Library of Congress system without dia-
criticals, for bibliographical materials in notes and for words
as words. Each title in the text, plot summaries, and Index is
accompanied by the date of the first publication; the bibliography,
however, gives the date of the edition used, adding whenever

applicable also the date of the original appearance. All translations of the quotations in the text are my own. To date, no
Russian or Western literary study dedicated to the Petrine novel
or to Peter's personality has ever appeared, though some studies
have been published (and several dissertations have been written)
on the general development, and separate periods of the Russian
historical novel as well as on individual writers.* The present
book is the first work that relates to the composite image of
Peter as it emerges from documents, anecdotic lore, and Petrine
historical fiction.

Books which are "firsts" in their fields are a challenge,
and writing them is treading a long rough road. It is no exaggeration to say that without the encouragement, the friendly advice, and the scholarly interest of Professor J. Thomas Shaw, I
might not have reached the end of that road. Thus my heartfelt
thanks go to him first. I owe a debt of gratitude to Professors
Michael B. Petrovich and James O. Bailey, who kindly read the
manuscript, and to my husband, Zygmunt J. Gasiorowski, who was
always forthcoming with constructive criticism and with moral
support. I also want to express my gratitude to the University
of Wisconsin Research Committee for research leaves and salary
support grants which enabled me to spend necessary time on work
in principal libraries in the United States and Europe.

The text is divided into three parts. Part I deals with the
genre of historical fiction, its interrelationship with history
and the anecdotic and undocumented materials known as *petite
histoire*, and the techniques which writers use in blending facts
with fiction. A biographical sketch of Peter's life is included
as it bears on the elements of monumentality and grotesque in
fiction's portrayal of him; and, within an outline of the development of Petrine novels, principal Russian literary, cultural, and
political trends have been noted. Parts II and III present the
characterization of Peter the Great in Russian historical novels
achieved, respectively, through his appearance and actions, and
through human relationships and environment.

The reign of Peter the Great is a watershed in Russian history, and his place in it may in many respects be considered
unique. No historical personage inspired such a rich anecdotic
lore, none is accorded so many works of scholarship and fiction,
few are so widely known. Peter's use of his autocratic power,

---

*E.g., A. Skabichevskii, *Nash istoricheskii roman v ego prosh-
lom i nastoiashchem, Sochineniia*, 2 vols. (SPb., 1890), II; S. Petrov,
Russkii istoricheskii roman XIX veka (Moskva, 1964); M. Serebrianskii,
Sovetskii istoricheskii roman (Moskva, 1936); Xenia Gasiorowska,
"Soviet Postwar Historical Novel," (AATSEEL Journal, 12 (1954), 70-79;
A. Belinkov, *Iurii Tynianov* (Moskva, 1965); M. Charnyi, *Put' Alekseia
Tolstogo* (Moskva, 1961); L. Twarog, "The Soviet Revival of a Nine-
teenth Century Historical Novelist: I. I. Lazhechnikov," *Harvard
Slavic Studies*, IV (1957), 107-26; M. Karpovich, Soviet "Historical
Novel," *Russian Review*, V (1946), 53-63; C. H. Bedford, *The Seeker:
D. S. Merezhkovskyi* (Lawrence, Kansas, 1975).

the grandeur of his statesmanship and the strange dichotomy of
his personality, the fear and admiration he inspired—all these
diverse elements went into the creation of his popular image. No
attempt will be made to decide whether the image is true to the
historical original: no scholar, so far, has written a *personal*
biography of Peter the man, nor has any fiction writer undertaken
a psychological study of him. It remains vague, elusive, and incomplete. An image is, of course, brought into being equally by
facts, legends, their presentation by a novelist, and the creative
vision of the reader.

If, therefore, the thin line dividing historical sources and
fiction's rendition of them appears occasionally blurred in these
pages, if Peter's image emerges as a blend of fact and fiction
which it has always been in the minds of his contemporaries as
well as of later generations—the reader is requested to accept
it as such, unreduced to the neatly classified basic components
of documents and fantasy.

Part I

1.   On Genre

The artistic representation of history is a more serious
pursuit than the exact writing of history. For the art
of fiction goes to the heart of things, whereas the factual report merely records details.
>   Aristotle, *Poetics*

Very deep is the well of the past. Should we not call it
bottomless?
>   Thomas Mann, *Joseph and His Brothers*

Chroniclers record contemporary events, thus preserving them for
posterity; historians present past events in pragmatic order,
emulating philosophers in their efforts to create a logically
structured universe; writers of historical fiction, using primarily the *petite histoire*—letters, anecdotes, and memoirs—
create images of epochs and people. Therefore, while they all
deal with basically the same materials, they differ in their ways
of handling them and in their goals, and whenever their paths
cross, the encounter is far from harmonious. And, of course, the
uneasy marriage between history and literature is not simply
cliché.

Historical fiction as a genre is a maverick, viewed with
some suspicion by literary critics and with some hostility by
historians. It is related to both history and literature, being
a direct descendant of legends and sagas, but its plots are no
longer tales of noble deeds, its protagonists no longer kings and
warriors, and it often is too akin to adventure fiction to hold a
distinguished place in the literary hierarchy. Besides, it takes
liberties with chronology; intermingles historical personages
with fictional characters, recorded facts and documents with
imaginary events; and, moreover, insists on its exclusive right
to all these infractions in both disciplines.

3

"The artist," says Alexey Tolstoy, "has the courage—or call it impertinence—to tell boldly and with assurance the story of an era solely on the basis of his imagination, intuition, and a few insignificant [historical] fragments. . . .   May one invent a biography for a historical personage?   One *should*, yet in such a way that what has been invented is plausible, so that if it did not happen, it ought to have.   Next, is it permissible to tamper with dates?   Some dates are brought about by the logic of historical events, the dialectics of History; others occur by chance and have no influence on the course of historical developments; these the artist can handle at will.   Thirdly: historical personages must think and speak in obedience to their era and its events."[1]

Yury Tynyanov, a distinguished historical novelist and critic, succinctly expressing the same idea, insists that he has no faith in "pompous documents [which] lie impudently, like humans . . . . Where the document ends is where I begin [my story]."[2]

The fact is that because the world of historical fiction is built of materials, either proven or alleged, in some manner recorded as having occurred in times past, it claims independence from certain general laws of the world of fiction, especially from the obligation of providing strict causal patterns for the plot and for the behavior of characters.   The reader of a novel reproducing contemporary reality cannot see these patterns in actual life: being *inside* it he sees and accepts events as they happen and people as they are.   But in relation to the world of fiction he is an outsider, sees the events and people's behavior in perspective, and will not give credence to anything chaotic or illogical about them, unless the event is openly acknowledged as miraculous, or is part of a fairy tale, or, in case of behavioral oddities, is explained by circumstances such as insanity, drug addiction, alcoholism, or similar deviations from the normal "This happened in real life" is not an argument for plausibility in the world of contemporary fiction, but in that of historical fiction it is a basic one, because many a strange thing is assumed possible in the uncheckable reality of the past, particularly since the period is usually chosen for its dramatic events and/or colorful setting.   Therefore, the reader, taking the author's word for the accuracy of his presentation, is free to allow himself an uncritical enjoyment of the exciting plot.   All he wants to know is what happened next, and the author, relieved from the responsibility of explaining why it happened, concentrates on showing how, since this is what really matters to them both.

The task seems easy, and it is for the majority of authors of conventional historical novels—in fact, too easy for those among them who treat the genre as a literary free-for-all.   The author has to observe certain rules, avoid certain mistakes, but otherwise is free to let his dramatis personae act in their predictable ways against the backdrop of decorations customary for

the given period, within a plot as fantastic as the author pleases.
But there are things he should keep in mind all the time—several
important dos and don'ts.

In the first place he must himself feel certain that this is
how things happened because he needs to convince the reader of
that. As was said, the reader is willing to assume that a historical novel is based on actual events and therefore tells a
true story. But he has a knowledge, however general, of these
events, and the author must not strain the reader's credulity.
To this end the plot should affect the fortunes of fictional
characters, occasionally those of obscure historical personages,
but never those of important ones. For example, Lucy and Charles
in *A Tale of Two Cities* may or may not escape death at Dickens's
will, but not Marie Antoinette and Louis XVI. Conversely, great
historical moments must involve the participation of fictional
characters to become integrated within the novel. It is to this
end, for instance, that Tolstoy brought the civilian Pierre
Bezukhov to the battlefield of Borodino. An exciting plot may
and should make the reader forget his historical foreknowledge of
its denouement. In *Woodstock*, Walter Scott piled dangerous obstacles so high on the path of Charles II and his fictional supporters that the suspense makes the worried reader forget the
comfortable certainty that the king is bound to escape the dangers
and eventually regain his throne. Nevertheless, the participation
of such important figures should be limited to a few appearances,
and the plot should definitely concern itself with the legitimate
inhabitants of the fictional world. Meetings and conversations
between the two are permissible: Louis XI engages the services
of Quentin Durward in the novel of that name, in *War and Peace*
Napoleon finds Prince Andrey lying wounded on the battlefield of
Austerlitz. Monarchs' intervention in the lives of protagonists
is a routine device—Peter the Great is so often cast as a *deus
ex machina*, it has become part of his image—and the reader expects them to act in a certain manner, according to what can be
termed their historic reputation. For example, since it is known
that Queen Anne was often guided by her whims rather than by
reason, Hugo in *L'Homme qui rit* makes her arrange, out of jealousy
and spite, the marriage of the lovely heroine and the monstrously
ugly hero.

Unfortunately, however, the reputation of historical personages is not established by scholarship alone. Anecdotes based
on hearsay and gossip, memoirs written decades after a distinguished person's death and containing involuntary or malicious
mistakes and misquotes, are documents' powerful rivals; and the
influence of these components of petite histoire cannot be stressed
enough. They have the appeal of what is known as "human interest"
and, when presented in the setting of the period and glamorous
fictional events, become indelibly impressed on the public's
imagination. A novelist does not consider himself obligated to
be objective—he selects whatever details he needs. Thus, it is
in vain that historians, armed with documents, try to change a
created image. In the eyes of the average reader, Mary Stuart,

by courtesy of Schiller and of Walter Scott, will forever remain
a lovely, innocent victim of her enemies' intrigues in spite of
scholarly evidence and several recent factual *vies romancées* sufficient to compromise any reputation, queenly or otherwise.   Conversely, Lucrezia Borgia, who was proved of late to have been in
actuality a rather placid matron, is invariably seen—even
in *Leonardo da Vinci* by Merezhkovsky, who usually relies on documents for his secondary characters—as a vicious beauty much given
to poisoning undesirable members of her court.[3]

One should, however, distinguish between creating an image—
a mental portrait—of a historical personage and tagging him with
a specific gesture, sentence, or physical feature.   This is done
not necessarily by historical fiction writers alone—witness
Karenin's jug-ears or Mr. Micawber's "waiting for something to
turn up"—and is done for a variety of artistic reasons which
cannot be discussed here.   But in a historical novel this device
serves the double purpose of rendering the atmosphere of a particular era and of helping the reader to recognize a secondary
character upon each of his reappearances in a crowded plot.   King
Arthur, we are forever reminded, had burned the cakes.   Darya
Arsenieva, Menshikov's wife, had once signed a letter to Tsar
Peter as "Darya the Silly"—and Darya the Silly she remained
thereafter in works and periods as different as those of Daniil
Mordovtsev's *The Tsar and the Hetman* (1879), Tynyanov's *The Waxen
Effigy* (1931), and Alexander Sokolov's *Menshikov* (1947).   Menshikov
himself seldom appears in Russian historical fiction without
carrying a tray of cakes either in the course of the plot or at
least in his own reminiscences or those of other characters.

The use of such "tags" as typical mannerisms or well-known
anecdotic events in the characterization of important historical
personages is not excluded from historical fiction.   But because
this tends to make them two-dimensional and colorless, it should
not be overdone, even in conventional novels where their personal
participation is limited.   In biographical novels such telling
details may serve to retouch the completed portrait: Tsar Peter's
staff ever ready for use in quick punishment and Queen Victoria's
"We are not amused" have become part of their image.

Fictional characters, whether cast as protagonists or in
secondary roles, should be above all *homines historici*, typical
representatives of their era.   So also should minor historical
personages, who, at any rate, once engulfed in the stream of the
plot have to blend into the surrounding world of fiction.   Great
historical figures remain outsiders in conventional novels where
their role is limited to ensuring in the reader's imagination the
authenticity of the period—Elizabethan, Victorian, or Petrine,
as the case may be.   But in biographical novels, where they are
protagonists and personalities whose image is of paramount importance, the plot becomes secondary and the milieu serves as a
mere backdrop.

Since the author of a conventional historical novel cannot
allow the reader's attention to flag or be diverted, he has to
keep the plot steadily moving, strong, and structured.   He

therefore avoids introducing secondary plots and is careful to satisfy the reader's (or the publisher's) curiosity as to the ultimate fortunes of his heroes. Sometimes, as Walter Scott explains in a postscript to *Quentin Durward*, he refuses to do so on artistic grounds, but generally he complies. Even Leo Tolstoy wrote an epilogue to *War and Peace*, though Natasha's admirers may wish he hadn't.

In a biographical novel the plot is provided by history, and its course cannot be altered at the author's will. It may stay open-ended because, as in real life, the protagonist's story can begin or end at any given moment—which, incidentally, is one of the main features distinguishing a biographical novel from a *vie romancée*, a fictionalized biography such as Lytton Strachey's *Queen Victoria* (1922) or André Maurois's *Edouard VII et son temps* (1933). *Peter the First* (1929-45), for example, interrupted by A. N. Tolstoy's sudden death, is nevertheless a complete novel because it is not necessary to its completeness that Peter should die in the last chapter: his death would merely end his life and his reign, and these are not the essence of the novel. Had Tolstoy ended it, as he had planned, with the Battle of Poltava in 1709, this would have left untold twelve glorious years of Peter's reign, but it would have told the story: how Peter brought Russia out of her mediaevalism. As it is, the novel ends with the siege of Narva in 1704, when the process was already in full swing, and thus its purpose is carried out. Secondary plots peopled with fictional characters are, of course, customary and necessary in historical novels and follow the usual conventional pattern, but they are not what these novels are about.

A word on the controversial question of whether every novel set in relation to its readers in a time past can be considered a historical novel. In this writer's opinion it cannot. Naturally, Mlle de Scudéry's *Le Grand Cyrus* (1649-53), Richardson's *Clarissa Harlowe* (1747-48), and Thackeray's *Vanity Fair* (1848) give perfect pictures of life and mores in their respective centuries, but they do not belong to the historical genre. They are novels contemporary of their period, whose atmosphere need not be re-created, whose plot's plausibility—or the lack of it—is obvious, and whose dramatis personae are the next-door neighbors of both author and reader. Reading them today is comparable to watching a play by Chekhov or G. B. Shaw in period costumes: we get a glimpse of life as it used to be in the author's time.

A novel still may be considered as belonging to the genre if it is set in a time recent to the author but historically completed and closed so that a perspective of events can be achieved and so that research becomes necessary. Such works usually reflect the author's political stance, as does Mikhail Sholokhov's *The Quiet Don* (1928-40), or a philosophical theory, like Tolstoy's antihistoricism in *War and Peace*. They are epic panoramas of a national upheaval, with a strong fictional plot not significantly involving historic figures. Generally, though, more time distance —of perhaps several centuries—offers a more useful challenge to an artist's skill in re-creating the atmosphere of the period.

The historic atmosphere in conventional novels is achieved primarily by a milieu which the reader has come to associate with a certain period. He expects to find wreaths of roses, slaves, and guests reclining on couches at Roman feasts, as he does in Sienkiewicz's *Quo Vadis?* (1896); silk purses filled with gold coins, swords, and velvet mantles at a Renaissance court, such as in Dumas's *La Reine Margot* (1842); sables and cloth-of-silver coats worn by the boyars of Ivan the Terrible and heavy oak furniture in their homes, as in *Prince Serebryany* (1861) by A. K. Tolstoy.[4] These archeology artifacts are designed to enhance the romantic glamor of the plot and to create an atmosphere stronger than reality, capable of overcoming the historical foreknowledge of the reader.

At this point one should note the necessity of distinguishing the characteristic features of conventional and sophisticated historical novels. This is not to imply inferior quality in the former. The conventional, Scottian novel is easier to imitate and therefore *has* been imitated by many inferior writers, but adoption of the method certainly in no way cheapens the work of Dumas, Hugo, A. K. Tolstoy, or contemporary writers of historical fiction (which of late has again become *en vogue* in Western literature). The difference between the two lies mainly in the degree of artistic depth and in the author's goal. Is he writing an epic or simply telling a story? Is he just entertaining the reader or endeavoring to promote a philosophical idea by creating the image of an era or (a frequent combination) fictionalizing a major historical personage? The degree of the artistic depth is usually evinced in the methods employed in creating the historical atmosphere. A conventional novelist is satisfied with describing the milieu; a sophisticate is pursuing ideal artistic truth. It is that truth, the typified historic reality, which presupposes his right to rummage in the recorded facts and objects, to reject some and select those he needs to reproduce the genuine mental and emotional climate, the temper of the era, its physical environment, and its people. To achieve the era's historic atmosphere the novelist needs an intuitive poetic vision.

Leo Tolstoy, who had done considerable research and assembled plentiful documentary materials in preparation for writing a Petrine novel, abandoned the project after several frustrating attempts. Among the manifold reasons for this failure offered by various critics and by Tolstoy himself, two bear on the point discussed here: Tolstoy's growing dislike for Peter as a person, and his acknowledged "inability to re-create in his imagination the everyday life of the Russians of that epoch."[5]

The artist needs to familiarize himself with customs and beliefs no less than with lodgings, furniture, and landscape of the era he has chosen to inhabit. This is what writing a serious historical novel amounts to: entering the era like Alice her Wonderland through a small door in the green tree of imagination and closing that door. The artist's overall purpose must be that of the Moscow Art Theater: creating on the stage a perfect illusion of reality, making

the reader feel a participant in the drama instead of an
onlooker.

The process is demanding since it is all too easy to shatter
that painstakingly created illusion. Having a candle belonging
to a different period lighted instead of an oil lamp, or introducing a character of a married Roman Catholic priest at the end
of the eleventh century though celibacy was established in its
middle, might go unnoticed except perhaps by a sophisticated
reader. But a pipe smoked by, say, Henry VIII, or a character of
a French serf in the time of Napoleon, would not. Of course,
such niceties are not observed by the majority of conventional
novelists, but their method of avoiding mistakes consists in using a standard stage setting—"Roman," "Mediaeval," or "Slavic,"
as the case may be—and a standard romance-and-adventure plot.

Living among historical artifacts is not simple either.
These should be, as they are in real contemporary life, within
easy reach, useful, and usable: linen stockings, wooden dishes,
beds built into the walls of manor houses in Sigrid Undset's
Kristin Lavransdatter (1920-22); the great brown loaf making the
rounds of the family at supper in their tiled-floor kitchen in
Reade's *The Cloister and the Hearth* (1861); a deep well under a
sacred tree, Rachel's magnificent multicolored veil, a night camp
fire lighted by the ten shepherd brothers in Thomas Mann's *Joseph
and His Brothers* (1934-44). There should be no cluttering because cluttering impairs the illusion of reality. For example,
Merezhkovsky's trilogy *The Death of the Gods* (1896-1905) and
George Eliot's *Romola* (1863) contain too many archeological details, museum pieces certified to be genuine and yet disappointing to the reader because fiction does not allow anything that is
not indispensable to environment or plot. This is what Chekhov
meant by his stage direction "if there is a gun in the first act
of the play by the fifth it should be fired." To sum up: archeological details should be introduced economically, selectively,
and unobtrusively.

So should documents. Michael Bulgakov in his *Life of Mon-
sieur de Molière* (1936) went so far as to obliterate all traces
of documentation, used instead a bare biographical skeleton, and
fleshed Molière out with an interpretation of his plays without
using a single quote. The result is that this *vie romancée* reads
like fiction; in fact, few historical novelists could claim having mastered Bulgakov's original technique.

Beside the intuitive vision of an era the artist needs what
may be termed personal experience in it. He has to steep himself
in its life style, become personally acquainted with its contemporaries, understand their world and make them fit into his own
order of the universe. A. N. Tolstoy insists that "after years
of groping for Peter's image, I came to see every grease spot on
his uniform coat but he still remained firmly planted in the
mists of history" until Tolstoy had clarified his own artistic
conception of the world—and produced *Peter the First* by "entering history through the gate of the Marxist present." Antoni
Gołubiew, author of the epic, multivolumed *Bolesław the Brave*

(1948-74) and a devout Catholic, makes a similar point: "Authenticity in a historical novel," he says, "consists of a truthful portrayal of a man submerged in the changeability of history, so that through that changeability we discover in him—in ourselves, that is—what is stable, unchangeable, human."   In short, in the words of L. Feuchtwanger, "the writers of great historical novels make use of history merely to express their own concept of the world."[6]

Still, a historical novelist should not become involved in an in-depth psychological study of the inhabitants of his fictional world: they are too remote for complete empathy.   He can report on their behavior, their words, or as omniscient narrator, on their thoughts and feelings, but he cannot know more about them than he would about his own friends and neighbors in real life.   Most historical personages are by the nature of things impervious to psychological analysis—Peter certainly proved to be—while conventional fictional characters, whose function is limited to promoting the forward movement of the plot, are of necessity flat.   However, a form of a psychological study of a fictional character can be achieved with the help of a flawless execution of historical atmosphere, as in *Kristin Lavransdatter*.   The plot of that novel is timeless—merely a life story of one woman, like Guy de Maupassant's *Une Vie* (1883)—and serves only for the protagonists' characterization.   It is also simple: Kristin, at seventeen, met and became mistress of the only man she would ever love, married him, overcoming her parents' opposition, bore him eight sons, stayed faithful to him through dark as well as sunny years, and surviving him, died, a nun, of the plague.

On the surface, *Kristin Lavransdatter* need not have been a *historical* novel.   Yet, the author's own certainty conveyed to the reader that this is how it all happened and could not have happened differently—in other words, the novel's artistic truth —is reinforced by the mediaeval setting and its spiritual and social atmosphere.   Everything counts—the magnificence of cathedrals, the monasteries with their hostels for travellers, the bustling crowds in the markets and narrow streets, the manors and villages scattered in the vast expanses of the land, a glimpse of the king's court.   These are not just a mediaeval stage set; they form the backdrop for a feudal society, a way of life permeated with respect for moral values, tradition, and above all, piety founded on unquestioning faith.   The depth of Kristin's passion is striking in that for its sake she readily jeopardizes not only her own and her family's honorable standing in this society but, in her earnest belief, the very salvation of her soul; she gladly makes penance for and bears the burden of her carnal sin to the end of her life.   Thus she is a genuine inhabitant of the fourteenth century not by Undset's creative whim but by Kristin's psychic essence.   Historical atmosphere takes over the role of a modern novel's psychological analysis.

Similarly, Tsar Peter's presence and even his active role in the torture chamber, as in A. N. Tolstoy's *Peter the First*, Dmitry Merezhkovsky's *Peter and Alexis* (1905), Valentin Kostylyov's

Pitirim (1936) and all of Konstantin Skildkret's novels, are possible not only because he was himself—Peter—but also because he
was a Russian tsar of the eighteenth century. Ivan the Terrible,
on the other hand, whether in *Prince Serebryany* or in Kostylyov's
trilogy bearing that tsar's name (1942-47), does not demean in this
way his dignity as an anointed Orthodox monarch of the sixteenth
century. Nor does Nicholas I—although an autocrat like his predecessors, with comparable strains of cruelty in his disposition—attend
the executions of, say, the Decembrists in *The Contemporaries* (1926)
by Olga Forsh. After all, autocrats were civilized in the nineteenth century.

Thus the typification of historic reality, independently of
the novelist's talent, is natural when applied to the legitimate
inhabitants of the world of fiction, but in the case of historical
personages the process involves their fictionalizing. When these
are distinguished and popular figures, it results in the creation
of a composite fictional image. This study, then, is dedicated
to a reconstruction of the composite image of Peter the Great
created by historians, the petite histoire, and Russian historical novelists.

2.   A Biographical Outline

And then—Peter.
Karamzin

Peter was the fourteenth child of Tsar Alexis (1629-1676),
Alexis's first by his second wife, Natalya Naryshkina. Peter was
born on May 30, 1672, into an atmosphere of court intrigues and
in the midst of a feud between the Naryshkins and the family of
Alexis's first wife, the Miloslavskys. He was only three years
old when his father died and Fedor, his eldest brother and godfather, ascended the throne.
Fedor always treated his stepmother with respect and his
little brother with kindness, but the influence of the Naryshkins
ended with Tsar Alexis's death and that of the Miloslavskys increased. At the head of the Miloslavsky party stood Peter's half-
sister, Tsarevna Sophia, a young woman of intelligence and powerful will who was to become Peter's political opponent and personal enemy. The struggle for influence at court was to become
further complicated by the intrigues of the relatives of Fedor's
widow, Martha. Two influential noblemen—Prince Vasily Golitsyn,
Sophia's lover, and Prince Ivan Khovansky—sided with the Miloslavskys.
At the moment of Fedor's death in April 1682, there were two
parties, backing, respectively, the candidacy to the throne of
Fedor's younger brother, the feeble-minded, fifteen-year-old
Ivan, and that of Peter. Peter's party won for the moment, and
the ten-year-old boy was proclaimed tsar. Then for the first
time the Streltsy came into Peter's life.
The Streltsy had been Tsar Alexis's favorite bodyguard and
had enjoyed many privileges during his reign. Well armed, well
organized, and comparatively well-to-do, they lived in time of
peace in suburban settlements (*sloboda*) and engaged in trade.
Their military profession was hereditary; they jealously guarded

their privileges, followed old Russian ideas and order, and were friendly to the Old Believers.[1]

Three weeks after Peter had been proclaimed tsar, the first bloody revolt of the Streltsy, instigated by Sophia, took place. His two maternal uncles, his mother's foster father, Matveev, and several other boyars were murdered before his eyes. For three days he saw the Kremlin overrun by the rioters. At their demand Peter's maternal grandfather, Kirill Naryshkin, was forced to enter a monastery; Peter himself was made to share the throne with his half brother Ivan as "the second tsar"; and Sophia became regent, as both tsars were too young to rule.

In spite of such immediate acceptance of their demands, or perhaps because of it, the Streltsy were slow to quiet down. They tried to reestablish the old church order, they made audacious demands that a monument be erected in Red Square to commemorate their revolt, and they looted rich boyars' homes. It was not until Sophia retired with both tsars to the Trinity Monastery and appealed to the nobility for help that the Streltsy were finally subdued and their commander, Prince Khovansky, executed without trial. The court returned to Moscow, and Sophia took over the management of state affairs. The Dowager Tsaritsa Natalya retired with the "second tsar" to the palace of Preobrazhenskoe outside Moscow. The first act of the Streltsy tragedy was ended and so was Peter's childhood.

Peter's adolescence and early youth were spent in an atmosphere of hostility and neglect created by Sophia, and in an atmosphere of resentment and fear created by Tsaritsa Natalya, who, though reportedly "carefully chosen by Providence to be the mother of Peter the Great," was, according to other sources, "a princess of mediocre intelligence." She would not admit scholarly monks, such as Simeon Polotsky, who had taught Peter's older brothers and Sophia, to the palace, lest they prove to be the enemies' spies. As a result, Peter's education never advanced beyond the elementary stage. He was taught reading, writing, church singing, the Holy Scriptures, and by means of picture books, some rudiments of history and geography. All this knowledge was imparted before he was ten by Zotov, the future "patriarch" of Peter's "most-crazy, most-drunken council (*Vseshuteishii vsep'ianeishii sobor*)."[2] At sixteen, at the insistence of his doting mother, who hoped to attach him to home and to a decorous, sedate way of life, he married Evdokia Lopukhina, a foolish, pretty, and thoroughly old-fashioned girl. He was seventeen when Alexis was born, and though he had two other sons within the next three years, both of whom died in infancy, Evdokia—unsurprisingly— failed to make her temperamental husband into a dedicated family man.

These peculiar circumstances of his early life and education gravely influenced the formation of Peter's character and his choice of occupations, amusements, and companions, then as well as later. It was during this time that, with the help of a few foreign officers, he organized his "play regiments" (*poteshnye*) the nucleus of the future new, modernized Russian army; with the help of foreign shipbuilders, laid the foundations of the future Russian fleet;[3] and, escaping from the unbearable tedium of his home, sought relaxation in Moscow's Foreign Quarter (*nemetskaia sloboda*).

This miniature Europe on the outskirts of Moscow must have indeed, as was rumored, cast a spell on the young Russian tsar. It opened fascinating vistas of the outside world, offered an outlet for his pent-up zest for life, and gave some satisfaction to his insatiable curiosity. The *sloboda* was inhabited by all the foreigners who had permission to stay in Russia—tradesmen, mercenaries in Russian service, occasional foreign envoys, as well as international adventurers and seekers of fortune. In comparison with the still mediaeval Russia it belonged not only to a different civilization but almost to a different century.

This was, of course, a most unsuitable milieu for a monarch to complete his education, to learn the arcana of diplomacy and court protocol, or to develop self-discipline. Peter learned there arithmetic, dancing ("without taking regular lessons," he explained; "from practice only"), and fourteen trades, of which he was very proud. With this education of a tradesman's apprentice he also acquired the tastes and manners of Dutch sailors, whom he admired, and habits as shocking in the eyes of foreign courts as they were in those of Russian boyars and the populace. It was this disregard for traditional proprieties (*istovost'*) that was at the root of Peter's unpopularity and did the most harm to his reputation. Even the hardships caused in subsequent years by his reforms and wars—taxes, slave labor, and recruiting—were borne with comparatively less resentment than the Tsar's carousing in low company. It was not his right to do as he pleased that was ever questioned—Russia was used to being ruled by an autocrat—but the unseemly character of his behavior, the low and unusual quality of his pleasures.

On a night in August 1689, the news of still another plot threatening Peter's life came to Preobrazhenskoe, and he escaped on horseback to the Trinity Monastery. The shock of this flight apparently seriously affected Peter's nervous system (though historians differ on this point, as do fiction writers) and originated the notorious facial tics, convulsions, and fits of insane rage which plagued him throughout his life. It also deepened his hatred for the Streltsy and for the elements of the old Russian order which they represented.

The majority of the army, however, proved loyal to Peter; the attempted coup resulted in the fall of Sophia and her favorites, and she was forced to retire to a convent. Officially, the regency was ended, but in reality it passed to the clique of Tsaritsa Natalya. Tsar Ivan was sickly and had neither the ability nor the will to rule, and Peter continued to train his regiments, build his ships, and seek amusement in the Foreign Quarter, where he had already found lovely Anna Mons and his friend, companion, and mentor Franz Lefort.

The military maneuvers which Peter organized in 1694 with his "play" regiments, by now regular army units, were followed by his first deeds of arms, the two Azov campaigns against the Turks. Both the failure of the first of these campaigns in 1694 and the success of the second a year later were important. They showed the urgent need for the creation of a modern Russian army and navy, and underlined the dangers and the possibilities of Russian foreign policy. They also brought out some of Peter's basic characteristics: his perseverance and courage in defeat, his boundless energy, his impatience, and his peremptoriness. They also increased his eagerness to learn more about the West and all it had to offer.

By this time he was free to act as he pleased: Tsaritsa Natalya had died in January 1694, and Tsar Ivan had died two years later. Thus, in March 1697, Peter sent Fedor Golovin and Franz Lefort on a tour of foreign courts as his "Great Envoys" (Russia had no permanent representatives but customarily sent special diplomatic missions); and he himself accompanied them, incognito, as "volunteer Peter Mikhaylov." He continued this strange, self-effacing practice throughout his reign, passing himself through all the military ranks, beginning with that of a bombardier in the army and a junior officer in the navy. The reason could have been anything from his much-vaunted modesty, to a deep-rooted feeling of insecurity which manifested itself abroad in attacks of paralyzing shyness, to a statesmanlike desire to magnify the importance of personal service and value above the nobility of birth which had been of paramount importance in Russia.

Eighty other "volunteers" had gone abroad six months before Peter; and thirty-five more, among them Peter's famous future favorite, Alexander Menshikov, formed part of the "Great Envoy" retinue. They all had to stay for a complete course of studies in navigation, shipbuilding, artillery, and military drill—subjects in which Peter himself was interested. "Volunteers" in their case was a misnomer, since these young men of the noblest Russian families had gone on Peter's orders, against their own will and that of their parents. Many of them, however, were to become Peter's helpers, the "fledgelings of his nest," and to take an important place both in Russian history and in Russian fiction. The practice of sending out volunteers was to continue throughout Peter's reign.

During the eighteen months of his first stay abroad (he revisited Europe in 1717-18), Peter visited Brandenburg, Holland, England, Saxony, Austria, and Livonia. He had several meetings of political importance: with Elector Friedrich of Brandenburg (from 1700, king of Prussia); King William of England; Augustus, elector of Saxony and king of Poland; and Emperor Leopold. He visited museums, factories, and shipyards; studied artillery and shipbuilding, the latter in Holland while working as a carpenter in Zaandam; observed military and naval maneuvers (at Riga he was refused permission to inspect the town fortress and subsequently used this affront as a pretext for declaring war on Sweden). Everywhere, he bought raw materials and tools needed for the establishment of Russian industry, hitherto nonexistent, and modern arms for the intended reorganization of the Russian army,

Peter the Great As a Young Man. *Portrait by Knoeller, 1698.*

and engaged officers, technicians, sailors, and engineers for
both these purposes. He also bought practically everything that
struck him as unusual and therefore likely to be necessary for
the Westernization of Russian culture and life. This included,
among other items, paintings (which in Russia, with the exception
of icons, were banned as sinful, as were mirrors) and, during the
second journey, exhibits for the future Museum of Natural Sciences
(Kunstkamera) such as stuffed animals and embryos preserved in alcohol. The latter items, as will be shown, came to play a significant role in Russian historical fiction.

Peter intended to visit Italy also but had to change his
plans as the news of still another Streltsy revolt reached him in
Vienna. He hastily returned to Russia and, in August 1698, though
the revolt had already been suppressed by that time, punished the
plotters in a series of mass public executions in which he—and
at his orders, some of the courtiers—personally took part.

This chapter in the story of Peter's life deserves attention, and it certainly has not been overlooked by fiction writers,
though the manner of its presentation varies. The threat of a
Streltsy plot, Peter's nightmare, had been ever-present since his
childhood. A plot to assassinate him arranged by a Strelets officer, Tsikler, was discovered on the very eve of Peter's departure on his European trip. Now, on his return, his throne was in
danger (the origin of the revolt had again been traced to Sophia
and her followers), perhaps his life, and certainly the future of
the reforms which were already taking shape in his mind. Peter's
reaction to both these plots revealed for the first time the
strain of savage and often grotesque cruelty which was to reappear
whenever, under strong provocation, he flew into one of his uncontrollable rages. It is in this connection that the macabre details
of the executions will be discussed in a later chapter.

The repression of the latest—and last—revolt of the Streltsy
was in the nature of Stalin's "liquidation of the *kulaks* as a
class" rather than that of a punishment. Thousands were sentenced
to death, thousands to exile and hard labor; Streltsy families
were expelled from Moscow. The accompanying atrocities shocked
foreigners even in a century not renowned for its humanitarian
principles. The public slaughter was preceded by unusually barbarous tortures. For five months corpses were left to rot at the
place of the execution, including those of the two hundred who
were hanged in front of the convent where Tsarevna Sophia was
confined. Three of them, hanged from the window of her cell,
held lists of their crimes in their hands. After a stormy investigation conducted by Peter himself, Sophia and her sister
Martha, an accomplice in the plot, were forced to take the veil.
Sophia remained in strict confinement till her death in 1707.

A month after his return to Russia Peter banished his wife
Evdokia to a convent and in June 1699 forced her to take the veil
—a time-honored way for Russian tsars to regain their freedom,
since a wife who became a nun became dead to the world and her
husband became a widower. Evdokia's son, the eight-year-old
Tsarevich Alexis, was given into the charge of Peter's sister

Natalya and was forbidden any communication with his mother.   It
had never been a happy marriage: Evdokia's hostility to everything new and foreign, the total incompatibility of the young
spouses, would have brought on a disastrous end in any case.
Peter's liaison with Anna Mons, daughter of a wine merchant from
the Foreign Quarter, which had begun even before his trip abroad,
probably precipitated matters.   Both women and their considerable
influence in the creation of Peter's fictional image will be discussed later.

The two years following Peter's return from abroad were
spent in the conclusion of the war with Turkey, Russia obtaining
fairly favorable truce conditions, and in the reorganization of
the Russian army in preparation for a war with Sweden, which began in August 1700.   That war lasted twenty-one years and resulted
in Russia's securing a firm foothold on the shores of the Baltic
Sea and in her ascendance as a great European power.   The most
important landmarks of that period include the Russian defeat at
Narva three months after the beginning of hostilities, followed
by nine years of fluctuating fortunes and strenuous effort in
building up a modern Russian fleet and army; the foundation in
May 1703 of St. Petersburg—Russia's new capital, port, and strong-
hold—on a desolate, marshy island in the estuary of the river
Neva; and the celebrated Russian victory at Poltava in June 1709.
After Poltava, came twelve years of indecisive fighting and complicated diplomatic games, at which Peter and his "fledgelings"
were becoming increasingly proficient, and finally in 1721, the
conclusion of the treaty of Nystadt, a great success for both
Russia's military force and her diplomacy.   Solemn church services, public pageants, and fireworks, with which Peter customarily
celebrated his successes, were held on this occasion on a truly
gargantuan scale.   Peter himself, in an ebullience of spirits,
danced on top of banquet tables—a detail usually omitted by fiction writers; on the other hand, his acceptance of the "promotion" to the rank of admiral granted by the navy, and of the
title of "Father of the Fatherland, Emperor, and Great" offered by
the Senate, seldom goes unmentioned.   The navy and the Senate
had, of course, been created by Peter himself as part of his
sweeping reform, along with practically every other modern institution in Russia.

Another significant date is that of the Russian defeat at
the river Prut, in 1711.   It was a political defeat rather than
a military one, since no actual fighting took place.   The Russian
army was surrounded by an enormous Turkish force; and in order to
prevent the capture of his whole army, Peter, who with his second
wife, Catherine, had also fallen into that trap, concluded a
treaty with the Turks forfeiting all his former gains on the Azov
and Black Seas.   This short-lasting, ill-starred confrontation
with Turkey had been brought about by the intrigues of Charles
XII of Sweden and the treason of the Ukrainian Hetman, Mazepa,
who had joined Charles in his flight to Turkey after the battle
of Poltava two years earlier.   Both Mazepa's treason and the
allegedly noble and courageous behavior of Catherine, who helped

to raise for the sultan a substantial ransom, including her own
jewels, are among the favorite topics of Russian historical fiction.

After the conclusion of the treaty of Nystadt, Peter waged
one more war: a short and successful war with Persia (1722-23).
The period between 1718—the year of the death of Charles XII,
which made the outcome of the Swedish war a foregone conclusion—
and Peter's own death on January 28, 1725, was dedicated to the
introduction of internal reforms in Russia.

A detailed discussion of Peter's reforms is beyond the scope
and subject of this study. Moreover, the reflection of these reforms in fiction and its influence on Peter's image were not
necessarily in direct proportion to the reforms' actual importance. For example, the ruthless taxes on practically everything
from beards to bathhouses have been presented in fiction as the
main cause of the "national lament," but the "census of souls"
conducted in 1719 in preparation for the "taxation of souls," the
poll tax introduced in 1721, has not. And yet, these two ukases
turned the peasants into personal property of the landowners:
previously, they had been attached only to the land, which was
considered as owned by the tsar, and only temporarily granted to
the nobility in exchange for military service. Likewise, the
branding of recruits to prevent desertions, which was notorious
among the populace as a "seal of the Antichrist," overshadows in
fiction the whole, all-important military reform, that basis of
Russia's naval, military, and diplomatic power. In short, the
reforms stressed by writers of historical fiction are, naturally
enough, those affecting the life style (*byt*) and fate of fictional
characters.

Peter had begun the reforms immediately after his return
from the European journey of 1698, but at least until the battle
of Poltava, they had the character of emergency measures geared
to the demands of warfare. At times, they were contradictory and
had to be altered or even cancelled later. Still, practically
all of them eventually became part of the structure of the new
Russian State. Peter, impatient over trifles, could wait in important matters and never completely abandoned a project even if
it had to be postponed indefinitely.

War, above all, required money; in Peter's words, "money is
the artery of war." Hence, in 1708, administrative reform started
with the division of the country into eight provinces (*gubernia*)
and continued with the establishment, in 1711, of the Senate,
whose main duty consisted in collecting taxes through a steadily
growing net of bureaucracy and in punishing both tax evaders and
corrupt officials. Corruption was universal, accepted as a way
of life, and seemingly ingrained into the fabric of the Russian
society. Peter was to fight it throughout his reign single-
handedly and in vain—a topic popular with anecdotists and fully
exploited by historical fiction. In 1718, after several false
starts, the organization of nine ministries (*Kollegia*) was completed, and their heads joined the Senate, bringing the number of
senators to twenty. In 1722 a ukase created a "table of ranks,"

a quasi-military hierarchy for Russia's by that time enormous
bureaucracy; it established stepping-stones for an administrative
career, which, as with the military, conferred hereditary nobility
above a certain rank.

War, of course, required a regular army, fed, clothed,
equipped with modern weapons, and drilled by professional officers. Hence, in 1699, the first permanent Russian army was created
by partial draft and a call for volunteers; then came compulsory
drafts, from 1705 on. A Military Regulation Code (*Voinskii Ustav*)
was worked out in 1716 and was followed in 1721 by a ukase con-
ferring hereditary nobility on all officers irrespective of birth.
The culminating point of the military reform was the ukase dividing the country anew, into ten provinces, and the army into ten
regiments which were to be quartered in and supported by these
provinces. This system amounted to a military occupation, since
the commanders were given considerable authority over local ad-
ministration and supervised the collection of taxes. Moreover,
officers were instructed to generally keep an eye on the behavior
of the population: Peter assumed a good officer to be automati-
cally fit for any nonmilitary job.

The building of the new capital, port, and fortress of St.
Petersburg, that "window on Europe" on the newly conquered Baltic
Sea, swallowed money and manpower as greedily as did the war itself. St. Petersburg's role in Peter's life and in the creation
of his fictional image are of such importance as to require
separate discussion in later chapters.

By the end of Peter's reign Russia possessed factories and
foundries, manufactured her own guns and cloth for uniforms, and
had built in her own shipyards a large mercantile fleet and a
powerful navy. The wealth of ores in the Urals could well be
called Peter's discovery, and the Demidov family, who developed
its mines, holds a prominent place in historical fiction, as does
—in modern fiction, at least—the slave labor they employed.
Yet, Peter did not wage wars for war's sake like Charles XII of
Sweden; warfare for him was a necessary part of Russia's Europeanization. He is not famed for his deeds of arms. While much
is made of his hat having been pierced by a bullet at the Battle
of Poltava, both historians and novelists skirt giving an explanation of his leaving the scene of the defeat at Narva in 1700. (He
simply returned to Russia and immediately began levying money and
building up a better-equipped army.) Instead, "the Tsar Laborer,"
"the Crowned Carpenter," building a ship, forging a piece of pig iron,
are endlessly stressed. There exists a rich lore of anecdotes relating Peter's simplicity of habits, his kindness to common people,
his thrift, his love of picturesque Russian customs and proverbs, of
cabbage soup (*shchi*), and of aniseed vodka (the latter, incidentally, was not originally Russian, but was imported by Peter himself
from Holland, as the samovar was later). When it came to changing
those aspects of lifestyle (*byt*) which made Russians look like
Asians—such as introducing foreign fashions in dress, shaving, wigs,
tobacco, participation of women in and dancing at social "assemblies" (*asambleia*)—Peter could be and was ruthless.

Pushkin, in the notes for his unfinished *History of Peter the Great* (1835) comments on the difference between Peter's permanent laws and his temporary, ad hoc ukases. "The first were created by a broad mind, full of wisdom and kindness; the second were mostly cruel and self-willed and seemed to have been written with a knout."[4] In other words, the first were those of a statesman, the second those of an autocrat.

Yet, Peter was not a typical autocrat—a tyrant, a despot—for he seldom acted to satisfy a personal caprice, even while assigning cruel punishments for disobedience in unimportant matters. Laws and ukases alike were meant to promote the cause of the state's welfare, which, Peter insisted, he himself served all his life. He even introduced a new form of loyalty oath—to the tsar (as usual) and to the state[5]—and was willing, up to a point, to explain his reasons for the measures: most of his ukases start with the word *because* (*ponezhe*). But he gave up no part of the monarch's privilege to decide on what constituted that welfare. In his words: "His Majesty is an autocratic Monarch, who never needs to give account of his actions to anyone . . . but has the power and the right to rule His realm and His lands as a Christian Sovereign, according to His will and good judgement."[6]

He had to be obeyed. His ukases, invariably reinforced by stiff penalties for disobedience, replaced time-honored customs and paved the way for a police state. They instructed the populace on the proper way to build houses, entertain guests, and bury the dead. Ukases regulated the cut and length of clothes, the width of linen towels, the breeding of sheep, and the position of women in society. A large body of informers (*fiskal*) was created to report on any cases of disobedience to the Tsar's decrees and of improper conduct, including embezzlement of state money and the hoarding of one's own. An *ober-fiskal*, the "Tsar's eye," had been appointed simultaneously with the establishment of the Senate to watch and report on the activities of that lofty body. The whole apparatus was strictly connected with the *Preobrazhenskii Prikaz*, established in 1697 as a kind of special security bureau, and headed by the awesome Prince Fedor Romodanovsky, a colorful personage as familiar to readers of historical fiction as are wily Menshikov or virtuous Prince Yakov Dolgoruky. After Romodanovsky's death in 1717, the institution was renamed "the Secret Chancellery" (*Tainaia Kantselariia*) and entrusted to Peter Tolstoy, notorious for his role in the trial of Tsarevich Alexis. The archives of the chancellery, transferred at the beginning of the nineteenth century to the state archives, have since (allowing for fluctuations in censorship policies) served as an important source both for historians and writers of historical fiction.

The task of fighting crime in the cities as well as generally supervising the orderly behavior of the inhabitants—including their attending court parties when invited—was entrusted in 1718 to the newly established police. "The police," Peter explained, "are the soul of civic life."[7]

The church had its own informers, called "inquisitors," headed by a "proto-inquisitor." As in the case of the Senate,

these watchdogs were appointed simultaneously with the creation of
the Holy Synod (in 1721) and for the same purpose.

Under Peter the church became firmly subordinated to the
tsar, though not in matters of dogma. Peter was interested in
various religions—witness his discussions with Protestant bishops
during his stay in England and with Jesuits in France—but he had
no intention of reforming Orthodoxy. He did not confiscate church
property outright, though he laid a heavy hand on the monasteries'
revenues, assigned modest sums for the maintenance of monks and
nuns (whom he considered loafers and freeloaders [*tuneiadets*]),
and restricted their numbers. In 1700, after the death of the
patriarch, he forbade the election of a successor and appointed a
layman (*ober-prokuror*) as head of the Holy Synod in 1722.

The inquisitors, then, were employed to report on schismatics,
on cases of unbecoming conduct in church—Peter believed in piety
in his subjects, though his own has remained a controversial
matter with both serious historians and authors of the petite
histoire—and, most important, on signs of opposition to the
Tsar's reforms and criticism of his person.

Peter lived to be fifty-two years of age; he reigned for
forty-two years and ruled for twenty-six. His life from adolescence to the day of his death was full of strenuous effort, movement, hard work, and tension; and in spite of his powerful physique
and apparently inexhaustible energy, his health was none too good.
As was mentioned, he was subject to nervous tics and convulsions,
numerous strange idiosyncrasies, and for the last ten years of his
life, several chronic ailments, caused apparently by his strenuous
as much as intemperate way of life. The direct cause of his death
was dramatic, as were all the important moments of his life: he
caught a severe cold while helping to rescue a group of soldiers
from a shipwreck near St. Petersburg on a stormy winter night.

His personal life was not a happy one. His numerous half-
sisters were hostile, several of them participating in plots
against him. His marriage to Evdokia ended in what may be called
a divorce; his first love, Anna Mons, apparently never had a
genuine affection for him. Though his second wife, Catherine,
whom he dearly loved, proved a good companion, even she was discovered to be unfaithful to Peter, as late as 1724, almost on the
eve of her coronation. And yet she, the Livonian servant girl
captured during the siege of Marienburg in 1703, owed everything
to him. Peter announced his marriage to her and adopted their
two daughters, Anne and Elizabeth, in 1712, and crowned her empress in 1724.

Nor was Peter fortunate as a father. Of the eleven children
he had by Catherine, only three daughters survived him—Natalya,
the youngest, by only one week. His eldest child, Alexis, son of
Evdokia, preferred the old Russian order and secretly opposed
Peter's reforms. In 1716 Peter demanded that Alexis resign his
hereditary rights to the Russian throne in favor of his infant
brother, Peter. Alexis complied but, fearing further persecutions from his father, escaped abroad in 1717 and sought refuge
with Emperor Charles VI, to whom he was related by marriage.

Peter succeeded in persuading Alexis to return to Russia, promising his son a full pardon. On his return, however, Alexis was
accused of high treason, tried by the Senate, found guilty, and
sentenced to death. He died before the execution, and the real
cause of his death has not been definitely established by historians, though a whole literature—part gossip, part documents—
exists and, as will be shown, has been extensively used by writers of historical fiction. Young Peter, the heir to the throne,
died at the age of three in 1719. In 1722 Peter issued a decree
establishing the right of Russian monarchs to appoint their own
successors, but he himself died without having appointed his successor, a circumstance which resulted in several palace coups
during the seventeen years following his death.

   Not only had Peter little happiness in his personal life,
but as a ruler he had to fight opposition to his reforms and to
himself throughout his reign. His wars, his private life and
manners, the changes he introduced in the Russian lifestyle were
incomprehensible, frightening, and shocking to the Russian people,
who were, moreover, ruined by heavy taxation and drained of manpower by drafts and forced labor. Hence the rebellions,[8] the
plots, and the wild rumors among the populace that Peter was a
changeling and the Antichrist. Hence also the hostility of the
old nobility and the clergy, who felt certain that the Tsar was
leading Russia and themselves to ruin. After the suppression in
Moscow of the last Streltsy revolt hostility did not flare into
open protest, but it smoldered under the surface, as was proved
by the trial of Tsarevich Alexis and by the numerous bloody protocols of the *Preobrazhenskii Prikaz*. Moreover, Peter did not
have reliable subordinates. All institutions were responsible to
the Tsar, and driven by necessity as well as by his temperament,
he participated in every matter, practically in every detail. He
did try to delegate authority—for instance, to the Senate in the
matter of taxes and to the military commanders, Russians and mercenaries, in the war. But he could trust or rely on no one. A
few talented commoners, able noblemen, and intelligent foreigners
who surrounded him were only executors of his will, not advisers
and companions. The whole enormous task of building the army and
the fleet, of directing the reforms, foreign policy, and military
campaigns—all was initiated, planned, and supervised personally
by Peter. No wonder he is so often referred to as "the Giant,"
and his physical height must have enhanced the weird impression
which his powerful personality and unlimited autocratic might had
on contemporaries.

   It is commonly assumed that Peter knew exactly what he was
doing: his goal, as he himself stated, was "Russia, living in
wealth and glory." That goal was to be achieved by Russia's
adopting Western civilization and joining the family of European
nations on equal terms. In that he succeeded, his reign creating
a new era and becoming a watershed in the history of Russia.
There is, however, no agreement among historians as to whether
his reforms were not introduced too violently, in too much of a
hurry, and at too great a cost to the nation. Another controversial and

unresolved question is whether such a complete change could best
have been achieved under the direction of a self-educated,
opinionated man, an oriental potentate of violent temperament—
in short, by Peter.

3.   Sources

Oh, lofty calling of History! One's heart trembles at
the sight of a powerful monarch . . . called to account
for his acts by the humblest of researchers.
            Pogodin 1860

Isn't the whole of Russia a veritable history and a
faithful mirror of the blessed deeds of Peter the Great?
            Krekshin, 1740

Historical sources necessary for the creation of the image of
Peter the Great *as a person* are few and above all unreliable.
There exist, of course, Peter's own letters and notes, his ukases
and orders—both those temporary and those later codified into
laws. There are dependable materials connected with his wars and
foreign policy and formation of the army and the navy, and the
whole vast edifice of his sweeping reforms. There are the archives of his ministries and the secret police. There are the
reports of foreign envoys to their governments.

All these primary sources have served Russian historians from
the nineteenth century on in their portrayal of Peter's reforms
and of Russia during his reign. Their evaluations of Peter's
statesmanship and the significance of his reforms vary with cultural and political trends and lie beyond the scope of this study.
But while the image of Peter the statesman arises from and dominates the history of his era, that of Peter the man eludes historians, remaining blurred and controversial and usually being
summed up in the ambiguous and not very enlightening statement of
the Duchess Sophia of Brandenburg: "He is a very good and a very
evil person." Peter's human image, which is the subject of this
study, has been created in part by nonfiction writers—minor historians interested mainly in the human aspect of historical
events—but above all, by writers of historical fiction.

The reason for this, besides the limitations imposed on Russian historiography first by tsarist censorship and later by the strictures of Marxism, is that, except for basic biographical facts, little is known for certain about the details of Peter's personal life—not even the real name of his second wife, the exact date of their marriage, or the circumstances of the death of his eldest son, Tsarevich Alexis. Nor do we know many particulars about his personality, the source of his famous convulsions, for instance, or why his childhood fear of water eventually changed into a passionate enjoyment of seafaring. Peter himself contributed to this scarcity of sources. "Writing behind closed doors" was punishable by severe penalties;[1] monks, whom he specially mistrusted, were forbidden to have pens and paper in their cells; the Moscow chronicles (*letopis'*) kept since the fourteenth century were discontinued. Thus, personal information handed down to posterity by Peter's contemporaries is based on hearsay and, while plentiful, is often of questionable veracity.

Most of the testimony of Peter's contemporaries as well as stories about him which sprang up immediately after his death, hagiographic and slanderous alike, are a tissue of misinterpreted facts and gossip. To repeat: too little was known about him; too much of it was incredible, contradictory, and baffling. Moreover, Peter's chroniclers were hopelessly biased. The Russians assumed an attitude of abject servility and religious worship of the Tsar's memory and his deeds; foreigners, in contrast, were too often malicious and almost invariably ignorant of the Russian language and customs. How can one trust, for instance, Peter Krekshin when he openly states that he, "slave of the most excellent Emperor. . . . should glorify his sainted deeds according to the duty of love and bondage and not wantonly dare to describe them in the guise of history?"[2] Or, conversely, of what value is the Chevalier d'Eon de Beaumont's information that "Peter, son of the second wife of *Michel Alexiowicz*," chose his bride from among hundreds of girls assembled for that purpose in the "grand hall of Moscow" and that "Evdokia, by her modest behavior, won the prize of the Emperor's uncertain vows"?[3]

Russians of the generation of Peter's father, Tsar Alexis, did not leave diaries or memoirs. This is most unfortunate because their memoirs would have been invaluable to Peter's biographer—those, for instance, of the chief of the secret police, Prince Fedor Romodanovsky, or his successor in that job, Peter Tolstoy, who had lured Peter's fugitive son, Tsarevich Alexis, back to Russia. Had Peter been taught, his educators could have contributed much information, but he had none, unless one counts Nikita Zotov, subsequently the "patriarch of the most-crazy council," or the easy-going and not too sober Prince Boris Golitsyn. Peter's own contemporaries or his "fledgelings"—with the exception of Prince Boris Kurakin, Ivan Neplyuev, and Andrey Matveev—either were kept too busy by the Tsas during his lifetime or perhaps did not consider it adviseable to record many of the events they had witnessed or some details of their own careers. Besides, many of them,

like Alexander Menshikov and Alexander Rumyantsev, were barely
literate.

Of the existing memoirs by Russians and by foreigners,
several are of doubtful authenticity. Those of Nartov, an uneducated wood turner in charge of Peter's personal workshop from
1712, were in all probability written at the end of the eighteenth
century by his son Andrey, on the basis of his father's reminiscences and some notes. Henry Bruce's memoirs were published in
1783 by his widow, twenty years after his death; and while he
claims having been tutor of the future Emperor Peter II, an eye-
witness to several secret court events, and a cousin of James
Bruce, Peter's favorite diplomat, he almost certainly was an impostor who may or may not have served for a time in the Russian
army. The memoirs discovered and published by Hallez in 1841, by
François Villebois, a French adventurer who made his career in
Peter's navy and at the court of Catherine I, were, serious
bibliographers insist, written by Marquis de Campredon, French
envoy to Russia from 1721 to 1728. There are others.

Diaries and especially memoirs left by foreigners are, on
the whole, of uneven quality and furnish little information on
Peter the man. Diplomats relied heavily on hearsay and—like
Korb, Bassevitz, and Bergholz—tended to record especially unfavorable facts concerning the barbarous nation and its tyrant
ruler. Others, like Weber, were more interested in various
peoples inhabiting the vast land which was undergoing such a
drastic change than in the personality of Peter. Hired foreign
specialists and mercenaries, like the British engineer John Perry
or Baron Huysen, would often vent their dissatisfaction by pub-
lishing accounts of their wrongs, real or imagined as the case
might be.

Most of the apocryphal anecdotes which materially contributed to the creation of Peter's image are contained in the famous
collection of Jacob von Stählin, a member of the Academy of Sciences for fifty years after his arrival in Russia in 1735 and an
habitué of the courts of four tsaritsas in succession. He
claimed to have obtained his anecdotes—published in 1784, sixty
years after Peter's death—from trustworthy persons who had
either themselves participated in the events described, or had
heard of them from their near relatives. The same claim, for
that matter, is made in the memoirs of Galizin (1863) and Dolgorukov (1867). Soulab d'Allainval (1745), Georg Helbig (1809),
François-Louis d'Escherny (1811), Alexis Eustaphieve (1812), and
even Golikov, who assembled an enormous collection of such materials, either confirm or, with insignificant variations and ad-
ditions, repeat Stählin. Osip Belyaev (1793) also uses some of
these anecdotes to illustrate his catalogue description of the
museum exhibits surrounding the life-size waxen figure of Peter.

Uncritical, haphazard compilations of these various materials proliferated throughout the eighteenth and into the early
nineteenth centuries and claimed the status of "histories of
Peter the Great." Bernard de Bovier Fontenelle (1728), John
Mottley (1939), and Eléazar Mauvillon (1742) repeat and enlarge

in their works the misinformation supplied by the voluminous opus (1725) of Baron Iwan Nestesuranoi, "le prétendu boyar," as Voltaire calls him. Nestesuranoi was in fact the French publicist Jean Rousset; mediocre but with a flair for sensation, he thus became, not, of course, the first biographer, but the first Western popularizer of the image of Peter the Great. This literary genus, though undoubtedly on a higher level, developed and flourished during the nineteenth century: the works of Daniil Mordovtsev, Mikhail Semevsky, and Kazimierz Waliszewski may serve as examples. Voltaire, Peter's first Western historian, in his *Histoire de l'Empire de Russie sous Pierre le Grand* (1759), at least concentrated on Peter's reforms, just as future Russian historians were to do and, like them, escaped many an inexactitude by avoiding an extensive discussion of the Reformer's private life and personality.

The ignorance of early foreign memoirists and would-be historians was aggravated by their nonchalant attitude toward establishing the reliability of their preferred information and by their scant (in many cases, nonexistent) knowledge of the Russian language. It would be impossible to offer here a complete picture of the historic and linguistic blunders of these contributors to the Petrine petite histoire, but a few samples may serve to give an idea of them. D'Escherny informs the reader that "after Tsarevich Alexis's tragic death, Tsar Peter had by Catherine another son whose name was *Petrovich* (*Peter* Petrovich, of course)"; that he loved his sister Sophia; and that he relied on "his *denchiks*, so-called from two Russian words, *den*, signifying day, and *chiks*, meaning servant, that is to say, servants for the day . . . whom he also used as cushions."[4] Villebois (Hallez, actually, it will be remembered) asserts that "Princess Marthe, whom some call Marie because she had two names, the Tsar's beloved sister," arranged his marriage to Catherine because she did not like Evdokia.[5] Nestesuranoi calls Evdokia "Ottokeza Lupochin," and Bruce and even Voltaire follow suit, though Voltaire later had the name right. Mauvillon maintains that Tsar Fedor, Peter's elder brother, married a Polish lady, "Marie Eufrosine Luproprini," and that the boyars, displeased with his choice, poisoned them both; that Sophia named her favorite, "Galliczin," grand chancellor and *Wrenimienk* [*vremenshchik*?] which means "Administrator of Temporal Affairs, a position approximately equivalent to that of the Prime Minister of State"; also that Sophia eventually had to retire to the Nunnery of the New Virgins" [*Novodevichii monastyr'*?].[6] All these authors emphatically stress the accuracy of their information.

These sources are widely used by minor historians, by authors of popular "biographical sketches," and by historical novelists. They are not, however, necessarily sought out by scholars, who, whenever forced to resort to them, do so with many reservations and individual interpretations. Historians' quest is for recorded facts (which they tend to consider synonymous with truth), while writers of historical fiction and popularizers of history look for stories involving human emotions, preferably but not

necessarily, confirmed by actual events. Thus, fiction writers
and popularizers readily and indiscriminately use both the
document-conscious *grande histoire* and the *petite histoire*, the
underbrush which grows around important events and personages in
the forest of history, such as gossip reported in letters and
memoirs, collections of anecdotes, and later compilations of unchecked information.

4.   On Petrine Fiction

> A novel should serve the author either as means of de-
> veloping some philosophical idea, or of helping him shed
> light on the mysteries of the human heart, or of leading
> to a better understanding of the character of a histori-
> cal personage.
>   Bulgarin, 1833

> This is my chapbook art gallery of an unforgettable era.
>   Kukolnik, 1846

There are no Western-style *vies romancées*, or fictionalized biog-
raphies, of Peter the Great. Alexey Tolstoy's *Peter the First*
and Dmitry Merezhkovsky's *Peter and Alexis* probably come the nearest to being that, but neither qualifies completely. In the
first place, they do not cover Peter's whole life; secondly, the
authors handle historical facts, documents, and chronology freely;
finally, these works contain fictional characters and secondary,
fictitious plots. These are, therefore, biographical novels or,
as Soviet critics like to call the genre, "historical chronicles."
Censorship has precluded the publication of a candid, factual,
and unbiased vie romancée of this controversial personality.
Under the tsarist regime many embarrassing facts about the an-
cestor of the reigning monarchs could not be revealed. Under the
Soviet regime a completely objective work would not meet the re-
quirements of Socialist Realism. Thus, there are in Russian fiction either what can be termed conventional Petrine novels or
novels about Peter.
     Conventional Petrine novels belong to the pattern estab-
lished by Walter Scott. This pattern calls for a fictitious plot
based on the adventures of imaginary characters, while a few historical personages (highly fictionalized) are introduced in

secondary roles in order to lend authenticity to the atmosphere of the era. Monarchs especially—Richard the Lion Hearted in *Ivanhoe*, for example, or even Queen Elizabeth in *Kenilworth*, who is cast in a less episodic role—serve to make the plot move forward and by their mere presence help the reader feel at home in their remote centuries; apart from that they have no other function.

Not so in the case of Peter the Great. Even when his appearances are few and of short duration his powerful personality dwarfs the fictional protagonists and dominates even the most fantastic plot. Not only does he revive the historical era, but he continues to create it, as in his lifetime. It is his war, his reforms, his eccentricities, in short, he himself that develops the plot and determines its denouement, especially since he often appears as a deus ex machina punishing vice and rewarding virtue. He does not simply lend authenticity to the atmosphere of the novel: he permeates it.

In novels about Peter, the ones in which he is the protagonist, these characteristics are, as can be expected, even more pronounced. Here, a thin fictional plot serves merely as a pretext for showing Peter in action, for picturing different sides of his personality, and for developing his relationship with fictional characters and fictionalized historical personages by whom he is surrounded. These range from works of the caliber of A. N. Tolstoy's *Peter the First* or Merezhkovsky's *Peter and Alexis* to those of Konstantin Shildkret's trilogy *Subjugated Russia* (1933-35) or Mordovtsev's *The Crowned Carpenter* (1883). Sometimes the entire plot consists of a dramatization of historical documents concerning an actual event from his reign, as in the case of Vsevolod Ivanov's *Tsar Peter's Night* (1968), which features the affair of Tsarevich Alexis and might be called a *document romancé* rather than a novel. Sometimes it is what might be termed an animation of an apocryphal anecdote or a piece of gossip reported in a letter or in the memoirs of a courtier or a diplomat. Several short stories by Nestor Kukolnik and Alexander Kornilovich belong to this category.

The vogue of the historical novel in Russian literature of the 1830's and 1840's owed its origins to the example and the popularity of Walter Scott, Victor Hugo, and Alexandre Dumas, and to Nikolay Karamzin, whose colorful *History of the Russian State*, appearing between 1818 and 1824, became a veritable treasure trove for writers of historical fiction. Karamzin's *oeuvre*, however, ended with the sixteenth century, and authors of Petrine fiction turned for materials to the *Original Anecdotes on Peter the Great* published in 1785 by a suave courtier, Jacob von Stählin, and to Ivan Golikov, an uneducated dilettante who had vowed "to dedicate his life to the saintly memory and glorious deeds of Peter the Great." Between 1782 and his death in 1801, Golikov had compiled a thirty-volume collection of heterogeneous and unchecked materials to that purpose.[1] Thus the aura of grandeur and adulation surrounding Peter in the last years of his life and his image in the eighteenth century was inherited from

the beginning by Russian historical fiction. Authors did not
take advantage of whatever foreign materials of *grande* or *petite
histoire* were available to them at that time.

Traditional Western historical novels in the nineteenth century were tales of adventure with an admixture of court intrigue
or—a heritage of the Gothic novel—of romantic mystery. Scott's
Quentin Durward (1823), Hugo's *Notre Dame de Paris* (1830), and
Dumas's *The Three Musketeers* (1844-47) can serve as random examples. Usually, their two-dimensional heroes, noble in character
and by birth, braved numerous dangers, overcame many obstacles,
and in the end married nondescript heroines. But, as always, this
Western pattern acquired a distinct Russian flavor when it was
grafted onto Russian literature. Thus, the hero of the Russian
tale was not necessarily poor, nor particularly eager to engage
in armed encounters, nor did he achieve fame and/or fortune by
the end of the novel. He usually settled down on his family
estate or continued in the service of his monarch. He was a Russian patriot and a firm believer in what was later formulated as
Uvarov's trinity: orthodoxy, autocracy, and nationality. Mikhail
Zagoskin's *Yury Miloslavsky* (1829) and Pushkin's *The Captain's
Daughter* (1836)—the latter considered here solely in that frame
of reference—can serve as examples.

In Petrine fiction this type of novel is first represented
by Kukolnik's *Two Ivans, Two Stepanychs, Two Kostylkovs* (1846)
and Zagoskin's *Russians in the XVIIIth Century* (1848); it continued to the end of the century in the works of Mordovtsev (*The
Tsar and the Hetman*, 1879), Grigory Danilevsky (*To India in Peter's
Time*, 1879), and Evgeny Salias de Turnemir (*The Wedding Rebellion*,
1886), to cite a few. This trend was interrupted during the
literary and historical upheavals of the twentieth century which
produced *Peter and Alexis*, by the symbolist (decadent, Soviet
critics insist) writer Merezhkovsky; several iconoclastic works
by modernists such as Pilnyak (*His Majesty Kneeb Piter Komondor*,
1919) and Tynyanov (*The Waxen Effigy*, 1931); and contributions by
Soviet antireligious propagandists, such as Kostylyov (*Pitirim*,
1936) or Shildkret (*Our Savior-on-the-Tallow Church*). The traditional type—with appropriate ideological readjustments, to be
sure—was reintroduced in Soviet literature under Socialist
Realism by writers like Yury German (*Youthful Russia*, 1952),
Evgeny Fedorov (*The Demidovs*, 1941), and Dmitry Petrov-Biryuk
(*Kondrat Bulavin*, 1946). Petrine mystery novels flourished in
the 1830's, thrilling the readers of Rafail Zotov (*The Mysterious
Monk*, 1834), or Faddey Bulgarin (*Mazepa*, 1833), but at the end of
that period died without issue.

The three main factors influencing the creation of Peter's
fictional image are the authors' personal attitudes towards him,
the use they make of historical materials, and Russian censorship. Of these, censorship needs the least elaboration. Established in 1792 by Catherine the Great, whose belief in enlightened
absolutism was shattered by the French Revolution, that institution exercised control over every printed word in Russia until the
Revolution in February 1917, when it was abolished by the

Provisional Government, but it was reimposed eight months later,
after the Bolshevik coup.

The strictness with which censorship was enforced fluctuated
with political developments and social trends. Throughout the
reign of Nicholas I (1825-55) Peter's fictional image was enveloped in an atmosphere of respectful awe and admiration. He
appeared within the plot like Jupiter (without, however, any of
the latter's embarrassing escapades), magnificent, wisely dis-
pensing rewards and punishments; one could almost see the lightning and hear the thunder in the moments of his always righteous
wrath. At the same time he deigned to be kindly, delighted humble
folks by visiting their homes to partake of their simple fare,
gave his nobles an example of combined thrift and progress by
wearing simple clothes of foreign design, and engaged in manual
work to teach his subjects respect for labor.

Under Alexander II (1855-81) the censorship was relaxed, and
much archival and documentary material became accessible to historians as well as to writers of "historical tales" and Petrine
novels. Nikolay Ustryalov's *History of the Reign of Peter the
Great* (1858-63), Sergey Soloviev's *History of Russia from the
Oldest Times* (1851-77);[2] monographs like Mikhail Semevsky's *High
Treason!* (1860), Mordovtsev's *Russian Women of Modern Times* (1874),
and Mikhail Pogodin's *The Trial of Tsarevich Alexis Petrovich*
(1860); numerous articles, memoirs, and anecdotes appearing in
the journals *Russia's Past* and *The Russian Archive*[3]—all these
and many other publications testify to awakened interest in the
Tsar Reformer. The scholarly value of many of these works was
uneven, Golikov's collection, for lack of better sources, was
still relied upon to a considerable degree. Reports of eighteenth-
century foreign envoys to their governments and memoirs of foreign
courtiers such as Georg von Bassevitz, Friedrich von Bergholz, and
Johann Korb came to be used extensively, but these often did not
rise above the level of gossip.

Much of the new material revealed, or at least made public,
certain strange and dark aspects of Peter's personality and tar-
nished his bright, heroic image. There were the stains of much
bloodshed: many notorious public executions, scenes in the torture chamber (*zastenok*), and other hints at the Tsar's personal
cruelty. There was the stigma of the Alexis affair, ending in
the death of the Tsarevich; the scandal of the meetings of the
"most-crazy, most-drunken Council"; Evdokia's banishment; Catherine's embarrassing past. There were stories of popular dissatisfaction and folklore tales about the Tsar (the foreign changeling,
the Antichrist). True, the memoirs of Prince Augustin Galizin
(1863) and of Prince Peter Dolgorukov (1867) still had to be published outside Russia,[4] but they were known there, as were also
many publications by foreigners, equally hostile to Peter. Prolific mediocre writers, like Mordovtsev, Danilevsky, Polezhaev,
and Vsevolod Soloviev, used this material whenever they could do
so without getting into trouble with the censor. But in the
period of tight censorship following the assassination of Alexander II in 1881, fiction for the most part prudently reverted

to the politically safe pattern of the 1830's and 1840's.

With the relaxation of censorhip on the eve of the first
revolution in 1905, Peter's image acquired new characteristics.
Peter and Alexis overflows with archeological details: Merezhkovsky managed to use in this novel practically everything that
had been published on Peter the Great in Russia up to that time.
But now the Tsar's image in it, besides radiating its traditional
Jovian majesty, inspires an eerie, mystical fear, which, while
seldom openly expressed, had always been felt by Peter's contemporaries and fiction characters, as well as by both readers and
writers of historical fiction. This had already appeared in
Pushkin's *Bronze Horseman* (1833) and in the fragments of the
Petrine novel Leo Tolstoy attempted to write between 1872 and
1873, and it lingers in Bely's *Petersburg* (1913), and haunts post-
humously in Tynyanov's *The Waxen Effigy*. It was not noticed by
serious historians like Vasily Klyuchevsky, Sergey Platonov, or
Mikhail Pokrovsky, who continued to concern themselves with Peter
the statesman, nor by Soviet writers, whose unemotional approach
has been similar to that of historians, if not quite the same.

In Soviet historical fiction Peter is neither a demigod nor
a mystical Presence. In fact, with the abolition of the censorship after the Revolution, much scandalous gossip found its way
into Petrine fiction—witness the works by Pilynak, Kostylyov,
and Shildkret. After World War II, however, he is presented as
a statesman and a reformer (not in capital letters), a good family
man of simple tastes, and a hard worker. Yury German in *Youthful
Russia* denounces the Tsar's dependence on foreigners and corrupt
nobles, but allows him in the end to realize this mistake and to
appreciate the wisdom and the expertise of simple Russian seamen.
In Fedorov's *The Demidovs*, this family of village smiths-turned-
millionaires ruthlessly exploits slave labor in Siberian mines
and foundries; they act with the full support of the wise Tsar,
whom they help to industrialize backward Russia. There is in
this novel much mutual respect, appreciation, and conviviality;
and Peter roars with laughter and drinks aniseed vodka much as he
did a hundred years earlier in Kukolnik's short stories. He inspires no fear, whether of the Jovian or mystical kind. And
though it was by then well known in Russia, no scandalous gossip
attaches itself to his image. As to A. N. Tolstoy's *Peter the
First*, this unique novel is about Russia and young Tsar Peter,
both shown within the inexorable and lawful (*zakonomernyi*)
process of historical change.

The authors' choice of historical material and of the period
in Peter's life in which they would set their works was not determined simply by fluctuating censorship restrictions. Cultural
trends also played their role—the conflicting stances of Western-
izers and Slavophiles on Peter's reforms, for example, or Symbolism's revival of the vogue for historical fiction. An author's
goal could be simply to entertain the reader—Masalsky bluntly
says so in *The Streltsy* (1832), and surely, Kornilovich, Kukolnik,
and Zotov had no other ambition—or to educate him, this being the

official duty of a Soviet writer, like Yury German. Pilynak may
have been trying to shock bourgeois sensibilities while delighting connoisseurs with a highly original style. Leo and Aleksey
Tolstoy and Merezhkovsky used this genre as a vehicle for pro-
pounding their respective philosophies. Above all, works on Peter
the Great and his era are born of the authors' enduring fascination with him. And having chosen his subject, each artist attempts to recreate the Tsar's image as he sees and feels it, thus
adding his contribution to the composite fictional portrait.

Basically, the period of his life in which the novel is set
does not materially affect Peter's image. He is equally regal
and awe-inspiring as a "child born to the purple" (*porfiro-
rodnoe ditia*) when upbraiding "in a thunderous voice" the rebellious mob in Zagoskin's *The Brynsk Forest* (1846), while leading
troops to battle at Poltava in Ilya Selvinsky's *From Poltava to
Gangut* (1949), or when standing at the helm of the ship (sym-
bolically that of the state) in *Peter and Alexis*. In practically
every work of fiction, Peter from childhood on, is subject to
nervous tics and convulsions and is restless and inquisitive. All
his adult life he builds ships, wages wars, relaxes at his lathe,
and never falters in his tireless pursuit of Russia's greatness—
from the time he confides this goal with boyish enthusiasm to
Lefort in *The Streltsy* to the time when he sacrifices his son's
life to it in Ivanov's *Tsar Peter's Night*. Still, not all periods
are equally popular with writers of historical fiction.

The struggle for the throne after Tsar Fedor's death in 1682,
the Streltsy's bloody riot incited by Sophia, her regency and
Peter's virtual exile to Preobrazhenskoe—all these events en-
compassing Peter's childhood and adolescence—were *en vogue* only
in the nineteenth century. Except for *Peter the First* and the
first part of Shildkret's trilogy *Subjugated Russia: The Rebel*
(1933), that period appeals less to twentieth-century authors.
The last years of Peter's life have attracted even less attention, though they were rich in vital new reforms, in the codify-
ing and streamlining of earlier ukases, and in military successes
(the triumphant end of the twenty-year war with Sweden, the vic-
torious war with Persia). Pushkin did give, in *The Blackamoor of
Peter the Great* (1828), a glimpse of the Tsar enjoying, two years
before his death, the fruits of his lifelong labors, the new and
growing Russia; and Kostylyov in *Pitirim* showed him, at approximately the same time of life, grimly fighting the opposition of
the masses and the corruption of his bureaucrats. But most
Petrine fiction is set in the two decades between 1698 and 1718.
It portrays the young Tsar's return from his first journey abroad,
full of energy, impatient to start reforming everything at once,
enraged at the mutinous Streltsy and anyone else who stood in the
way of his giant reforms. The war with Sweden looms large: the
Narva defeat, the Poltava victory, the building of ships and recruiting of soldiers. Factories and mines are founded in Siberia;
St. Petersburg rises from the swamps by the Baltic Sea. Much attention is given to Peter's liaison with Anna Mons and the rise
of Catherine and of Menshikov; even more, to the compulsory

shaving of beards and women's novel participation in social life.
Public executions, torture chambers, scandalous pageants, and the
meetings of the "most-crazy council" are introduced with varying
degrees of discretion.   Finally, about 1880, attention turns to
the case of Tsarevich Alexis, never mentioned before and seldom
omitted since.   Merezhkovsky's *Peter and Alexis*, the third part
of Shildkret's trilogy: *The Eagle Cup* (1935), Polezhaev's *Tsarevich Alexis Petrovich* (1881), and Ivanov's *Tsar Peter's Night* are
completely dedicated to it.   The image of the incomprehensible,
awesome genius, revolutionizing with autocratic ukases the lifestyle and fate of Russia, was created mainly against the background of the middle part of Peter's reign.

Just as there are popular periods, so there are also favorite anecdotes, documents, and quotations whose choice by writers
depends on practically the same reasons as their choice of various
periods.   Ingenuous writers of the type of Zagoskin or, later,
Polezhaev and Arseniev or, later still, of Sokolov and Yury German
found it easier and safer to use materials which would not contra-
dict the established image of Peter, and thus in turn helped im-
press it on the readers' imagination.   In such works Peter is
readily recognizable, does not interfere with the simple plot or
overshadow fictional characters, and helps create the historical
atmosphere readers expect to find in Petrine fiction.   For these
writers the anecdotic lore was, in the words of Keats, "fancy's
casket, unlocked to choose."   Conversely, sophisticated writers,
such as Pilnyak, Merezhkovsky, and Tynyanov, conscious of the
duality in Peter's personality and looking for new approaches to
and interpretations of his image, chose from "fancy's casket"
items which startled the reader by revealing unknown and alien
features in the familiar figure of the Tsar.   The rendition of
Peter's image as a demigod by the loyal Kukolnik and Kornilovich,
and as an ogre by the Soviet writers Shildkret and Kostylyov with
a distance of a hundred years between them, had the same crude-
ness and the same reason: he was a tsar.   They could not visualize him as a person.

Nothing can compete in popularity with Peter's making mandatory the shaving of beards and the wearing of European-style
clothes.   Several ukases on this subject were issued between 1701
and 1705,[5] but novelists' favorites are the scenes of Peter's
personally snipping off the beards of the most distinguished
boyars.   This was one of his first acts after returning from
Europe in 1698, simultaneous with the beginning of the reprisals
for the recent Streltsy revolt (another popular topic).   The impact of that particular reform on fictional characters and plots
alike inspired Zagoskin and Kukolnik, Mordovtsev and Polezhaev,
Alexey Tolstoy and Shildkret; Masalsky dedicated a play to it:
The Shaving of Beards (*Borodobritie*) (1837).   Kukolnik, picturing
both events together in "The New Year," says:

> The crowd [awaiting Peter's appearance] had many reasons
> to grieve at the moment.   Thousands of their relatives,
> the Streltsy, had died on the scaffold; thousands were
> still in prisons awaiting ignominious death. . . .

Another reason, however, perhaps stronger than all the
rest, depressed the ignorant, foolish populace: the war
declared on beards and old-fashioned dress filled them
with panic and fear. . . . [Peter appears, accompanied by
his retinue in foreign dress: the boyars are beardless,
their wives and daughters are without veils.] Loud,
joyous greetings changed into a single hollow groan.
Many in the crowd broke into sobs and tears.[6]

"The foolish, ignorant populace" is seldom if ever shown
lamenting over the "census of souls," which reduced peasants to
the status of the landlords' property, or over taxes imposed on
salt, on coffins, or, for that matter, on their own beards, which
they, unlike the boyars, could keep if they paid for that privilege. Generally, although Soviet Petrine novels have portrayed
the oppression of the masses by monks and foreigners and their
exploitation in mines, traditional novels kept to the grudges of
old-fashioned nobles and merchants: the masses were allowed to
stay as old-fashioned as they pleased.

Many anecdotes well known to the non-fiction reading public
were found unsuitable in fiction. For example, the story of
Peter's discrediting the miracle of a lachrymose icon by publicly
displaying the trick it involved is often introduced as proof of
his being free from superstition. But the anecdote telling how
Peter, shown the stain on the wall where Luther had thrown an
inkstand at the Devil for interfering with the translating of the
Bible, is not. Yet Peter, on that occasion, not only commented
ironically on the freshness of the ink stain, but expressed surprise that a wise man like Luther could have believed in the
Devil.[7] Peter's love of surgery is consistently shown in scenes
where he pulls a healthy tooth of the wife of one of his aides,
in spite of the patient's protests; but the story of his operat-
ing for dropsy on the merchant Borst's wife, who died the next
day, goes unreported except in the story of Merezhkovsky's Fräulein Juliana.[8] Peter's severity in executing Catherine's maid of
honor, Marya Hamilton, for killing her illegitimate child, has
been prominently used in fiction of the periods of relaxed censorship, but the anecdote on the Tsar rebuking villagers for mal-
treating a girl who had had a child out of wedlock and his ukase
establishing orphanages for such "shameful infants" (zazornyi
mladenets)[9] went unnoticed.

Obviously, the choice of appropriate materials was greatly
influenced by how colorful they were: the establishment of, say,
the town councils (burgomisterskaia palata) in 1699, as part of
Peter's first reforms, could have but a scant appeal for writers
of historical fiction or for their readers. Yet, such omissions
had a profound impact on the fictional image of Peter the Great.
Besides, many materials were simply unmentionable in Russian
literature; some, at certain periods, as were Peter's sexual
habits, others permanently, as was the enormous apparatus of his
lay and clerical secret police. Finally, much in the creation
of Peter's image depended on the quality of the materials themselves.

5.   How It Is Done

Get your facts first and then you can distort them as
much as you please.
     Mark Twain

Fiction writers given a choice between bare, recorded historical
facts—often skimpy and almost certainly devoid of juicy details
—and the colorful lore offered by petite histoire and its popularizers invariably and understandably choose the latter. The
case of the termination of Peter's long and steady liaison with
Anna Mons can serve to illustrate this important point.
    The facts as provided by Soloviev in his prestigious,
voluminous *History* are that in 1794,

> It was rumored that the belle [Anna] had contracted a
> close relationship with the Prussian envoy Keyserling and
> accepted his proposal of marriage. Whether Anna was
> motivated by love or, in the face of Peter's growing in-
> difference (he already had two children by the future
> Catherine I), by a desire to secure an honorable position
> by means of such a prestigious union, *we do not know.*
> *All we know* [italics mine] is that together with her
> sister (Mme) Balk, she fell into disgrace and was put
> under house arrest. . . . Two years later, Keyserling
> begged permission for Anna to attend church, explaining
> his solicitude by gossipers' "attributing her misfortune
> to him" and his request was granted. (VIII, 369.)

For Soloviev the matter is closed—Anna's subsequent fate is
not even mentioned—and this minor episode in the history of
eighteenth-century Russia, or more specifically, in that of the
reign of Peter the Great, has no sequel. But not for minor historians, petite histoire, and the writers of historical fiction.
"All we know" is what happened in 1704: the liaison of Peter and

Anna was broken. But why did it happen and especially how? At
this point, the dull nakedness of the fact is enveloped in the
mantle of imagination richly embroidered with gossip.

Ustryalov, though a bona fide historian and author of a six-
volume *History of the Reign of Peter the Great*, goes into more
detail—and immediately becomes enmeshed in petite histoire and
its inconsistencies. He relates Peter's anger at Anna's "unfaithfulness," cunningly disclosed by Menshikov; his taking away from
her of his portrait set in diamonds, "since a mean slave has been
preferred to the original"; and his "overwhelming her with reproaches" though allowing her to keep numerous other liberal
gifts. "After a time," Ustryalov continues, "Anna married Keyserling but, distressed by the Tsar's disfavor, fell ill and died
within the same year."

This version is based almost verbatim on Nartov's reminiscences and on those of Alexander Gordon, a Scot who had served
in the Russian army from 1696 to 1711 and wrote his memoirs in
1755. Ustryalov also mentions the report of the Austrian envoy,
Pleyer, that Keyserling was recalled in 1704 because his marriage
to Anna had made him a *persona non grata* at the Russian court; and
a report of Peter's minister, Golovin, that Keyserling, back in
Moscow in 1706, was asking permission for Anna to attend church.
She died, he concludes, still in the same Foreign Quarter in
Moscow, in 1714. (Ustryalov, IV/1, 149-150).

Thus, according to historians, Anna apparently would have
married Keyserling in 1704, immediately after Menshikov's dis-
closure of her engagement, in the same year Keyserling was recalled, and she died "of grief" ten years later. Did she continue
to live in the Foreign Quarter under house arrest as Keyserling's
wife? The wording of his appeal to Peter makes this unlikely.
Did she—as Helbig claims a century later—deprived by a rancorous
Peter of all his former largesse, marry Keyserling on his deathbed
in 1711 and spend the rest of her life as a widow, in dignified
retirement? Or did she in fact become engaged to a captive
Swedish officer, Miller, who after her death was accused by Anna's
brother of having stolen some of her jewelry? That story is reported by Semevsky and by Mordovtsev, who does not mention his
sources, and by Waliszewski, who is satisfied to quote both as
his sources.[1]

The authors of "historical tales" are given to rather fantastic interpretations of dry documents. Anna willed some jewelry
to a little orphan girl; wasn't the child her daughter by Peter,
suggests Mordovtsev? A small boy cried pitifully at her funeral;
her son by Keyserling, perhaps? But fiction writers do not have
to make guesses: they have a right to choose (though not to invent) any historical event, any evidence, however slim, or even a
piece of gossip and build a solid fictional structure on them.

Another version of how the famous liaison was terminated is
introduced by Lady Rondeau's *Letters* (1732). Quoting "a sensible
woman" member of the Russian court in Peter's time, she relates
how Anna's romance with the Saxon envoy Koenigseck was discovered
by Peter when the envoy drowned at Schlüsselburg in Peter's

presence and Anna's love letters were found on his body. Peter, though deeply affected (even to tears!) showed great magnanimity and liberally provided for Anna, whom he married "to someone who had employment at a distance."[2]   The story, ignored by Soloviev, and rejected by Ustryalov and even by Semevsky, was unreservedly accepted by Waliszewski and also by Mordovtsev, who used it in his novels *The Tsar and the Hetman* and *The Crowned Carpenter*.

For the purposes of this study—as a detail of Peter's image —the presentation by fiction of the manner of his parting with a former mistress is more important than the truth about Anna's actual fate. Lady Rondeau's dramatic version appealed not only to Mordovtsev but also to A. N. Tolstoy, who used it in "Martha Rabe" (1931) and in *Peter the First*, while Shildkret, in *Our Savior-on-the-Tallow Church*, chose as the cause of Anna's undoing Menshikov's informing Peter of Anna's desire to marry Keyserling. All three writers accept Nartov's report on Peter's demanding the return of his bejewelled portrait, although Semevsky and Mordovtsev say this report is incorrect, since the portrait was found among Keyserling's possessions after his death in 1711, and among Anna's in 1714.

The differences in the manner of handling the episode are informative.

> "So—," said Peter [having finished reading Anna's fateful letters]. He leaned on the table, staring at the candle. "Well, what do you know?" He shook his head, smiling. "She would rather have him. I can't understand. She lied. How she lied, Alexashka! All life long, from the first moment, did she? I just can't understand it." . . . He filled his pipe, rested his elbows on the table. "I climbed fences to get to you, kept on repeating your name . . . fell asleep on your warm shoulder, trustingly . . . Fool, fool that you are, you should be minding chickens, you are too stupid for anything else. . . . Well, all right, that's all over now." And as if curtly dismissing the whole affair with a gesture of his hand, Peter got up, flung away his pipe and throwing himself down on his creaking camp-bed, pulled his sheepskin coat over him. (*Peter the First*, pp. 611-12.)

Mordovtsev's Peter, whom he likes to call the "Tsar Laborer" and the "Crowned Wrath," lives up to this exalted image on this occasion as on others. He even decides on the spot to build St. Petersburg, his new capital, on the ruins of his old Moscow love:

> "Where are Koenigseck's papers?" asked the Tsar. . . . "Poor Koenigseck—Ah! What is that? . . . Anna. . . . Her letters, I know her handwriting. . . . So that is how! The snake! Ah!"—Something crashed.—A chair fell.—"To the rack! To the scaffold! She should be impaled, the German breed!"—The Tsar's voice was frightening; he paced the tent upsetting everything he met on his way. . . .

He muttered brokenly: "I never loved Moscow; now I hate
it! They wanted to kill me in Moscow, and now I have
been cheated there.—The devil take Moscow! I have a new
seat for my nation's capital, and from now on it is going
to be my paradise and that of the whole Russian realm.
. . . And then Martha—what eyes! So pure, so innocent.
Perhaps she will really love me.!"[3]

And this is Shildkret's version of how Peter, according to
Nartov and Ustryalov (IV, 148), overwhelmed Anna with reproaches:

"So this is how you love me, you profligate vermin!" He
struck Anna the moment she opened the door. Raging, the
Tsar tore the woman's dress, dragged her naked into the
street, and there kicked her until she stopped giving any
signs of life. "Give me back my portrait," he yelled when,
after long efforts, Anna had been brought back to consciousness. "You don't need it any longer, vermin.—Take
that! And that!"—[he struck her, screaming obscene
oaths]—"since you have preferred a mean slave to its
original!" Anna Mons was deprived by the Sovereign of
all her land and henceforth was considered by him as
dead.[4]

The choice of materials, then, depends on the author's vision
of Peter's image. The process of evaluating the materials and in-
corporating them into the novel is a matter of individual technique.
The world of historical fiction is inhabited by people who
owe their existence solely to their author's skill and by those
who can claim some degree of historical authenticity. The latter
retain the names of historical personages, which conveniently
serves to distinguish them from fictional characters assumed to
be figments of the authors' imagination. In fact, however, they
all are fictional characters, whether or not some of them are
mentioned in historical documents or still have a tombstone mark-
ing the place where they were buried centuries ago. The difference, such as there is, consists in the artistic devices used in
their characterization. Otherwise, they are all mixed freely,
share the lifestyle of the period, are subject to the same laws
of history and fiction, and are involved in the same plot.
Fictional characters in Petrine novels are composite types
created to fit in with their historical counterparts, a *commedia
dell'arte* troupe. Peter's opposition—the boyars, Pushkin's
Lykov and Rzhevsky in *The Blackamoor of Peter the Great*, Zagoskin's
Prokudin in *The Russians in the Eighteenth Century*, Buynosov in
A. N. Tolstoy's *Peter the First*—allowing for differences in artistic value, belong to one traditional type. Their enlightened
sons—Peter's supporters—such as Yury German's Ivlyov in *Youthful
Russia*, or Danilevsky's Kasatkin in *To India in Peter's Times*, belong to another. Wicked elders (*starets*) who have escaped the
fierty death in Old Believers' settlements after having talked

their victims into taking this form of escape from Peter the Anti-christ—Mordovtsev's Yanuary, Zagoskin's Pafnuty, Merezhkovsky's Kornily, A. N. Tolstoy's Nektary—follow the same pattern, though Merezhkovsky volunteers the opinion that their motives were not always selfish: some escaped to continue their mission elsewhere.[5]

The resemblance typical fictional characters bear to their historical prototypes varies and is in direct proportion to the artistic skill of their creators. Though Kukolnik's dissatisfied boyars are interchangeable with those of Zagoskin or Masalsky, the grumbling voice of A. N. Tolstoy's Prince Buynosov can be distinguished in their monotonous chorus. His Sanka Brovkina does not resemble any of the cardboard "liberated women" in Petrine fiction: she is one of Tolstoy's charming contemporary heroines whose existence in the Petrine era is also possible and therefore, by the laws of historical fiction, plausible. She is Peter's contemporary as much as was, say, Marya Rumyantseva (née Matveeva), and she dances with the Tsar, shares his grief at Lefort's death, is married by him to a semihistorical character, Volkov, as naturally as if she and her life story had been recorded by *petite* and *grande histoire*, like Marya's. In fact, she is more real than Marya, because while fictional characters are simply created by the author, historical personages are interpreted by him, are reflected (sometimes distorted) in the mirror of his own personality —in short, they are *images*, and not necessarily valid ones.

Of course, historical personages as important to Peter's image as are Catherine, Menshikov, or Tsarevich Alexis have fully developed images of their own, often sharing with the Tsar the elements of duality and the grotesque in a mutual exchange of characteristics. In their cases, which will be fully discussed separately, data (however controversial) and anecdotes (however unreliable) are plentiful and authors have to use them with some discrimination. But historical personages of secondary importance are often treated as unceremoniously as are fictional characters. A few examples may be useful to make this point.

Afrosinya, Alexis's beloved mistress, who had accompanied him in his flight abroad and whose testimony at his trial proved to be the most damaging, emerges as a different person in each novel. In *Peter and Alexis* she is the red-headed "white she-devil," pregnant by Alexis, whom she hates for having raped her when she was a servant girl of Prince Vyazemsky—a detail Alexis had long forgotten. She takes pleasure in betraying his plans of treason to Peter. In Shild-kret's *The Eagle Cup*, except for a hint that she had poisoned Princess Charlotte in order to marry Alexis, her role is insignificant, and her fatal testimony can hardly be considered voluntary, since it was given on the rack. Polezhaev in *The Throne and the Cloister* (1881) makes her a goldenhaired beauty, reciprocating Alexis's love to the bitter end with the simple devotion of a serf girl; there is no mention of rape. Finally, Mordovtsev in *Realists and Idealists* (1878) is the most generous: his Afrosinya is not a serf at all, but a ward of Vyazemsky, beautiful and "pure like a dove," and dies (a suicide) a virgin, having refused to marry Alexis and lived abroad with him as a sister.

We have the word of Soloviev (*History*, VIII, 507) that
Tsarvena Natalya was Tsar Peter's favorite sister. The fact that
Peter, after banishing Evdokia, gave their son Alexis over to
Natalya's care and the affectionate tenor of his letter humor-
ously assuring her that "he is not going out of his way to meet
the bullets but cannot promise that they won't try to meet him"
seem to support this statement. She died unmarried, however, at
the age of forty-three, though Peter had been very active in arranging matches for his nieces, daughters, and mistresses (so
that his interest in matchmaking became a feature in his characterization). Natalya's role in fiction is insignificant, her
character indistinct. Merezhkovsky mentions her in Fräulein
Juliana's diary as "an old maid, the world's meanest creature"
(*P. & A.*, I, 93). Yet, Alexey Tolstoy, reportedly having studied
a miniature of her, not only describes her as a "full-bosomed,
pink-cheeked blonde, affable and merry" but even involves her, a
fairy-tale princess, in a chaste romance with a fictional character, Gavrila Brovkin. He remembers Natalya's interest in Western
theater and her efforts to introduce it in Russia, but not her
age, making her three years Peter's senior at the time of her
mother's death in 1694, and then allowing her to say in 1704 that
she is "only five years younger than dear brother Peter" (*P.F.*,
pp. 242 and 738). Actually, she was born eighteen months after
Peter, in 1673.

Most authors tend to cast Tsarevna Sophia as a villainess,
or at least as a power-mad, passionate, and vindictive woman.
There is, however, considerable disagreement as to her appearance.
Ivan Lazhechnikov, Zagoskin, and Vsevolod Soloviev call her
lovely[6]—after all, a tsarevna, whatever her shortcomings, is always beautiful in Russian folklore. Polezhaev cautiously remarks
that "she could not be considered beautiful since she was af-
flicted with scrofula" (though the affliction escaped the attention of historians). Shildkret calls her fat (she was), and A. N.
Tolstoy, plain. Leo Tolstoy, who strongly disapproved of sensuous
and self-willed women, refers to her as "ugly and profligate."[7]
Her liaison with Golitsyn and sometimes that with Shaklovity
figure prominently in Petrine fiction; Zotov in *The Mysterious
Monk* also makes her propose marriage to Golitsyn, to Prince
Khovansky, and even to her maternal uncle, Ivan Miloslavsky—all
married men. Kurakin does say that Sophia was "a princess of
great intellect," and Matveev, that she was "a maiden endowed
with excellency of mind and subtlety of understanding surpassing
those of a man,"[8] but she was Peter's archenemy, so naturally, in
novels set in his early years she is usually cast as a monster.
Moreover, she is considered responsible for Peter's convulsions
and possibly for his morbid suspiciousness; this could not but
adversely influence his image as an adult, as well as her own.

Strangely enough, Ibrahim (Abram Petrovich) Hannibal, a
colorful historical personality and one of Peter's "fledgelings,"
owes his fame in Russian literature only to Pushkin's *Blackamoor
of Peter the Great*. Hannibal was born in 1696, kidnapped by
slave-traders in 1703, and two years later brought to Russia as a

gift to Peter by one of his diplomats. Peter stood sponsor to
the little Negro, who thus owes the Tsar his names and the patronymic, and made him his page: Shklovsky, in one of his miniature
Novellas mentions Hannibal's keeping in readiness tablets for
Peter to make notes on in case of insomnia. He was eventually
sent abroad to study engineering, saw action with the French army,
and had a passably successful military and administrative career
after his return to Russia in 1723. His family life was rich in
scandals, including bigamy and white as well as mulatto children,
one of whom, Joseph, became the maternal grandfather of Alexander
Pushkin. Hannibal died in 1781. He is mentioned by A. N. Tolstoy
in a fictitious letter from Vinius to Peter abroad, dated April
1697: "The Negro Hannibal has quieted down, thank God, is no
longer chained to the wall, and is learning Russian" (*P.F.*, p.
291). Hannibal at that time would have been one year old and
still living happily in his native Africa, but as we know, Tolstoy
took liberties with unimportant dates. Hannibal's other appearance
in Petrine fiction is in Selvinsky's play *From Poltava to Gangut*
(1949). He is described as a youth of about fifteen (at the siege
of Poltava, in 1707, he would have been eleven) whose eyes are
"full of ineffable vivacity"; he is dressed in military uniform
and discourses (in verse) at Peter's side on the omen represented
by a field of blood-red poppies. Zagoskin's Prokudin in *Russians
at the Beginning of the XVIIIth Century* says bitterly: "I was
told that the Tsar found for his godson, some kind of a blackamoor, a noble and wealthy bride."[9] Fiction preferred to make no
reference to Hannibal's marital troubles, though they are fore-
shadowed in *The Blackamoor of Peter the Great*.
    The fewer the available data, the freer the handling of his-
torical personages. In the play just mentioned, Selvinsky also
introduced Peter's court jester, the engineer Ivan Balakirev,
whom, presumably for euphonic reasons, he names Dorimedont.
Selvinsky's Balakirev is slim, young (born in 1699, he would have
been very young indeed at the feast celebrating the victory at
Poltava in 1709), witty, and impudent. He gives much sound
though unsolicited advice to generals, Tsarevich Alexis, and Peter
himself. In another play, *Jester Balakirev* (1940) by Anatoly
Mariengof, set in 1723, he is still the honest, wise jester, this
time helping the Tsar to eradicate corruption among the bureaucrats, especially among the inspectors supervising tax collectors.
Balakirev accompanies Peter on his travels, making sure in advance that the houses where they stop for the night are free from
cockroaches because, in his words, "fools are afraid of snow-
storms, thieves of the Tsar, and the Tsar of cockroaches." (This
is one of the few references in fiction to Peter's strange idiosyncrasy, which will be discussed with the others later.) Actually, Balakirev is known only for his involvement in Catherine's
romance with Willim Mons—as a go-between, lavishly bribed for
his services. He was indeed a jester under four successive
sovereigns,[10] but his fictional reputation of unusual wit and
certainly that of honesty have no confirmation in historical
documents. Nevertheless, he has been quite a favorite with

novelists and cracks jokes in Fedorov's *The Demidovs* in 1941 just
as he used to in "The Black Casket" by Masalsky or in *The Last
Recruit* by Lazhechnikov, in 1833.

Data on another jester, Yakov Turgenev, are even scantier,
but he figures prominently in fiction, his role and person changing according to the needs of different authors in their characterization of Peter. He is created out of Kurakins' mentioning
him among other court jesters as "old, harmless, and feeble-
minded" and of Zhelabuzhsky's description of his wedding in
January 1694. The latter is famous in its own right, since it
became in Petrine fiction the prototype for all the bizarre,
clownish processions with which Peter liked to shock the populace.
The bride, according to Zhelabuzhsky, was the widow of a petty
clerk—and, three weeks after the wedding, also Turgenev's.[11]
A. N. Tolstoy supplies her with a name (*Shushera*, meaning
"rabble"), escessive makeup, and embonpoint. Kukolnik, in *The
Sentinel*, goes farther: she is Charlotte, a charming young Fräulein from the Foreign Quarter, and her bridegroom "Yasha Turgenev,"
a witty, dashing youth, the Tsar's trusted companion and jester;
the couple is understood to have lived long and happily ever
after. Shildkret in *Mamura* (1934) preceded the wedding with a
scene in which Peter, irritated by Evdokia's stolidity, vents his
rage on Turgenev by kicking the old man unconscious.

Historical personages scantily supported by documents have
always been considered fair game by fiction writers. Some of
them—usually cast in episodic roles—are created out of a mere
name, historical clay into which the artist's imagination breathed
life. Not every writer of historical fiction has that magic
power, but a few samples of its workings can be provided by
several characters of Alexey Tolstoy. Two of them were born out
of an entry in a list of names which Kurakin made in 1723 as "information on names needed in the History," the latter being *The
History of Tsar Peter Alekseevich*, which unfortunately remained
unfinished. One entry was "*pop* Bitka,"[12] the other simply
"Vytashchiv." In *Peter the First* "young *pop* Bitka, Peter's
drinking companion," is seen asleep in the ornate carriage of the
newlyweds Turgenev; in "Martha Rabe," with several other members
of the "most-crazy council," he accompanies Peter on a visit to
Menshikov, "shaggy, skinny, his eyes swollen, attired in a soiled
surplice." He mildly answers "amen" to the profane invocation
(part of the "most-crazy council" services) intoned by "an enormous glum man with prominent cheek-bones, dressed in a homespun
coat with silver braidings. The man had a wreath of leaves on
his close-cropped head and held in his arms a small barrel of
vodka. This was the notorious Stepan Vytashchi, who has been
[Peter says] drunk for the last six days."[13] This appearance
covers the entire span of the man's life in fiction: having
served as a detail in Peter's characterization in "Martha Rabe,"
Vytashchi, provided by Tolstoy with the first name which he lacked
in Kurakin's entry, returned to the ashes of historical oblivion.
He did not rise again in *Peter the First*.

The clay from which Varenoy Madamkin is created is Peter's

authentic letter to Apraxin during the Azov Campaign in 1694.
The letter (addressed, in *Peter the First* to Romodanovsky) advises
that Peter and his companions "lead a life of untiring martial
labors and drink your health in vodka and even more in beer."
Among the several practically illegible signatures are those of
"Petrushka Alexeev" and "Varenoy Madamkin" (p. 267). The latter
is, of course, a nickname; it translates roughly as "hardboiled
chaser of hussies," which is probably the reason for Peter's
vouching elsewhere in the novel for Madamkin's expertise in find-
ing camp followers for the officers' entertainment (p. 270). A
few pages later the reader meets him in person: "Preceding
Peter, who solemnly marched at the head of his company, gamboled a
huge man with a nose like a bear's and with thick lips, clashing
brass cymbals. This was the Tsar's new drinking companion, a
cymbalist answering to the name of Varenoy Madamkin, an unsur-
passed debauchee and a drunk" (p. 271). Before the end of the
Azov campaign Tolstoy had him "fall in an attack with his skull
shattered, a few paces from Peter" (p. 281). He had already
served his purpose.

Some names never become actual historical personages, remaining shadows, conjectures, but nevertheless a part of the plot.
Such is the unborn child of Alexis and Afrosinya, to whom they
referred by a pet name, "Seleblyany," in an exchange of letters
in 1717 (Ustryalov, *History*, VI, 422-25). At that time Alexis
had started with his captors, Peter Tolstoy and Rumyantsev, on
the fatal return journey to Russia, Afrosinya following at a
slower pace. It is known that upon her arrival Afrosinya testi-
fied against Alexis under torture and also in a confrontation
with him in Peter's presence, and that she gave birth while in
prison and was set free after Alexis's death. There are even
stories about her marrying later and of the Tsar's giving her a
dowry in recognition of her services at the trial, but no trace
remained of the child except that pet name in its parents' letters. For historical novelists the name sufficed.

Ivanov in his novel supplies a sentimental detail to the
fugitives' romance: "They had a costly fur-lined coverlet ready
for the arrival of Seleblyany" (p. 145). Merezhkovsky, on the
other hand, had Afrosinya assume a cynical attitude toward
Alexis's joyous hopes for his future son and heir.

> You are my golden one [Alexis says to her] and he [lisp-
> ing tenderly] he is going to be our silver baby
> [*Sel(r)ebl(r)yanyi*]. You will be the tsaritsa and Sel-
> eblyany the heir to the throne. . . . We will call him
> [Ivan] Vanichka, the most pious, most autocratic Tsar of
> All the Russias, Ioann Alexeevich. (*P. & A.*, II, 27.)

To this Afrosinya lazily reminds her lover that she is a
serf who has no earthly chance of becoming a tsaritsa—and continues to relish an unusually juicy peach.

The images of Alexis, Afrosinya, and Peter are sharply
etched in the powerful confrontation scene in which Afrosinya

repeats in Alexis's presence her testimony on his high treason.
When she leaves, kindly dismissed by Peter, the stunned Alexis
suddenly realizes that she is no longer pregnant and demands to
know what became of the child. Peter says curtly that the boy was
stillborn.

> The Tsarevich clasped his head in his hands. His face
> grew purple and distorted. He recalled the Tsar's custom
> of having stillborn babies preserved in alcohol, and send-
> ing them in jars to the Kunstkamera, with other "monstra."
> "In a jar! In a jar of alcohol. The heir of the
> Tsar of All the Russias is swimming in alcohol like a
> frog!" he shouted and suddenly burst into a laughter so
> wild that it made Peter shudder. Again he thought "This
> is a madman," and experienced the same feeling of revul-
> sion, the weird fear which he always felt at the sight
> of spiders, cockroaches, and other such vermin. (*P. & A.*,
> II, 202.)

There follow the scenes of Alexis's refusal to testify further and of the savage beatings he received which terrified the
whole palace and left both father and son on the threshold of
death, Peter having immediately afterwards suffered unusually
severe convulsions.

Merezhkovsky had more than his imagination to help him create
that scene. The Kunstkamera was a museum of arts and sciences
founded by Peter after his return from his second journey abroad.
Destined to become a grotesque mausoleum to his memory by housing
his mannequin, it has long fascinated anecdotists, historians,
and writers. Anecdotists like Stählin and Feoktistov treat it as
another proof of Peter's genius and of the wide range of his interests. But minor historians and memoirists like Dolgorukov,
Semevsky, and Mordovtsev reveal many a strange rumor about it,
which, in turn, are perpetrated in Petrine fiction. Two stories
figure prominently among these rumors. One is that after the executions of Marya Hamilton and Willim Mons, their heads, by
Peter's orders, were conveyed to the Kunstkamera as exhibits,
where they were eventually discovered in a cellar during the reign
of Catherine the Great, who had them buried. The other is that
exhibit No. 27, reputedly an excellently preserved head of a young
boy, was in fact the lovely head of Marya Hamilton.[14] Both versions were indignantly denied by Belyaev. There is still another
rumor, possibly started as an analogy to the historically documented fate of a fetus miscarried by the wife of Marshal Olsufiev
as a result of a large amount of pepper brandy she was forced to
drink at one of Peter's parties. This one asserts that Afrosinya's child died mysteriously at its birth in prison and, like
the Olsufiev baby, joined, in a jar of alcohol, the Kunstkamera's
collection of "monstra."[15] Tynyanov, in *The Waxen Effigy*, lists
Seleblyany as *"Pueri Caput No. 70."*

This head is yellow and solemn—that of a small child but

also like that of a petty Mongolian prince.   Its expression is peaceful, the heavy lips unsmiling.   He was
brought, this boy, from a cell in the Fortress of St.
Peter and Paul.   Which cell? Nobody knows.   How many
women were imprisoned there at that time?   Three.   And
the third one was a captive Finnish wench, Efrosinya
Fedorova by name.   She had been arrested in connection
with the trial of Peter's son, the Tsarevich Alexis.   She
was his mistress and also the one who betrayed him.   She
gave birth in the fortress.   So, does this mean the Pueri
Caput No. 70 is Peter's grandson?   Nobody knows anything
for sure about that.   He looks at everything from under
heavy eyelids, sullen, solemn like a petty Mongolian
prince, and squints as if the sunlight is bothering him.
(*Effigy*, p. 30.)

No other Petrine novel introduces Sebleblyany.   Historical personages created out of a shadow of a name did not appeal either
to nineteenth-century writers or to those writing under the rules
of Socialist Realism.

Still, history has a way of proliferating sensational rumors,
which, unchecked and unauthenticated, tend to persist and, finally,
to acquire a life of their own.   Such were the several stories of
miraculous survivals: that of Tsarevich Dmitry, which doomed
Boris Godunov and placed an impostor on the Russian throne; that
of Peter III, which gave its leader to Pugachev's mutiny; that of
Tsarevich Alexis, which stirred unrest at home and caused acute
embarrassment to Peter abroad.   There were also countless vague
rumors and conjectures about the deaths of Catherine I (allegedly
poisoned by Menshikov) and Alexander I (said to have died in old
age in Siberia, a hermit).   There are defamatory stories on the
birth of Peter I (allegedly son of Boyar Streshnev or of Patriarch
Nikon), Peter III (son of Colonel Baumer), and Paul I (son of
Count Saltykov, or even a Finnish baby hastily substituted for a
stillborn child of Catherine II).   Many other stories, just as
fantastic, originated in court gossip or in the imagination of an
embittered populace.   Because they had the appeal of human interest and of the sensational, some of these rumors found support among minor historians and attracted historical novelists.
Even a serious historian like Kostomarov produced *Kudeyar* (1875),
a novel about the adventures of a son of Ivan the Terrible born
in a convent to this tsar's estranged wife, Solomonida, forced to
take the veil some months earlier.   The story was completely implausible, since Ivan got rid of Solomonida precisely because she
was barren, and a son born shortly after her entering the convent
would have been welcomed as legitimate heir to the throne, even
while the mother would have had to have remained a nun.   But at
the time there were some such rumors, and Kostomarov used them
for his plot.

Some Petrine novels dispense not only with facts, or rumors,
but produce yarns and characters based on what may be termed lack
of negative evidence.   Thus, the mysterious Valdemar in

Lazhechnikov's *The Last Recruit* (1833) is revealed at the end of the novel to be a son of Tsarevna Sophia and Prince Golitsyn. It has not been proven historically that no child was born of that liaison, but it is known that Sophia's sisters had had several abortions—so, Lazhechnikov seems to imply, why not a Valdemar? In Danilevsky's novel *To India in Peter's Time*, Peter, faithful to the memory of his friend Lefort, is generous and kind to Lefort's daughter, his ward Dunya, a fictional character. Given Lefort's reputation, one can assume that he did have illegitimate offspring —so why not a Dunya? Probably the most ridiculous of all is the story of Grisha in Zotov's *The Mysterious Monk*. A foundling brought up in the home of Prince Ivan Khovansky, he is discovered to be not only the same noble Strelets who saved Peter from the assassin's knife at Trinity Monastery in 1689, but a grandson of Hetman Mazepa, son of his (fictional) daughter Elena and Hetman Doroshenko, who, when Elena married Prince Khovansky, became the mysterious monk of the title. Zotov does not make it clear whether Grisha was born out of wedlock or Elena had committed bigamy, but since readers did not expect historical accuracy in every detail, the novel in its time was a success.

Finally, some characters are completely fantastic. The best example is Xenia, the wife who, in Eustaphieve's play, accompanies Alexis in his flight abroad. Xenia was substituted for Afrosinya, the author explains,

> because my respect for the virtues of the sex, and deep,
> pleasing conviction of their excellency will never permit
> me to bring them before the public in the polluted garb
> of infamy; besides, by representing Xenia as a lawful
> character, I have gained for my tragedy the sympathy of
> love, the effusion of tenderness, the tears of repentance,
> and an instructive moral, [16]

—elements which he considers more important than historical accuracy.

While monarchs' appearances in historical fiction are limited, minor personages, whose claims to historical authenticity are often based on anecdote, freely associate with fictional characters and participate on equal terms in the plot. This is a legitimate device, since these personages serve to convey the spirit of the era and, having been unimportant in real life, can be used in the plot at the author's convenience.

For instance, young Konon Zotov, son of Peter's Prince-Pope Nikita, is in love with Danilevsky's fictional Dunya and polemicizes with Pilnyak's fictional priest in *Kneeb Piter*. Fedora Rodimitsa, the authentic faithful servant of Tsarevna Sophia, has a fictional daughter who befriends Lyuba, the heroine of Vsevolod Soloviev's *The Tsar Maiden* (1878). The historic Fedor Sklyaev, celebrating his return from Europe, became involved in a tavern brawl, was arrested, and was handled rather roughly by Romodanovsky. This story is known from Peter's angry letter demanding the immediate release of his "fledgeling," who was badly needed and

impatiently awaited in the shipyards.   There is an episode in
Peter the First in which Peter makes fun of the chastened and embarrassed Sklyaev, but Sklyaev proves to be better in shipbuilding
than Peter's highly paid foreign engineers—a favorite topic of
Soviet authors.   But Mordovtsev uses Sklyaev for a different purpose.   In *More Enlightenment* (1881) the young man rescues the fictional heroine, Fima, kidnapped by Old Believers, and marries her
with the blessing of Peter, who makes a short and timely appearance for that purpose and also makes a speech on the need for
"more enlightenment."

The three doctors Blumentrost, father and two sons—actual
historical personages—appear in most Petrine novels almost as one
composite character.   Lavrenty Blumentrost, a man with a German
medical diploma and an excellent reputation, became Tsar Alexis's
personal physician in 1668 and also served Fedor, Sophia, and
Peter in this capacity, until his death in 1705.   His sons,
Lavrenty, Jr., and Ivan, both born in Moscow, completed their
medical educations abroad at Peter's wish and on their return
long held similar positions with Peter and other members of the
royal family until their careers were ended by court intrigues
in the reign of Anna Ioannovna.   In Petrine fiction a Dr. Blumentrost treats not only Peter, Natalya, Tsarevich Alexis, and various court personalities, but is also summoned to the beds of fictional characters whenever medical help is needed.   This too is
a legitimate device, because while no author seems to know which
of the Blumentrosts he is using, one of them was sure to be around
at any given time and could plausibly be sent for.   Conversely,
in *Russians* Zagoskin entrusts to the protagonist, Simsky, the
farewell letter which Peter sent to the Senate from his besieged
camp at the Prut (Soloviev, incidentally, denies the authenticity
of the document [*History, VIII*, 388] but petite histoire and the
novelists accept this fine gesture as indicative of Peter's
statesmanship).

Similarly, we do not know whether James Bruce ever played
chess with Peter, but it is quite possible he did, so that such
a scene in *Peter and Alexis* raises no questions in the reader's
mind.   Nor do we question Bruce's befriending Tikhon, a fictional
character in the same novel who was orphaned as a child during
Peter's executions of the Streltsy and later became a victim of
cunning Old Believers.   In *The Blackamoor of Peter the Great* another Strelets orphan, Valeryan, is similarly befriended by Prince
Rzhevsky; he falls in love with Rzhevsky's daughter, Natalya, and she
with him, but her father would have opposed their marriage even if
Peter had not asked for Natalya's hand for his favorite, Ibrahim.
No seams show in the fabric of the plot where these eminently historical personages join the members of the fictional Rzhevsky
household: in the world of historical fiction all the inhabitants
breathe the same air and are subject to the same laws.   In the
hands of a master like Pushkin or A. N. Tolstoy, one cannot tell
them apart; in less inspired hands the fragile fabric of the plot
can be suddenly torn and the illusion of the whole cloth disappear.
The art of good historical fiction is subtle and demanding.

Another demand on the novelist's skill is the incorporation
of historical materials—documents, anecdotes, gossip—into the
world of fiction. Again, as in the case of historical personages,
it has to be done unobtrusively, so that no connecting seams are
visible. An anecdote should become a part of and develop with the
imaginary plot; a document has to be adroitly inserted into a
conversation or transformed into a scene. Petrine novels whose
atmosphere is permeated by Peter's actions, words, and personality
are especially dependent on this process. Mordovtsev and Masalsky,
who like to vouch for the authenticity of their documents in footnotes, or Zotov and Kukolnik, who, like a Greek chorus, inter-
polate the narrator's opinions into the plot, offer examples of
how the historical atmosphere should *not* be created in a novel.

Documents which are inserted verbatim or made into a scene
are almost without exception Peter's ukases and correspondence.
In *Peter the First*, Peter's impatient reading of letters from his
mother and his "unworthy wife Dunka," both timidly requesting his
return home, illustrates his growing estrangement from that home
and themselves. So does the scene of Evdokia's writing another of
these "unwanted little messages" blotted with tears she cannot
restrain. The ukase on submitting to the Kunstkamera any "living
or dead monstra" is used *in extenso* by Tynyanov and by Merezhkovsky; the ukase on the assemblies is read and commented upon by two
of Kukolnik's fictional characters, who wonder whether their rank
is high enough to gain admittance. The visit to the Foreign
Quarter by "Tsarevnas Katka and Mashka" in *Peter the First* is
lifted in its entirety from Soloviev's *History*, who has it from
Ustryalov. The letters between Peter and Alexis before the Tsarevich's flight abroad, as well as extensive excerpts from his
testimony during the trial, are introduced unchanged by Merezhkovsky, Pogodin, and Ivanov.

Anecdotes and rumors, though extensively used, are seldom, if
ever, directly inserted into the narrative. Instead, they are
usually introduced as episodic scenes, sometimes for the sake of
historical atmosphere but mainly, as will be shown in subsequent
chapters, because of their pertinence to Peter's image. They may
be transformed into complete stories: Kornilovich and Kukolnik
specialized in this literary form, reminiscent of animated car-
toons. To cite a few examples, Kornilovich's "God Remembers a
Prayer, the Tsar—Faithful Service" (1825) is an animation of
Nartov's anecdote (no. 37) on how the Tsar, posing as Peter
Mikhaylov, was hospitably received in the modest home of a retired soldier, whom he rewarded by giving his daughter a dowry and
her fiancé a promotion. In "Avdotya Likhonchikha" (1843) Kukolnik
tells how Peter, touched by the tears of the mother whose three
Streltsy sons had been sentenced to death, allowed her to choose
one son whom he would pardon, explaining that respect for law forbade him to pardon all three. This anecdote is from Golikov (no.
8) who, like Kukolnik, shares the mother's anguish but admires
Peter for such a stern yet humane decision. Kornilovich, in
Andrey the Nameless (1832), and Kukolnik, in "Kapustin," also
share a happier example of Peter's justice, the source of their

inspiration again being one of Golikov's anecdotes (no. 113).   It is a story, told with slightly differing details, of a young nobleman deprived, through a false accusation of illegitimacy, of his fiancée, his estate, and his very name; owing to the Tsar's astuteness in judicial matters, the hero is rehabilitated, and all his misfortunes become a thing of the past.

Anecdotes and rumors, the latter occasionally supported by documentary evidence or by historical analogy, may serve as the nuclei of purely fictional plots. Stälin's anecdote (no. 65) on a talented youth who is sent abroad by Peter to study and returns as an accomplished painter inspired Masalsky's mediocre yarn "The Black Casket" (1833), and is reflected in the appealing life story of Andryushka Golikov in *Peter the First*. *The Wedding Rebellion* by Salias de Turnemir has as its point of departure the false rumor of a ukase forcing all Russian girls to marry foreigners, which indeed resulted in hasty mass weddings in Astrakhan in 1705; Salias's fictional lovers took advantage of the rumor and obtained their reluctant parents' consent to their union. Soloviev (*History*, IX, 513) mentions Captain Vasily Levin, alias the monk Varlaam, mentally ill and an epileptic, who announced from a rooftop that Peter was the Antichrist, was arrested, and was executed in 1723. Basically following that outline, Mordovtsev, in his *Idealists and Realists*, endowed Levin with passionate allegiance to old Russia and to Tsarevich Alexis, and provided a fictional heroine, Xana, whom Levin rescued from drowning and fell in love with. When Peter orders Xana to marry his orderly Orlov, she takes the veil instead. This causes Levin to develop epilepsy and a paranoiac hatred of Peter, and to become a monk, dedicating his life to denouncing the Tsar-Antichrist and his reforms. He perishes at the stake, with Xana, now a nun, witnessing his death. Mordovtsev takes the liberty of giving Levin's decapitated body to the flames and sending his head in a jar of alcohol to the Kunstkamera, there to join other "monstra."

The Locks of Epifan (1927) by Andrey Platonov is built on a historical analogy. Captain John Perry, hired by Peter in London in 1698 to build a waterway, spent sixteen frustrating years on that task and, back in London, published a candid and highly uncomplimentary account of his experiences: *The State of Russia under the Present Tsar* (1716). Platonov's engineer, Bertrand Perry, a wholly fictional character, comes to Russia in 1709 to build a canal connecting the Don with the Oka. He fails to overcome the tremendous difficulties of work in Petrine Russia and finally meets with a catastrophe while building the locks at Epifan, for which Peter orders him executed. Platonov's style and the gory details of the unfortunate Perry's life and death are reminiscent of the prose of Pilnyak, Shildkret, and Kostylyov; and Platonov seems to share their antagonism to Peter. All the works discussed above are traditional Petrine fiction in their plots and characters, and in that their historical atmosphere is created by Peter's influence on conditions and events rather than by his personl participation. The Tsar grants one short audience to Perry in *The Locks of Epifan*, attends an "assembly" and the

execution of Marya Hamilton in *Idealists and Realists*, and does
not appear at all in the *Wedding Rebellion*. In this respect
Platonov's novella, modernistic and hostile, resembles the old-
fashioned and loyal novels by Zagoskin and Lazhechnikov, in which
Peter's image emerges not from his acts and personality but from
life in the Russia he is reforming.

Certain historic sayings reappear as leitmotifs throughout
Petrine fiction. Many of them are Peter's own, like his advice to
a protegé on how to win over an old-fashioned nobleman: "Contrive
to flatter his boyar vanity by leaving your carriage outside his
gate and walking to his house bareheaded"; or to a *petit maître*,
fresh from Paris: "See that these velvet pants of yours do not
cause an argument between us; I myself don't own anything so elegant, and after all, I am richer than you are." Both of these remarks, quoted by Golikov (*Anecdotes*, nos. 110, 120), were used by
Pushkin in *The Blackamoor of Peter the Great*, as was Neplyuev's
report on Peter's saying to him: "Look, I'm your tsar and yet
there are callouses on my hands."

Other phrases remained anonymous: "Petersburg will lie
waste" has become a symbol of discontent and unrest among the
populace. Still others are attributed in fiction to persons
other than the actual speakers. In *Peter and Alexis*, for example,
the Tsar, arriving at a party in ill humor and unable to control
one of his nervous tics, finds the room too hot and personally
forces open a window which had been nailed fast to keep out the
winter cold. This feat earns him a compliment from the suave
Austrian diplomat Pleyer: "Your Majesty has opened a window into
Europe." Actually, the famous sentence, which became part of
Peter's historic reputation, belongs to Count Algarotti, who used
it in his *Lettres du Comte Algarotti sur la Russie* in 1769, while
the episode is a historic one, reported by Bergholz.[17] It was
Peter himself, not Alyoshka Brovkin, as Tolstoy has it in *Peter
the First*, who refused to grant free passage to the wives of
officers in besieged Noteburg. Tsarevna Marya's rebuke to Alexis,
who said he dared not disobey the Tsar and visit Evdokia in her
convent—"A man should be willing to face hardships for his
mother's sake"—is quoted by Ivanov, Polezhaev, Merezhkovsky, and
Selvinsky, who, however, has it said by Evdokia's brother, Abram
Lopukhin.[18]

There is an entry in Prince Kurakin's *History* which both
A. N. Tolstoy and Merezhkovsky applied in the characterization of
different historical personages. Says Kurakin:

> During my stay [in Venice in 1708] I was *inamorato* with a
> certain *cittadina*, Francesca Rota, famous for her comeli-
> ness (*khoroshestvo*), whom I had for my mistress. And I
> was so *inamorato* that I could not spend an hour away from
> her, who cost me in these two months 1,000 ducats. And I
> parted from her with greatest sorrow and tears, and even
> today this *amor* will not leave my heart, and I doubt it
> ever will. (*History*, p. 78.)

In *Peter the First*, having dispatched Yaguzhinsky to bring
the pretty captive Livonian girl he had seen in the camp after
Marienburg had been taken that morning, the elderly Field Marshal
Sheremetev

> sighed and shook his head. What could one do? There was
> no way to live without sinning, no escape from it. In
> Naples back in 1697, a slip of a girl, a little black-
> haired thing, had won his heart completely, unmercifully.
> He had climbed Vesuvius and looked down into the fires
> of hell, scaled the terrible rocks of Capri Island, visited
> the pagan temples of the Roman gods, thoroughly inspected
> Catholic monasteries. . . . [saw] many other astonishing
> and wonderful things. Nothing mattered except that bright-
> eyes chit Julia, singing, dancing with a tambourine. He
> wanted to take her back with him to Moscow and grovelled
> at the wench's feet. Oh dear Lord! Oh dear. (pp. 593-
> 94.)

In *Peter and Alexis*, at a garden party, surrounded by ladies,

> Peter Andreevich Tolstoy opened a mother-of-pearl snuff-
> box. . . . offered it to pretty Princess Cherkasskaya,
> took a pinch himself, and said with a languid sigh, "Dur-
> ing my stay in Naples—how well I remember it!—I was
> *inamorato* with a certain *cittadina*, Francesca, famous for
> her comeliness. She cost me more than 2,000 ducats. This
> *amor* still refuses to leave my heart." . . . Tolstoy was
> seventy but did not look over fifty, being robust and
> vigorous. He had charming ways with the ladies. . . . Vel-
> vety softness of movements, voice, and smile; velvety,
> thick, black eyebrows (dyed according to some). . . .
> Still, Peter himself, not given to caution in dealing with
> his "fledgelings," maintained that with Tolstoy you had
> better keep a rock—hidden but handy. (*P. & A.*, I, 24.)

The snuffbox, the velvety speech and eyebrows, and the cold
astuteness are also noted in *Peter the First* during Peter Andre-
evich Tolstoy's only appearance: they are part of his established
characterization as a historical personage in Petrine fiction.
It was Merezhkovsky's and A. N. Tolstoy's authorial right to use
Kurakin's reminiscences for the psychological makeup of two of
his contemporaries: all three were typical Russian aristocrats
of their time and so was the language of his entry.
    This language, spoken by Peter's entourage in the later years
of his reign—by courtiers and diplomats, men as sophisticated
and traveled as any of their European counterparts—is a pre-
requisite in Petrine fiction, as indispensable as their wigs,
snuffboxes, and high-heeled shoes. Its rendition is the artistic
touchstone of a Russian historical novelist and a nightmare for
a translator. It lends itself easily to caricature, either for
grotesque effect, as by Pilnyak or Tynyanov, or for ridicule, as

by Zagoskin or Yury German. It is the vernacular of eighteenth-century Russia, spoken alike at court or in the village *until* Peter's return from his first European journey. We cannot attempt here to follow its subsequent development in modern Russian. For the purposes of this study it suffices to emphasize the linguistic impact of technical terms brought about by Peter's wars and the reforms they necessitated.

Foreign specialists—army officers and sailors, architects and engineers, mechanics and carpenters—had to be brought to backward Russia at considerable expense until they could be replaced by the Russians whom Peter had sent to be trained abroad. There is an apocryphal and much quoted statement by Peter in that matter: "We need Europe for a few decades, after which we can turn our backs on her."[19] Peter lived to see his hope realized, but in the meantime, Russian was assimilating Dutch, German, and English words, distorted and Russianized, creating a mélange incomprehensible to most of his subjects. The language of the newly developing educated class and that of science, scholarship, and bureaucracy fared no better. Translators of medical and mathematical books and of Puffendorf's *History* (translated from Latin in 1718 and about the only book to be found in the world of Petrine historical fiction) discovered that the Russian language simply had no words into which these books could be translated and that unless they created their own approximations of foreign terms, their task was impossible. Since Peter did not recognize the existence of impossible tasks if they had been ordered by him (one unfortunate translator committed suicide rather than face the Tsar's anger), new words were created. Peter's own contribution to the modernization of Russian culture was significant: he personally designed a simplified Russian alphabet modifying and replacing the Church Slavonic characters in use until his time.

Of the young Russians sent abroad to study, many learned only "to drink, smoke a pipe, and play the bassoon," like the navigator whose frank admission earned him the amused Peter's pardon and a nickname of Prince-Bassoon. Many became what they imagined to be *petits-maîtres* and also acquired a smattering of Italian and French; still others really learned a foreign language, as, of course, did the Tolstoys, the Kurakins, and the growing contingent of Russian envoys to the foreign courts. Nevertheless, all of them contributed to the formation of that strange new language which was spoken by Peter's "fledgelings" and which provoked the shocked disapproval of Peter's opposition.

Efforts of less talented novelists to reproduce this language as part of the historical atmosphere, other than in ridiculing the native *petits-maîtres*, are always failures, sometimes amusing ones. Peter's letter to Baroness Segevold in Lazhechnikov's *The Last Recruit* is a fair sample:

> Min Frau! I, *Caesar* and Colonel of the Russian Guards undertook to be the matchmaker on behalf of Captain Gustav Traufetter. He likes your daughter, she likes him, so

what else is needed?   Please do not have any *pretensie*.
As her dowry I give her all your Livonian estates which
you have lost in the war, and allow you to manage them
till your death.   In time I promise you and your son-in-
law my special attention as Tsar.   In our common interest
I allow you to correspond with me directly in matters
concerning your Fatherland; for good news I will be always *reconaissant* to you.   As a wedding present, I give
you a snuffbox with my *persona* and 1,000 rubles.   I sup-
pose I have tolerably contented you, so why should you
be obstinate any longer?

> Piter.
>
> (*The Last Recruit*, p. 525).

A few writers find it necessary to support samples of such style
with footnotes, explaining that these are, at least in part, excerpts from historical documents; Mordovtsev, for instance, does
so in *The Crowned Carpenter* (p. 81).   Otherwise, it is apparently
assumed that a sprinkling of the Russian equivalents of "prithee,"
"tush," "marry," and "methinks" will suffice to recreate the
genuine historical atmosphere of the era.   Generally though,
Petrine novels (modernists' works excepted) are narrated in the
language of the period of their writing, from Pushkin's *The Blackamoor of Peter the Great*, begun barely a hundred years after Peter's
death, to Merezhkovsky's *Peter and Alexis*, published about the
two hundredth anniversary of the victory at Narva.   Soviet writers, being under the obligation of interpreting any era as a
Marxist stage of historical development and remembering the limited
vocabulary of the laboring masses for whose education they write,
use practically the same style in contemporary as in historical
fiction.   A. N. Tolstoy achieves a polyphonic effect in *Peter the
First* by constant shifting of the point of view: one can *hear*
Peter's voice barking orders and his wooden laughter, Evdokia's
nagging, and the mincing accents of Anna Mons.   For purposes of
archaization he finds eighteenth-century expressions in their contemporary sources: correspondence and diplomatic papers for gems
of the new court lingo, protocols of the Secret Chancellery for
the speech of old-fashioned nobility and the populace.   The nar-
ration is couched in the language of Tolstoy's own childhood,
both that of the educated class and that spoken by the peasantry,
who, in language as well as in customs, had preserved intact many
characteristics of the pre-Petrine era.

The narrator in Russian historical novels is omniscient and
omnipresent, relating what he sees and occasionally even intruding
with his commentary into the plot.   He is a storyteller, here
more than in any other fictional genre, since he speaks in the
reader's immediate present from out of a distant past.   The narrative proceeds along a simple temporal line with an occasional
explanatory flashback.   For example, Ivanov's Peter reminiscing
about his early years in the dead of the night and Merezhkovsky's
Alexis dreaming of his childhood serve to clarify the events leading to the Tsarevich's trial and death.   This device is not used

by A. N. Tolstoy: *Peter the First* is like a river, and rivers do
not flow backwards. Cautious intrusions into the future are made
—cautious because the author has to camouflage his foreknowledge
of historical events and tries to make the reader forget his. In
Peter the First Tsarevna Natalya says in 1705 that she will, if
necessary, send dragoons to bring the audience to her projected
theater (p. 633); she did not, but anticipates by analogy similar
measures taken by Peter in 1717 to ensure the attendance of the
"assemblies." In *Peter and Alexis* (I, 33) everyone shouts, "'Long
live Peter the Great, Father of the Fatherland, Emperor of All the
Russias!' lifting up glasses of Hungarian wine. The title, not
yet announced in Europe or even in Russia, was already in use
among Peter's fledgelings." Indeed, the title was granted to
Peter by his Senate in 1721, but the toast, made in 1715, stresses
the servility of the Tsar's entourage and his enjoyment of it.
Hence the need for Merezhkovsky's remark absolving himself from
chronological inaccuracy.

Merezhkovsky takes the same precaution in the case of the
sacrilegious behavior of Alexis's confessor, who reports to Peter
the details of the Tsarevich's flight revealed during a confession. Historically, Alexis broke down at the trial and revealed
everything, implicating himself and scores of others. The ukase
concerning matters of high treason was issued only in 1722, four
years after Alexis's trial and death;[20] thus Merezhkovsky had to
make Peter Tolstoy read to Alexis at the time of the trial in
1718 "the ukase, still secret but later made public at the time
of the establishment of the Most Holy Synod" (*P. & A.*, II, 114).
The impact on the pious Alexis of the Tsar's duplicity shown by
this blasphemous act serves to emphasize the depth of the rift between the father and the son and offsets their contrasting images.

Mordovtsev hints at the inevitability of that tragedy by
making Alexis at the age of five express his desire to retire to
a monastery and at the age of thirteen say contemptuously, "What
do I care for a throne!" Lazhechnikov's dwarf jester angrily
tells the giant Bourgeois that he will end as a stuffed "monstrum"
in the Kunstkamera (he did). Danilevsky and Merezhkovsky arouse
Peter's suspicions of a romance between Catherine and Mons in
1717, which, besides being seven years too soon historically, is
completely implausible psychologically: no man was ever less
likely to act as *mari complaisant* than Peter. Zagoskin's boyars
Kurodavlev and Buynosov discuss the changes which Tsar Peter, at the
time aged ten, is going to introduce in Russia when he grows up.[21]

There are outright prophecies. Yaguzhinsky foretells as
early as 1704 the ukase of 1716 changing the law of succession in
Russia because he overhears Peter saying that he hopes for a son
by Catherine who would take the place of "that sludge, Alexis."
How terrible, he muses, will be the struggle of these two forces,
those of the Crowned Wrath and the opposition backing Alexis
(*The Crowned Carpenter*, p. 134). Merezhkovsky's prophecy is the
strangest, and he makes it twice: both the Old Believer Dokukin
and the Tsarevich, each at the hour of his impending death, warn
Peter not to execute Alexis.

You will be the first to shed the blood of your son, the
blood of the Russian tsars, on the scaffold [says Alexis]
and that blood will fall on the heads of all the future
tsars down to the last one, and our family will perish in
blood. Because of you, God will punish Russia! (*P. & A.*,
II, 209-10).

The liberties authors take with chronology occur too often
to be listed, but a few of the more obvious may be pointed out.
In *Peter and Alexis* Alexis reminisces about the pageant for the
Azov Campaign of 1696, at which Tsaritsa Natalya is present, "a
little old woman with a deeply lined face, sitting in a gilded
coach." Actually, she probably would have looked better at forty-
four had she not died two years earlier. She is also present
when Peter banishes Evdokia in 1698 (*P. & A.*, I, 230, 235). Peter,
attending the dwarf's funeral procession in 1724, has in his pocket
Peter Tolstoy's letter announcing Tsarevich Alexis's arrival in
Russia: the letter is authentic, dated October 3, 1717, but at
the time of the dwarf's funeral, Alexis had been dead for six
years. In Kukolnik's "The New Year" the Tsar marries his favorite
orderly Rymyantsev to Marya Matveeva, who, born in 1698, would
have been two years old on that New Year's Day, 1700. In A. N.
Tolstoy's *Peter's Day* the day described is evidently March 18,
1722, the date Varlaam was arrested for announcing the coming of
the Antichrist; moreover, Peter Tolstoy, who is in charge of the
Secret Chancellery (he was since 1717), mentions the rumor of the
apparition (*kikimora*) in the church belfry, which was said to have
occurred in the same year, and St. Petersburg is already a growing capital. Yet, Franz Lefort, dead in 1699, is leading the
dances at the assembly at Menshikov's, attended by Peter between
investigations in the torture chamber. In *Peter the First*, Varlaam is arrested for the same offense in 1703; and Peter sends
sundry "monstra" from Europe in 1697, though historically he
started buying them on his second journey in 1717.

The reader is unlikely to notice such small chronological dis-
crepancies, and in A. N. Tolstoy's opinion, a writer not only may
but *should* feel free to adjust unimportant dates to the demands of
his plot or characterization. A special case can be made for con-
tractions in time in order to give a telescopic view of a character.
Fraülein Juliana's fictional diary, written between 1716 and 1717,
includes, in the opening chapters of *Peter and Alexis*, anecdotes and
sundry historical events from both before and after these dates.
Merezhkovsky's purpose here is not to use the diary as a device
in the plot development but from the start to create Peter's awesome image in the reader's mind. The outcome of the conflict
between the superhuman will of the Tsar and the all-too-human
weakness of Alexis thus becomes as inevitable as is the shatter-
ing of a fragile object thrown against a stone wall. The same
technique is used in Pilnyak's *His Majesty Kneeb Piter Komondor*
and in A. N. Tolstoy's *Peter's Day* (1918); both authors, intent on
the portraiture of Peter, mix their paints out of any serviceable
material and are unconcerned about chronological accuracy.

A. N. Tolstoy, however, alone among the authors of "historical chronicles," deliberately shows the flow and the passage of
time. *Peter the First* is a novel about change: Peter is the
force changing Old Russia and is himself being changed in the
process, growing up, becoming a statesman. The pace of events is
uneven, determined by their relevance to the creation of Peter's
image. Some scenes—Peter's meeting abroad with Kurfürst Friedrich, for instance—are recorded in minute detail; but a whole
year out of that European journey is condensed into two pages of
excerpts from the Tsar's correspondence with Romodanovsky. Fictional and historical characters are carried along the flowing
stream of time, their lives and personalities subtly changed at
each of their reappearances at Peter's side: they have no existence independent of Peter's characterization. Members of the
fictional Brovkin family make fairy-tale careers, but these are
no more fantastic than the real-life career of Menshikov, which
is shown developing parallel to theirs. The glories of the
princely house of the Buynosovs dwindle into poverty and ridicule. Andryushka Golikov's thorny path of physical and spiritual
starvation leads through the Old Believers' hermitage, army camps,
the barracks of St. Petersburg workmen to—by the grace of an omnipotent Tsar—the miracle of a painter's career. Tsaritsa
Natalya, old friends like Lefort and Gordon, and enemies like Ivan
Miloslavsky and Tsarevna Sophia die. Evdokia is replaced by
Peter's side by Anna Mons; Anna, in turn, by Catherine. Even the
ignoble story of the episodic character Mishka Tyrtov is traced
from his frustrated existence as an impecunious young squire to
highway robbery to the gallows. Nothing is forgotten or swept
away, but nothing stays the same. Within the changeable fortunes
of Peter's wars, battles are lost, then won. Icy winds sweep
over ruined, exhausted Russia and over peasants starving in their
dark huts as they have for centuries. Yet a fresh breeze blows
from the newly conquered outlet to the sea, St. Petersburg rises
from the marshes, life has been changed, and goes on changing.
What else matters to Peter, who lives only in the present, looking
to the future?

There is one brief moment in the novel in which Peter returns to the past, led from the side of their mother's deathbed
by his sister Natalya to her own little room (*svetelka*) upstairs.

> Peter sat down by the small window with the multicolored
> panes. Nothing had changed here since the days of their
> childhood. There were the same little coffers and rugs;
> silver, glass, and stone animals on the shelves; a small
> heart-shaped mirror in a Venetian frame; colored prints
> from the Scriptures; and shells from foreign lands.
> "Natasha," he said in a low voice, "where is that Turk,
> remember? The one with terrible eyes whose head had
> been broken off?" Natalya Alexeevna thought a little,
> then opened a little coffer, and from its bottom
> brought up the Turk and his head. She showed it to
> her brother, and her eyebrows quivered. She sat down

at his side, embraced him, and they wept together.
(*P.F.*, p. 243.)

The night of his mother's death was the last Peter spent in the old Kremlin—and the last in the past.

Part II

6.   The Bronze Statue
and the Waxen Effigy

> I take a piece of life, meager and coarse, and out of it
> create an exquisite legend. For I am a poet.
>   Sologub, *The Created Legend*

> He's awesome in his misty shroud.
> What thoughts conceals his brow so proud?
> What ruthless force in him is bound?
> His horse is fire, daring, speed—
> Where dost thou gallop, noble steed
> And where thy hooves will touch the ground?
> Oh, Fate's own lord, to power wed!
> 'Tis thus that Russia, slow and idle
> Was, jerked by thee with iron bridle,
> Across the chasm of future sped.
>   Pushkin, *The Bronze Horseman*

In this study both the fictional characters and the historical
personages of Petrine fiction are treated as a collective *homo
historicus* of that era, contemporaries who experienced the impact
of Peter's personality, shared in events which were to influence
his image, and became part of that image themselves. It was impossible for them to put their tsar's gigantic goals in perspective: they were standing too near him. Unlike historians, who
perceive in Peter mainly the greatness of a statesman, these contemporaries, along with writers of the petite histoire and of fiction, see first of all the peculiarities in his personality and
behavior. These were striking and numerous enough to secure
Peter a unique popularity in Russian fiction comparable only to
but not equalled by that of Ivan the Terrible.
    The peculiarities include Peter's physique—his giant height
and enormous strength, his handsome features distorted by nervous
grimaces—as well as his restlessness and inexhaustible energy.

The Bronze Horseman. *Monument of Peter
the Great by Falconet, 1782.*

The Waxen Effigy of Peter the Great.   *By Rastrelli, 1725.*

He had an insatiable inquisitiveness, eccentricities at times
dangerously bordering on insanity, strong phobias, and outbursts
of rage alternating with manifestations of benevolence and
exuberant merriment. He was equally capable of exquisite cruelty
and endearing kindliness, of magnanimity and pettiness. His
genius as statesman was beyond doubt to both friends and enemies,
as was the brilliance of his intellect, yet his amusements were
both coarse and childish. The grandiosity of his undertakings
was in sharp contrast with the simplicity of his tastes and habits.
He appeared to be simultaneously apocalyptic and divine: he was
strange, incomprehensible.

Thus, while to historians he became for better or worse Peter
the Great, the Reformer of Old Russia, his portrayal in fiction
isolated the elements of duality—a Dr. Jekyll and Mr. Hyde syndrome—the monumentality and the grotesque. Pushkin, the greatest
of Russian poets, conceives of the Tsar as a symbol of triumphant
autocracy: a fearless ruthless rider case in bronze, a demi-god
reigning in subjugated Russia on the brink of a future known to
him alone. A century later, a distinguished historical novelist
Tynyanov, viewed Peter's life work as futile, and him as a waxen
effigy, a mannequin enthroned in the Kunstkamera, the museum of
oddities and monstrosities he founded in 1714. Tynyanov is ex-
plicit: after Peter's death his reverential heirs tried to find
a suitable place for the Tsar's sculptured *persona*. Finally, "it
became obvious: yes, he should be installed with other 'monstra'
in the Kunstkamera as an object exceptional, intricate, and extremely rare from the viewpoint of the arts as well as of statesmanship. It was there that he belonged."[1]

The equestrian monument of Peter the Great in St. Petersburg
is the work of Ernest Falconet. The sculptor in correspondence
with his friend, Diderot, and his employer, Catherine II, left no
doubt as to the symbolism of the statue, but he rejected the additional allegoric adornments in vogue in that century, insisting
that "Peter the Great is in himself a subject and his own symbol."
The horseman's clothing, draped loosely about his body, has a
short mantle about the shoulders—in Falconet's words it is "a
heroic attire, belonging to all nations, all men, and all times."[2]
He has a sword at his belt, a bearskin for a saddle, and wears a
laurel wreath on the abundant locks of his proud head. Models
for the head were several portraits and the mask made in 1719 by
Carlo Rastrelli for a bust the Tsar had ordered. Peter's im-
perious, piercing gaze is turned toward the Neva, conquered but
rebellious, forever threatening the city with disastrous floods.
His right arm is outstretched in a masterful gesture, while with
his left hand, firm but relaxed, he reins in his mount. The
steed, rearing at the edge of a cliff, is trampling a serpent
with his hind hoofs. The base of the monument is a rock carved
out of a huge meteorite. Twenty-seven feet tall and weighing
fifteen hundred tons, the meteorite was, with tremendous difficulty, brought by land and water from a bog in Finland. It was
known as the Thunderstone because it had been struck by lightning.

The monument was unveiled in 1782 in the presence of the
Empress, her court, and enthusiastic crowds amidst celebrations
including fireworks, gun salutes, and a military parade. A contemporary writes:

> Let me guess the ideas which guided the sculptor of this
> image of Peter the Great. The steep rock represents the
> obstacles Peter overcame in achieving his goals; the ser-
> pent in his path—cunning and malice seeking his death in
> revenge for establishing the new order. The ancient at-
> tire, the bearskin, and the simplicity of form of the
> horse and the rider symbolize the coarse ways and ig-
> norance Peter had found in his people whom he strove to
> enlighten; his head is crowned with laurels because he
> was a conqueror before he became a lawgiver; his form is
> manly, powerful, and strong—that of a Reformer . . . and
> the outstretched arm shows that the great man, having
> eradicated the vices frustrating his efforts, now offers
> protection to all those worthy of being called his chil-
> dren.[3]

The monument's aura does not substantially change with the
passage of time:

> Almost at the foot of St. Isaac's Cathedral, on the square
> enclosed on two sides by the calm, lofty buildings of the
> Admiralty, the Synod, and the Senate, washed on the third
> side by the majestic Neva, stands the monument of Peter
> the Great erected by Catherine the Second: *Petro Primo
> Catharina Secunda*. Should one happen to be near the monu-
> ment on an inclement autumn evening, when the chaotic sky
> descends toward the turbulent earth, the granite-
> imprisoned river groans and tosses, and buildings seem to
> stir in the uncertain lights of wind-swept lanterns—then
> let him look at the Bronze Horseman, that fire transformed
> into metal, its outlines sharply thrust against the sky.
> What power, passionate and stormy, will be revealed to
> the visitor, beckoning him into the unknown? What great
> power will overwhelm him, what troubling question will
> arise in his mind, what promise does the future hold?
> Will it be victory or the abyss of perdition? The Bronze
> Horseman is the *genus loci* of Petersburg.[4]

Just as the statue of Pushkin's Bronze Horseman still towers
over Leningrad as the Tsar did over the St. Petersburg he had
created, so Tynyanov's waxen effigy, as of this writing, is still
on exhibit at the Leningrad State Museum, the *Hermitage*. Peter
himself had ordered this posthumous mannequin to Rastrelli. Waxen
effigies were unknown in pre-Petrine Russia, where human statues,
even those of saints, were considered "graven images" forbidden by
the First Commandment. They had been, however, quite customary
in Europe since the Middle Ages, and Peter almost certainly saw

some of them in museums during his second journey abroad.[5] The
mannequin of Henry IV of France, standing dressed according to the
latest fashions of his period, was later destroyed, along with
several other such royal statues, during the French Revolution;
the mannequin of Friedrich of Prussia, enthroned with all his re-
galia in Castle "Mon Bijou," is mentioned by Bergholz in his *Diary*
in 1721, and is still in existence.

Peter's mannequin has his waxen postmortem mask for face, a
wig made of his own hair, and wears the only costly costume that
this tsar ever owned: a coat of grosgrain blue silk embroidered
with silver sequins by his wife and resoled shoes of cheap, coarse
leather. According to an anecdote, Peter personally bought these
shoes at the market with the money he had earned forging a piece
of iron at the newly established Olonets foundries in 1724, a few
months before his death. They were chosen as part of the effigy's
costume as an emblem of his love of work and thrift.

Osip Belyaev, longtime custodian of the Kunstkamera, where
the waxen effigy was transferred in 1732, describes it in his
Cabinet of Peter the Great (1793) as seated in an armchair on a
platform under a canopy of crimson velvet with golden braid. On
both sides of the platform are glass cabinets preserving for posterity (and for historical fiction) Peter's green military uniform, his leather coat, and the tricorne pierced by a bullet
at the Battle of Poltava. Nineteenth-century novelists did not
seem to notice in the cabinets some of the other items less suitable for the Hero's image; Merezhkovsky in *Peter and Alexis* is
the first to show Peter wearing the rough blue cloth trousers,
the grey socks darned with black and yellow wool, the round
steel-mounted glasses, and the white cotton nightcap with a green
silk tassel. And Alexis remembers how, as a child, ". . . playing
with this tassel he once happened to tear it off, but Father did
not get angry at that time; interrupting the writing of a ukase,
he immediately stitched the tassel to the nightcap with his own
hands."[6]

In Belyaev's time, beside the cabinets surrounding the effigy, there were stuffed animals—two pet dogs, a parrot, the
horse Peter rode at Poltava—and stuffed humans—the giant French-
man Bourgeois and a Russian peasant, Foma, a dwarf with two toes
and two fingers on each limb.[7] There were also jars containing
numerous human fetuses and a severed head, all preserved in alcohol. The free use made by fiction of all these "rarities" was
discussed in the previous chapter. There are also collections of
medals, apothecary's instruments, and a lathe (working wood and
ivory was Peter's favorite hobby). "Many etchings, instruments,
tools and artifacts, that used to belong to an active man of many
skills, a hard worker,"[8] are charitably noticed in 1785 by
Shklovsky's fictional visitor at the Kunstkamera. A brass nail is
driven into a door frame seven feet above the floor, the exact
height of the late tsar.

The waxen effigy stares out of wide-open eyes made of gold
leaf; the lips are closed in repose; the features preserve the
last moribund swelling, reproduced by the postmortem mask. Belyaev

maintains that "the face expresses dignity, severity, mercy, and
solicitude." Tynyanov, describing Rastrelli at work on this mask,
sees it differently:

> . . . the artist stroked the spasm with his warm finger,
> and the mouth became as it used to be in life: a proud
> mouth denoting thought and knowledge, lips revealing
> spirit and glory. He rubbed the steep brow, the muscle by
> the temple, as one does to relieve a headache in a living
> man, and rubbed away the thick vein sprung of anger, but
> still the brow did not express friendliness, just obstinacy
> and perseverance. He bent further the curve of the wide
> short nose, and the nose became sensitive as though sniff-
> ing the path of the attainment of excellence . . . the
> head grew heavy as if thoughts were being poured into it
> instead of wax. "No anger"—said the Master—"no joy, no
> smile. . . . He seems to be listening to the blood which
> is pressing on him, strangling him, from deep inside."
> . . . There was something like fear in the corners
> of the mouth, and the Master did not attempt to rub it away.
> (*Effigy*, nos. 2, 11.)

Tynyanov's novella *The Waxen Effigy* has an unusual plot in
which the protagonist is not only dying but dead; it also contains
most of the grotesque elements in Peter's characterization. It
seems needless to discuss here the controversial definitions of
the grotesque as a genre, but it is legitimate, in fact necessary,
to point out how its basic features relate to the image of Peter
the Great created by Russian historical fiction.

The image has strong elements of the mysterious, the supernatural, and the absurd, which causes a displacement of the levels
of fantasy and reality. It has the spiritual and physical dis-
harmony of a *sensed* genius and a *perceived* absurdity of deport-
ment. There is also present a degree of dehumanization, sometimes
animalistic, typical for a grotesque object. For example, the
Tsar, with his round face, bristling moustache, and cruelty, is
often compared to an enormous cat, the favorite devil's familiar
of Russian fiction. "A black cat, a changeling (*oboroten'*), jumped
on the Tsarevich's neck and began to strangle him, its fangs
scratching his heart," says Merezhkovsky, in *Peter and Alexis*
(II, 217). The grotesque aspect of the image is also enhanced by
Peter's convulsions, nervous tics, and precipitous gait—the
mechanical movements of a human figure manipulated ("possessed")
by external forces. "The devil twists him," said his subjects;
and in *The Waxen Effigy* the mannequin rises to greet one of his
living "monstra" and to banish his former favorite, Yaguzhinsky,
from his presence. [9]

The gargoyles and chimeras on the outside of Gothic churches
symbolize the evil spirits expelled by the Holy Ghost from the inside, which is graced by statues of martyrs and saints—the duality
of negative and positive counterparts of the same image. These
grotesque monsters, abstract yet palpable, frightening yet

ludicrous, their features dehumanized though not completely animal, were meant to evoke a mystical, eerie fear similar to that
which saturates the atmosphere of *Peter and Alexis*. That fear is
an integral part of Peter's image, as is the "paradise" he raised
on a marshy island, the fog-enshrouded St. Petersburg, Russia's
first Baltic port and powerful bastion, the mirage city of Russian
literature. The fear generated by Peter's presence is not, however, always grotesque; its varieties will be discussed at some
length later. He did inspire awe as well—an admiring, respectful awe—by the very same qualities of strangeness, incongruity,
and supernatural power. And this too is reflected in his image.
Contemporaries and nineteenth-century authors alike bestowed on
him the titles of Father of the Fatherland, Crowned Wrath, and
Fate's Powerful Master. Soviet authors, impervious to things
mystical and wary of imperial greatness (witness the title chosen
by Alexey Tolstoy—*Peter the First*), acknowledge in his representation statesmanship and love of work, but neither awe nor
fear. They dismiss strangeness: are not all persons in some way
eccentric?

Soon after the Revolution, during the short no-man's-land
period in Russian literature, appeared two novellas: Boris
Pilnyak's *His Majesty Kneeb Piter Komondor* (1919) and *Peter's Day*
(1918) by A. N. Tolstoy. Unusual in technique, these telescopic
portrayals of Peter the man were also novel in their attitudes
toward Peter the Great. In an agglomeration of behavioral and
physical details most of which tsarist censors had never allowed
to be made public, in a foreshortened view of the events of his
whole reign completely disregarding chronology, the novellas
presented a startlingly new tsar: a spiritual and physical caricature. Pilnyak saw a grotesque monster, a madman, on the throne:
A. N. Tolstoy, still a decade away from writing *Peter the First*,
was no less abusive but noted, in fact stressed, the impossible
burden of state carried by that lonely, coarse, and terrifying
autocrat.

This sudden attack on the image of the Reformer coming from
the camp of historical fiction (seldom a favorite with scholars)
provoked an angry rebuttal from a distinguished historian, Sergey
Platonov, who, explaining in a preface that he "no longer had the
patience to watch the distressing disintegration of the presentation of Peter the Great in Russian literature," wrote his own
telescopic vision of Peter's reign. His excellent *Peter the
Great* (1926) is the shortest, most concise history of the Reformer
in existence. Professor Platonov is objective and factual, he
even makes liberal use of the petite histoire, but no personal
image of Peter arises from his pages. Creating living legends—
whether true or false ones, no matter—is the unalienable privilege of fiction.

7. Personality: Appearance and Behavior

Truly, all the deeds of Peter the Great are glorious, precious, and admirable. . . . His main features were Faith, Hope, and Charity.
Malgin, 1811

A man completely devoid of a sense of responsibility and despising everything, a man who to the end of his life understood neither the logic of history nor the physiology of national life.
Pilnyak, 1919

The characterization of Peter the Great in Russian historical fiction favors the externals. The reader sees him as he appears to the other dramatis personae and reacts with feelings much the same as theirs. Both observe the Tsar's movements and hear him speak, but no one has access to his thoughts and emotions. Even the traditionally omniscient narrator does little more than report Peter's actions, words, and gestures—usually merely quoting from documents and scraps of anecdotes, using labels attached to his historic reputation and leaving nothing to the imagination. At the same time he is a vulnerable human being, by turns kindly and dangerously irascible, and an awesome presence, a god to be served and obeyed, inscrutable like Fate and just as final in his decisions. Neither the varying, often biased use of documented materials by individual authors, nor their presentation of close-ups of Peter and of his participation in fictional events materially affects his image. The strange combination of the predictable and the mysterious in that image helps the reader to visualize the Tsar but precludes his being understood by fiction as a whole or within separate novels.

Physically, Peter's appearance does not change, unless the time of the novel is his childhood and early adolescence (not a frequent case; *Peter the First* by A. N. Tolstoy is a notable exception) or the last several years of his life.   During the latter period, especially during the time of the flight and death of Tsarevich Alexis, as in Merezhkovsky's *Peter and Alexis* and Ivanov's *Tsar Peter's Night*, his health is failing, and his face becomes puffy and yellow like a death mask.   But at all times he is statuesque and monumental.   His towering (Merezhkovsky and Mordovtsev say nonhuman) seven-foot height is, naturally, the most striking feature of his external appearance.

Peter is presented in a wide range of ecstatic descriptions as "a royal Scythian of gigantic height and wild grandeur" in *The Last Recruit* by Lazhechnikov, "a Cedar of Lebanon" in *The Crowned Carpenter* by Mordovtsev.   A bronze statue of a horseman come to life, he pursues an audacious lunatic along the nocturnal streets of the St. Petersburg of Pushkin's poem and alights at the house of Bely's delirious revolutionary in *Petersburg*, slowly to ascend the stairs that disintegrate under his colossal weight.   In Fedorov's *The Demidovs* he appears as an animated copy of Antokolsky's 1872 statue of Peter the Great—"the monarch standing on a lonely seashore, erect, a cane held in his outstretched hand, a tricorne on his head, his piercing gaze scanning the misty horizon." In Shildkret's *Our-Savior-on-the-Tallow Church,* Peter's face in the torture chamber resembles a rusty cast-iron tombstone."[1]

Writers of fiction seem to have faithfully studied his portraits and sculptures and have reproduced the impression conveyed by Rastrelli's 1723 bronze bust, allegedly the best of Peter's likenesses:

> The head is proudly turned in a swift motion, the eyebrows are contracted in a frown, protruding eyes gaze peremptorily, and the lower jaw, slightly pushed forward, lends the face a cruel and stubborn expression.   Soft, curly hair seems to be swept back by a gust of wind, as is the lace of his neckerchief . . . the bust conveys all of the monarch's characteristic traits: rashness, stubbornness, and inexhaustible energy.[2]

One Soviet playwright, taking advantage of the theater's ability to create a strong visual, almost palpable image, provides in his stage directions a characterization of Peter closely resembling that bronze bust:

> Peter enters surrounded by courtiers.   He is very tall and very thin.   His features are too small for his gigantic figure, but the spiritual image they convey is majestic and awe-inspiring.   The narrow brow seems to be bulging from the pressure of the powerful ideas behind it.   The brown eyes are rather small but full of brightness and shine with intoxicated inspiration.   Small, red lips seem ready to utter words crashing like a thunderbolt.   Clenched teeth, tensed jaws.   His whole person, even in repose, radiates tenseness and impetuosity.[3]

This description also echoes Pushkin's poetic vision of Peter in *Poltava* (1829) issuing orders at the beginning of the battle: "Surrounded by favorites, Peter leaves his tent. His eyes shine; his countenance is awesome; his movements are precipitous. He is magnificent; he is like God's own storm."

Peter's powerful personality is manifest in his features, his precipitous movements ("unnatural in such a massive body," remarks a foreigner), and his fast, uneven gait ("a soldier's stride," say smiths and courtiers alike).[4] People accompanying him have to run to keep up with his pace. A grotesque 1907 painting by Serov shows a goggle-eyed, tight-lipped giant rushing on stiff, thin legs along a wind-swept, muddy strand of St. Petersburg. He is followed by a dwarf-like retinue trying to catch up with the monarch. So, too, is he seen by fiction. Shildkret in *Mamura* has Peter boasting of his endurance at the end of a walk in Moscow and pointing to his tired companions lying in a row on the ground. Danilevsky in *To India in Peter's Time* shows him merely surprised when an exhausted courtier on the verge of tears begs for a moment's rest.

A soldier in Leo Tolstoy's unfinished novel is overwhelmed by his first glimpse of the Tsar, with his

> steep, bulging brow; black eyes lusterless but clear and strange; a restless mouth . . . the stooping, ungainly figure; huge hands and feet; the awkward gait moving the whole pelvis and dragging one foot; and above all the hasty, uneven movements and an equally uneven voice, suddenly changing from bass to shrillness. But only when the Tsar laughed and it was not funny but frightening did Alexey comprehend him, to know and to remember forever.[5]

Peter's nervous facial tics and his convulsions are another prominent feature of his physical portrayal. Historians have not established their origin, and the anecdotic material used by fiction writers is even more apocryphal than usual. Stählin relates, from hearsay, a story of Peter's miraculous escape from a would-be assassin in the church altar of the Trinity Monastery during the Streltsy revolt of 1682. The anecdote is denounced as false by Ustryalov, but Stählin and, after him, Golikov and several foreign authors blame the convulsions on the Streltsy revolt, on the fright young Peter suffered in that episode, or even on poison secretly administered by the Regent Sophia.[6]

The latter version did not appeal to fiction writers, though. Zotov got several melodramatic effects out of Stählin's anecdote by casting the hero of his novel *The Mysterious Monk* in the role of the villainous Strelets, as did Lazhechnikov in *The Last Recruit* and Masalsky in *Streltsy*. In *The Throne and the Cloister* Polezhaev, discounting Ustryalov's opinion, describes the nervous tic appearing on the face of the boy Peter at the sight of the rioting Streltsy in 1682, and on his own responsibility remarks that from then on the tic became permanent. A. N. Tolstoy, in *Peter the Great*, shows Peter frightened at the time but not to the point of convulsions; but at fourteen his head is already jerking uncontrollably, and a year later Menshikov holds him during a fit which, Peter himself tells him, is epilepsy.[7] He is seventeen when introduced by Leo Tolstoy in another fragment of that unfinished novel: "The Tsar, his huge, long body bent almost double, was whittling a block of wood held between his legs. His head twitched, as did his mouth, and jerked to the left."[8] Generally, all writers of historical fiction seem to follow the instructions a Dutch carpenter who had worked in the Tsar's shipyard in Russia gave to his compatriots in Zaandam during Peter's incognito visit there in 1697: "Look for a very tall man with a small wart on his cheek, his head shaking, and his right arm flinging as he walks."[9]

The gaze of Peter's large, protruding eyes is frightening, both on a metaphysical level, since they seem to penetrate a man's secret thoughts, and simply as a physical threat, whether when "sparkling angrily and brightly" as in Yury German's *Youthful Russia* or when "crushing with their somber immobility" as in Kostylyov's *Pitirim*. Pilnyak, Merezhkovsky, and even Alexey Tolstoy agree that Peter's gaze is burning with insanity, and this is not just poetic license. One diplomat reported that it was "painful to bear," an archbishop complained that it had almost struck him down, and a German princess fainted.[10]

Macaulay, writing on the reign of William the Third, describes Peter's visit to England and draws the image of the Tsar as he would have appeared to curious Europeans. Discounting the exotic accessories which the nineteenth-century historian thought appropriate for a portrait of "volunteer Peter Mikhaylov"—the jabbering fool, the grinning monkey—the likeness is recognizable:

> Such was the prince whom the populace of London now crowded to behold. His stately form, his intellectual forehead, his piercing black eyes, his Tartar nose and mouth, his gracious smile, his frown black with all the stormy rage and hate of a barbarian tyrant, and above all, a strange nervous convulsion which sometimes transformed his countenance, during a few moments, into an object on which it was impossible to look without terror, the immense quantities of meat which he devoured, the pints of brandy which he swallowed, and which, it was said, he had carefully distilled with his own hands, the fool who jabbered at his feet, the monkey which grinned at the back of his chair, were, during some weeks, popular topics of conversation. He meanwhile shunned the public gaze with a haughty shyness which inflamed curiosity.[11]

Much is made of Peter's great physical strength, a quality which contributes to the element of grotesque in his fictional characterization. He is almost nonhuman, this often malevolent giant out of fairy tales, the hero (*bogatyr'*) of Russian folk epics (*byliny*). His booming voice gives trepidation even the rich and powerful, and to humble folks it sounds like the archangel's trumpet.[12] He bends silver plates with his hands at

feasts and stops windmills by seizing them by the wings, in anecdotes and fiction alike.[13] Like the *bogatyr'* Svyatogor he seems
ready to move the earth from its foundations, if only he can find
"the navel of the earth," grasp it firmly, and pull.

He does fell trees, and sometimes, while inspecting work in
the shipyards, moves enormous weights. Bulgarin's description of
such a scene in *Mazepa* is characteristic: "Several workmen were
struggling to bring a big piece of timber down to the side of the
structure. Peter approached, shouted, 'get out of the way!' and
when the men let go of their load, put his shoulder to it, pushed
—and the heavy beam blew down like a feather. The Sovereign
smiled and continued on his way." (p. 249.) Few novels fail to
show the Tsar in a smithy forging a piece of iron to be treasured
by history and extolled in anecdote. He was genuinely proud of
his workmanship, say Stählin, Nartov, and Golikov, and on one occasion demanded a smith's pay for such a piece from the owner and
bought a pair of shoes with the money. In novels the smithy is
owned by various fictional characters or by secondary historical
personages such as Nikita Demidov. Their reactions to the
monarch's deigning to busy himself with work routinely performed
by lowly mortals may, depending on the date of publication, differ
in form but not in substance. Arseniev in *Arisha the Ducky* (1889)
relates enthusiastically:

> "Give me a hammer," the Tsar ordered one of the workmen.
> He took the man's place, swung the hammer like a mere
> feather and . . . while a leather apron was being put on
> him, struck . . . the piece of iron with the hammer so
> that sparks flew in every direction. . . . It is impossi-
> ble to describe the feelings of those witnessing this re-
> markable scene, when he who sanctified all work and labor
> with his royal hands took his place among the smiths!
> "Astonishing! Incomparable! He is the miracle of
> our era." . . . Tears were welling in the smith's eyes
> . . . a deafening "hurrah" resounded under the low ceil-
> ing. The smith . . . kissed in reverence the kingly
> workman's hand. (pp. 7-9.)

The master smith Nikita in Fedorov's *The Demidovs* treats the
Tsar with something like camaraderie, but both he and the author
view Peter's interest in manual labor with approval:

> Nikita, on seeing the Tsar in his smithy, did not bat an
> eye; he calmly went on with his work.
> "Good day!" said Peter.
> "Good day, your Majesty!" Nikita bowed with dignity
> and hid his grimy hands under his leather apron. . . .
> Peter . . . seized the hammer. . . . Sparks flew. Peter
> hammered steadily, seemingly well, but when he showed the
> finished piece to Nikita, the smith made a grimace, and
> spit on the floor.
> "Good for nothing, Sire. I wouldn't hire you as my

lowest help, with this kind of work."
    The Tsar rolled up his sleeves, put on a leather
apron and roared:
    "Give me another piece!"
    The Tsar was glad that . . . the work in the smithy
went on meanwhile in the usual way.   (p. 17.)

These displays of strength are not always benevolent. Polezhaev notes the ease with which the Tsar's powerful hands chop off
the heads of the condemned Streltsy: he wields the heavy axe as
if it were a feather while the clumsy courtiers cause their victims to suffer unnecessarily (The Throne, pp. 433-35).   In Shildkret's Mamura (pp. 85, 201) Peter pounds a wall in anger, and all
the windowpanes fall out simultaneously; a single blow of his fist
breaks a table.
    Peter's manners, notorious for their coarseness among foreign
memoirists, run the gamut from unconventional to eccentric among
the Russians.   There exist numerous anecdotes of his unceremonious
behavior abroad.   The best known are his refusal to stay in the
magnificent apartments at the Louvre, sleeping in a servant's cubi-
cle instead—as he had done in Amsterdam in 1697, according to
Scheltema (p. 14); his visiting the octogenarian Mme. de Maintenon
in her bedroom; and his hugging the prim little King Louis XV, who
paid Peter a ceremonial visit—all in 1717 (Stählin, no. 15).
Only Danilevsky, however, made use of this material, in his To
India in Peter's Time.
    Peter is shown on various occasions fishing meat out of a
dish with his fingers, tearing apart a roast chicken with his
teeth, and munching a dripping dill pickle held in his hand.[14]
Some writers—especially Pilnyak, who disliked Peter almost as
thoroughly as did Leo Tolstoy—make such scenes repulsive, but
many others see them differently.   Among the latter, it is ad-
mitted that his manners were shocking, even at official ceremonies,
as was his slovenly attire (Peter was indeed, for instance, seen
wearing soiled gloves while taking the Queen of Prussia to dinner).
Yet it is felt that the Tsar, tired and hungry after a day's work
in a shipyard or a long journey over impassable roads, absorbed
by current, always urgent affairs, may well be forgiven lack of
proper table manners and inattention to clothes.   Peter simply
does not care what he eats, certainly not how he looks: he is
busy doing important things and has no time for trifles.
    His huge, calloused hands with dirty nails—the hands of a
laborer or a sailor but not those of a monarch—are invariably
mentioned.   They are seen with repugnance by Pilnyak as one of
the characteristics of a mad monster on the throne—"he ate with
his hands—enormous, greasy, and calloused,"—and by A. N. Tolstoy
—"Peter pried open the lid of his watch with a dirty black
nail"; with approval by Yury German—"the Tsar's enormous hand,
blackened by soot and tar" is strong and kind"; and with reverence
by Mordovtsev in homage to the Royal Carpenter—"Peter extended
his enormous, heavy hand, rough and calloused. 'These, Sire, are
not callouses but precious stones,' said Menshikov in a low voice."[15]

He eats often and heartily—his preference for simple national fare such as cabbage soup (*shchi*) and buckwheat porridge (*kasha*) is approvingly noted—but never immoderately, preferring snacks to meals. He also likes pungent Limburger cheese and lemons, fresh and pickled, and fiction writers remember that too. He has a curious aversion to fish, which is awkward since fish is Russia's staple Lenten food. This idiosyncrasy (Peter became sick whenever he tried to overcome this aversion) has gone mostly unnoticed in fiction, regrettably so because it was deep enough to be inherited not only by his daughter Elizabeth but also, in the third generation, by Peter III, son of his daughter Anne (Stählin, no. 109).

The simplicity of his clothes is endlessly stressed in Russian fiction and by anecdotic lore, and is routinely accepted as part of his characterization. Head and shoulders above the crowd, he looks regal and yet, unlike the popular image of the tsar, shockingly, strangely ordinary. "A tall man in a green uniform with a clay pipe in his mouth," says Pushkin; "tall and lank with large, dark, slightly protruding eyes, smelling of strong tobacco, vodka, and pungent sweat, dressed in a well-worn dark-green uniform with brass buttons," echoes the Soviet writer Fedorov more than a century later.[16] That green military coat, the worn robe and nightcap, the woolen stockings knit and/or darned by Catherine —indeed, on one occasion in *Peter and Alexis* darned by Peter himself—are faithfully recorded. So is the much-used pipe and, adding a pathetic note as Peter grows older and sadder, glasses in a round wire frame.[17] Pilnyak in *Kneeb* (p. 108) and A. N. Tolstoy in *Peter's Day* (p. 389) insist on his slovenliness, particularly evident in Peter's dislike of clean linen. Shildkret, in *Mamura* (p. 222), agrees ("He changed his shirt only on important holidays"), and Polezhaev more charitably adds that on such occasions the clean shirt had pitifully narrow lace cuffs—proof that the Tsar did not care for frills (*Tsarevich*, p. 55). Belyaev, incidentally, describing the lavish lace cuffs and jacket worn by the waxen effigy in the museum, specifically states that Peter was very fond of clean, handsome linen (*The Cabinet*, p. 14), but no writer took advantage of this bit of information.

Historians from the sycophant Krekshin to the more judicious Ustryalov, Platonov, and Brückner have pointed out the engaging simplicity of a potentate who could have surrounded himself with luxury, as had his predecessors.[18] But Fräulein Juliana, Merezhkovsky's *advocatus diaboli* in his case of Peter versus Alexis, accuses Peter of being a poseur (*P. & A.*, I, 122). Whatever its source, Peter's attitude towards clothes was pragmatic: their purpose was warmth, not adornment. He must have felt the same way about housing. The house Peter rented in Zaandam in 1697 had a kitchen also serving as a dining room and a small, windowless alcove for a bedroom, which A. N. Tolstoy makes the Tsar share with Menshikov. There was also a garret, where Tolstoy located two fictional characters, Alyoshka Brovkin and the jolly priest Bitka (*P.F.*, p. 310). Peter had a three-room "palace" in St. Petersburg, in which, in historical fiction, he never fails to stay, and small houses all over Russia, each complete with a

stock of food, where he could stay overnight during his travels:
a house to Peter was a roof over one's head. He preferred to
have his parties and the meetings of the "most-crazy council" in
the houses of Lefort or Menshikov, which he sometimes built for
that purpose himself, or in later years in Catherine's palaces.
For Catherine, after their marriage was announced, says Scheltema
(pp. 285-6), in contrast to her husband's studiously modest dress,
was "literally covered with diamonds" on a state visit to Holland
in 1717.

Such luxury, of course, developed only in the later part of
Peter's reign and was prompted by the necessity of upholding
Russia's prestige abroad, when the country already had its diplomats stationed at foreign courts and at home had foreign envoys
busily writing reports to their governments. At the beginning of
her career Catherine was by no means pampered and spoiled by
Peter's generosity, a fact understood by fiction writers, since
Peter considered spending money on women wanton waste. An anecdote about an English actress who was disappointed by the unexpectedly modest parting gift from the Tsar is used by A. N.
Tolstoy in a jocular exchange between Peter and Menshikov, but
that is about all; fiction writers are very reticent on Peter's
amorous adventures, a topic which will be discussed later.

Nor is his notorious thrift—some like to call it stinginess
—on other occasions much used by writers of historical fiction.
Stählin, Nartov, d'Escherny, Waliszewski, Galizin—practically
every memoirist or collector of Petrine anecdotes—tell how the
Tsar, kindly visiting the wives of his officers and soldiers to
congratulate them on a new baby, used to present them with a
ruble or a golden ducat, depending on the husband's rank, but
never more;[19] how he made gifts to foreign envoys of furs rather
than of money, as was customary, because in Russia it cost less,
and rewarded his courtiers with gifts of land and titles rather
than with money, which was needed for war, for industry, and for
St. Petersburg; how he appreciated a host's gifts to the servants
who accompanied him on a visit, explaining that their salaries
were too small for them to live on (Stählin, no. 81). There is
also the famous anecdote of his measuring leftovers of his favorite
Limburger cheese with a pair of compasses to make sure that
Velten, the cook, did not steal any; and another about his scold-
ing Catherine for embroidering a blue silk coat which Peter was
to wear at her coronation with silver sequins: two of these, he
said, cost as much as a year's pay for one of the grenadiers.
There are more.[20] Not so in fiction; writers avoided using such
anecdotes in spite of their spiciness—or because of it. Pettiness does not fit Peter's image, whether created by friend or by
foe. Danilevsky remarks on "thrift shown by the Tsar in matters
of small everyday expenses" (To India, p. 5); in Youthful Russia
Yury German cannot resist using the cheese and Velten story (II,
497-8) and introduces one episode in which Peter makes a courtier
tip foreign fiddlers so as to avoid doing it himself (I, 230-31)
and another in which the Tsar generously rewards a brave Russian
sailor, to the great surprise of his aides (II, 412).

He was always busy, always doing something, and enjoyed using his hands hammering, turning, and measuring. In spite of his convulsions and nervous tics, he had a sure eye and a steady hand, never parting with his cases of mathematical and surgical instruments, for, to the terror and danger of those near him, Peter was fond of extracting teeth and performing, not always successfully, surgical operations. He also never parted with his notebook, which would be a fascinating object for a modern psychologist to study, assuming that the latter could read it, because the notebook as well as Peter's letters are almost illegible. The hand which had mastered fourteen trades was apparently unable to draw one line of correctly spelled words in properly traced letters. He omitted whole syllables, put in wrong letters, coined new words, half Russian and half Dutch—the last habit widely represented in fiction.

Erratic spelling and jerky handwriting could also be easily ascribed to impatience, another of Peter's outstanding characteristics. He would grow impatient at theatrical performances (quite insipid and boring, to be sure); liked to act as master of ceremonies at weddings, an honor which involved constant moving around; had been known to give the baby for which he was standing sponsor to someone else to hold in the middle of a christening ceremony and to have ordered priests to cut short wedding services when he found them too long.[21]

Peter's notebooks bear witness to the chaotic way in which he implemented his reforms, to the abundance of his ideas, and to his complete disregard of any hierarchy in their importance. Stählin notes his anxiety not to forget any of his sudden ideas and his habit of jotting them, with the date, on any scrap of paper that happened to be at hand. The memoirist reports on an opportunity to read Peter's remarks pencilled in the margins of a paper outlining a project of the Academy of Sciences to be established in St. Petersburg. Some of the remarks concern the details of the project. Others are memoranda, on, for example, the need for checking on the progress of young Russian nobles studying abroad, on introducing wool manufacturing and issuing a decree that for this purpose landowners in the Ukraine should raise sheep instead of cattle, on the necessity of the regular translation of books from foreign languages, and on the utilization of old oak casks for the production of potash (Stählin, no. 66).

Merezhkovsky shows Peter checking one such memorandum already entered in a notebook and another one that had been jotted down during the night on a slate always hanging at the Tsar's bedstead for that purpose (*P. & A.*, II, 67). Shklovsky, in his *Novellas* (1941), mentions the habit and the slate, the latter handed the Tsar in the middle of the night by the little Blackamoor, Ibrahim Hannibal, whom the writer and the memoirist Bruce allege to be an exceptionally light sleeper. But otherwise, the wealth of ideas crowding Peter's mind in waking hours and in sleep have gone unrecorded by fiction.

One of the ways Peter's restlessness was displayed was, as could be expected, in his sleeping habits. Russian and foreign

memoirists relate that he was up at four o'clock in the morning,
winter and summer, and had a two-hour nap in the afternoon.   He
expected everyone to follow his example, had his secretary as well
as sundry dignitaries report on current affairs by 5:00 A.M., and
is known to have received foreign envoys at that hour, dressed in
his robe and nightcap.   Peter's early rising has not been forgotten
by fiction writers:

> The sun was slowly rising, and long, violet shadows were
> falling on the crooked Moscow streets. . . . Tsar Peter,
> wearing a short nightgown and a coarse linen nightcap,
> stood at an open window and admired the fine military
> bearing of his soldiers marching past the house. (*Bulavin*,
> p. 89.)

or:

> A dark, low-ceilinged room was filled with the sound of
> snoring—difficult, low, whistling, and gurgling . . .
> abruptly, it stopped, and a man rose to a sitting position
> on the creaking bed.   In the barely starting morning
> light, looking through the small panes of a long, narrow
> window, one could distinguish a swollen, big face under a
> nightcap, strands of dark, greasy hair, and a rumpled
> shirt open at the chest. (*Peter's Day*, p. 388.)

and:

> Peter got up early.   'The devils themselves are still
> asleep,' muttered his sleepy servant, starting the fire in
> the stove.   A black November morning lay outside the win-
> dow.   The Tsar, in a nightcap, and a leather apron over a
> robe, sat at a lathe by the light of a tallow candle turn-
> ing an ivory censer . . . working with such zeal that one
> would have thought he was earning his daily bread in this
> way. (*Peter and Alexis*, II, 64.)

Peter never had more than four hours sleep during the night,
interrupted, moreover, by sudden awakenings.   He took notes on his
strange, vivid dreams, mostly nightmares, which could have fur-
nished interesting materials for psychoanalysis.[22]   He was also
subject to convulsions in the night, accompanied by fits of acute
anxiety, and would often sleep with his hands on the shoulders of
an aide or, during his campaigns, with his head propped on the
stomach of a soldier.[23]   There is a lone instance of Peter's dreams
being discussed by a group of courtiers in *Peter and Alexis*, and
in *Peter the First* he falls asleep after one of the seizures with
his arms around Menshikov, holding on to him for safety.   But
aside from malicious hints of homosexuality by such notorious
gossipmongers as Villebois and Waliszewski,[24] neither petite histoire nor fiction pays much attention to Peter's dreams, his
anxieties, or the strange bedfellows they made necessary.

Peter's inquisitiveness—his need to see, to touch, or to acquire everything Western, from a natural science museum to a navy—is rendered in fiction as a burning desire to gain information in general (*liuboznatel'nost'*) and as a drive toward Russia's greatness. Leo Tolstoy, however, sees this characteristic as mere curiosity and condemns it unconditionally:

> A frightful curiosity, about vice, crime, miracles of civilization, how far can it go? And he is curious only about material things. He tampers with all the old roots in life and yet for his own purposes wants to make use of them: of faith, oath, ties of blood. It's a fateful thing, such a passionate desire to experience everything to the utmost limits. He is restless like a man "possessed." (*Materials*, p. 437.)

Tolstoy's criticism has not been shared by fictional characters, except those supporting the old order, usually cast as villains by Zagoskin and Kukolnik and by their Soviet counterparts Fedorov and German. Peter's inquisitivenss and its importance for Russia are, on the other hand, extolled by positive characters in the works of these writers and in juvenile historical novels and are, of course, reverently cited by anecdotists like Krekshin and Nartov. Peter himself mentions with pride his discovery at the age of fourteen of a small sailboat which for years had been gathering dust in a barn at Izmaylovo Palace. This foreign toy belonging to one of the Tsar's ancestors was destined to become the "grandfather of the Russian Navy" and a museum exhibit.[25] There is also the popular story of an astrolabe brought from abroad by a Russian envoy at the request of the ten-year-old Peter and thus setting the stage for all future sciences imported into and developing in Petrine Russia. There are reports by foreigners, diplomats, and gossipers alike telling of the Tsar's travels abroad and of his tireless interest in industry, shipbuilding, religion, sciences, arts, customs, and political institutions, as well as of his purchasing everything and hiring anyone that could be of use to his reforms. These indiscriminate and yet purposeful errands are used as details for Peter's characterization by A. N. Tolstoy and by Danilevsky, but since theirs are about the only works in which Peter travels abroad (in 1698 and 1717, respectively), his fictional image fails to convey much of that quality of passionate curiosity.

And for the same reason, Peter's morbid shyness does not significantly affect his fictional image. Apparent only when he was travelling in foreign countries, that shyness—stemming from an acute inferiority complex and startling in an all-powerful autocrat—made him flee curious mobs, abruptly leave receptions given in his honor by Western monarchs, and become paralyzed in the presence of these rulers. A. N. Tolstoy does show Peter struggling with such an attack of shyness during his meetings with the future king of Prussia and again with the two German duchesses, but these scenes serve only to convey the favorable impression made on these sophisticates by a giant child of Nature, potentate of the mysterious Eastern realm, and do not detract from fiction's image of the great Reformer.

If Peter's tenseness and the psychological factors underlying his tireless activities were little reflected in his fictional image, their visible outlet—his amusements—were utilized to the point of exaggeration. Undoubtedly, he needed relaxation and an opportunity to get away from the mental and physical strain of attending to the medley of tasks and details of his immense reforms. Perhaps, too, he needed momentary distance from that picture better to perceive the whole, invisible to others and overwhelming at times even to himself. And, of course, his amusements were shocking to foreigners and Russians, historians and fiction writers alike—as was everything else about him—because of their scope, intensity, and coarseness. The pageants he organized on any plausible pretext, personally attending to the minutest details; the parties he liked his favorites to give and in the later years of his reign gave himself; and especially the sessions of "the most-crazy, most-drunken council" whose statutes he had authored himself—all inevitably and significantly enhance the element of strangeness in his image.

If foreigners—whether the haughty Korb or, later, the malicious Helbig—were shocked, they were also amused in a condescending manner: what, after all, could be expected of an exotic monarch of a barbarian country? But the Russians—whether a Prince Kurakin or a Monk Avraamy[26]—were not amused; and the populace had only one explanation: Peter was not, could not possibly be, their anointed monarch, their pious, Orthodox Russian tsar (*blagochestivyi, pravoslavnyi, russkii Tsar'*). Hence the rumors that he was either a foreign changeling or the Antichrist in person.

The Russian people, Peter's contemporaries, could not themselves claim high standards of conduct, certainly not refined manners. Russians, Golikov remarks, "had been drinking since the time of Father Noah." Serious historians agree that drunkenness, violence, brutal treatment of women, cruelty, sexual licentiousness, and even perversions were appallingly prevalent in Russian society of the time.[27] Thus, coarseness among their equals would seem to be the quality least likely to shock Peter's subjects. But their tsar, almost godlike in his remoteness and in the Byzantine splendor and ceremony with which he was surrounded, could not afford, autocrat though he was, one thing: unseemly behavior (*neistovoe povedenie*). In creating Peter's image fiction writers have accepted a later meaning of the word *neistovyi*: "frenzied." Peter's amusements were frenzied.

They were also gargantuan, gaudy, and coarse. Grotesque. It was not as if Peter were the first tsar to preside at feasts which ended with most participants drunk under the table; his own father, Alexis the Meek, had been known to do that, not to mention Ivan the Terrible. But these monarchs did not themselves drink to unconsciousness and, a certain school of fiction writers chooses to assume, neither did Peter. Arseniev, Kukolnik,

Lazhechnikov, Kornilovich, and Masalsky, even Soviet writers such
as Fedorov, Petrov, and Yury German, jealous to preserve the lofty
image of the Great Reformer, picture him a guest of some humble
subject, enjoying a glass of his favorite aniseed vodka and a
krendel (a doughnut-like pastry). Mordovtsev, not always an ad-
mirer of Peter, makes it a jug, not a glass, of vodka (*Tsar and
Hetman*, p. 289); Fedorov, perhaps in recognition of the element
of hugeness ever present in the atmosphere surrounding Peter,
makes him on one occasion drink a whole jug of mead (*The Demidovs*,
p. 18). Zotov mentions Peter's being "tired after the victory
and its day long celebration"' Shklovsky guardedly asserts that
"drinking was not a part of Peter's daily routine"; and as for
social drinking, the Tsar's admirers prefer to see him as Nartov
did: enjoying a gay party but himself drinking in moderation.
(Kurakin, a reliable memoirist, says it was "debauchery defying
description.")[28]

But the majority of fiction writers show a different picture,
and this difference in view blurs this aspect of Peter's fictional
image. The Tsar drinks heavily or presides at orgies and "mon-
strous feasts" in works by Pilnyak, Shildkret, Merezhkovsky, and
Mordovtsev; and is brought home dead drunk in those by A. N. Tolstoy and Yury German.[29]

Historians disagree. Pogodin insists that Peter was never
really drunk, even when surrounded by drunken people at parties;
Platonov, polemicizing with detractors of that monarch in contemporary fiction, protests that "Peter did drink a lot, but in
no case was a drunkard."[30] Yet, the narrator in Tynyanov's *The
Waxen Effigy*, regretfully reminiscing at Peter's deathbed about
"last Thursday's glorious drinking," is historically correct; ten
days before his death Peter attended his last riotous, farcical
wedding, that of the servant of one of his aides, which was followed on the next day by the birth and christening feast of the
newlyweds' baby. And Villebois attributes the Tsar's death to
the excesses committed at that particular orgy (*Mémoires*, p. 51).
Doctors are said to have warned the monarch that he risked drinking himself to death, the populace called him a sot (*kutilka*), and
he himself reports in many a letter that "we had a hefty battle
with Jack the Hop (*Ivashka Khmel'nitskii*), and the Hop won."[31]

Whether or not he cared much for hard drinking, Peter was
certainly fond of forcing it on others. The old general Gordon
and the diplomat Bergholz complained of invariably being sick
after attending the Tsar's parties which—Korb, Just, and Bergholz
testify—were a nightmare for his guests, as nobody was supposed
to decline the invitation or leave unauthorized: the entrances
(or rather, the exits) were guarded by soldiers. Drinking hard
spirits—particularly pepper brandy (*pertsovka*)—was mandatory
for men and women alike, and the effects were often disastrous:
Old Prince Dolgoruky died of it, jester La Costa almost did, and
the wife of Marshal Olsufiev miscarried. He established a ceremony of drinking a quart-size "cup of the Great Eagle", as
punishment for breaking the rules of a whimsical protocol mandatory
at his court balls. Many a fictional character, beginning with

Korsakov in Pushkin's *The Blackamoor of Peter the Great*, contributed to the forced merriment of these "assemblies" (which merit a
separate discussion later) by stumbling away from the dance floor
after paying this fine for their social faux pas.   And many novelists—Merezhkovsky, A. N. Tolstoy, and Kostylyov among them—
glimpse the giant, sinister figure of the Tsar wandering among
his carousing courtiers listening to their drunken criticism of
reform, or plots against the Reformer, or hints of new embezzlement in high places—as was Peter's wont in real life.

In spite of his own numerous phobias (of which later) Peter
not only showed little consideration for those of others, but took
pleasure in forcing people to do or suffer things they particularly disliked or found repellent.   Fiction writers contribute
less to this aspect of his image than do memoirists and historians.
Most anecdotists, like Stählin, provide no examples; some, like
Nartov, treat them as playful tricks—as, for instance, Peter's
customary dunking of reluctant courtiers on their first sea voyage
(no. 94).   Ustryalov tells of Peter's serving a "chicken" stew that
turned out to be turtle meat and made several guests sick (III,
276); a Dutch contemporary cites the Tsar's making his "volunteers" tear the muscles of a corpse with their teeth in an anatomical theater during his first visit abroad (Scheltema, *Anecdotes*,
p. 146).   Korb was present at a party when the Tsar almost choked
old Golovkin, who disliked jelly, by personally stuffing it down
his throat (*Diary*, pp. 190-92).

Not much of this finds its way into Petrine fiction except
for descriptions of the meetings of the "most-crazy council."
The compulsory drinking of the "eagle cup" is even treated humor-
ously, as in *The Blackamoor of Peter the Great*.   But during the
garden parties in *His Majesty Kneeb Piter Komondor* and in *Peter
and Alexis* buckets of pepper brandy are carried around by grenadiers and ladled under the stern eye of the host to everyone from
young ladies to oldsters of both sexes.   Both novels also make
use of the anecdote about Peter choking a man with food forced
down his throat.   Pilnyak's victim is old Prince Trubetskoy,
plied with sweet jelly because he liked it (*Kneeb*, p. 118);
Merezhkovsky's, young Golovin, choked with fish jelly because he
hated it (as, it will be recalled, did Peter himself).   A. N.
Tolstoy uses the anecdotes about the turtle meat and the scene in
the anatomical theater in *Peter the First*, and in *Peter's Day* has
the Tsar pour pepper brandy into the mouth of old Prince Shakhovskoy, the court jester, simply because he is in vile humor that
day (p. 410).

If this giant with twitching features, jerky movements, and
strange, hypnotizing eyes is so striking a figure in ordinary
circumstances, any sudden sensation or emotion has the immediate
effect of intensifying these peculiarities.   In Alexey Tolstoy's
Peter the First, during a pleasant visit with the Duchesses of
Hanover and Brandenburg in 1697, Peter complains of the opposition he faces in Russia: "Abruptly his mouth twisted, his cheek
twitched, and for a moment his protruding eyes became glassy, as
if what they saw was not a well-spread table but a blood-stained

room in the Preobrazhenskoe." In Ivanov's *Tsar Peter's Night* the
memory of the Streltsy mutiny scorches him like fire and makes
his cheek twitch twenty-six years later. And when, enjoying a
merry feast, Peter is told secretly of bad news from Livonia, "he
obviously was trying to control himself, but when the next course
was served, he began spasmodically to jerk his knife and fork,
missing the plate and jabbing himself in the face."[32]   In *To India
in Peter's Time*, Peter, having learned during a parade of the
elopement of his favorite ward (both the event and the character
fictional), "for a moment was stricken dumb. Blood rushed to his
head, red patches appeared on his cheeks. Everyone saw the Tsar's
cheek and the right corner of his mouth under its short, shaggy
moustache twitch convulsively, his curly, statuesque head begin
to shake. Trembling all over, his teeth clenched, Peter slowly
put on his gloves; his burning, wrathful, unseeing gaze swept
around; . . . he ordered a horse and silently galloped away" (p.
36).

The most telling example, perhaps, of such paroxysms is
Merezhkovsky's rendition of Peter's slow and inexorably developing
certainty of Catherine's unfaithfulness with Willim Mons. Catherine, realizing that Peter is watching her and Mons, whom he had
personally invited to dinner for that purpose, is in turn watching
her husband for signs of an impending outburst and tries to mollify
him with talk about his shipbuilding and about their little son
in a mellifluous voice, looking into her husband's eyes with a
sugary smile: "Peter did not reply but suddenly looked at her
and Mons in such a way that everyone present felt a shudder of
panic." After dinner Peter sits down to a game of chess with
James Bruce but, raising his head, suddenly sees in a mirror the
reflection of Catherine and Mons deep in conversation: "Peter
jumped up, overturning the chessboard with his foot and sending
the pieces tumbling to the floor. His face twitched convulsively.
The pipe fell out of his mouth; burning ashes scattered around.
Bruce, terrified, jumped up too; the Tsaritsa and Mons turned
around at the noise." (*P. & A.*, II, 75-79). This, however, was
not an attack: Peter apologizes to Bruce and leaves the palace.

Catherine was not alone in watching Peter's behavior for
signals of a gathering storm in an effort to prevent it. Menshikov
reportedly made his fantastic career by mastering this dangerous
skill: "Alexashka," says Tolstoy, "kept glancing at Peter's
hands, which were clenching and relaxing in turn" (*P.F.*, p. 332);
and "he immediately noticed that a corner of *min Hertz's* mouth
was twitching, and was hurriedly figuring out what could be the
matter" (*P.F.*, p. 662). In Yury German's *Youthful Russia*, Menshikov is seen surreptitiously setting fire to some ribbons of his
clothes in order to distract Peter's attention from an act of in-
subordination and so to forestall an attack of uncontrollable
rage, usually culminating in a semi-epileptic seizure (I, 287).
Menshikov did not always succeed, nor, of course, was he always
at Peter's side, and fiction takes full advantage of the sensational possibilities these attacks provided.

The circumstances leading to these dangerous attacks have

been fairly well established historically. They were news of
plots and rebellions, foreigners' insulting attitudes toward Russia, and, most often, irritation at the reprehensible performance
of bureaucrats or the military, ranging from petty lies to embezzlement, bribes, and theft. Peter's admirers like to stress that
none of the causes for these fits of rage are personal and that
Peter could and occasionally did master the irritation or hurt
caused by them. But in fiction there are many scenes of similar
attacks prompted by jealousy (as in Shildkret's account of Peter's
parting with Anna Mons), by anger over disobedience to or simple
misunderstanding of the autocrat's orders, and especially by an
ever-present fear of assassination.

   Thus, A. N. Tolstoy had Peter "speechless with rage," spitting in the face of the old boyar Streshnev and kicking him for
inefficient army supply during the Azov Campaign (*P.F.*, p. 265).
And Pilnyak shows him in an epileptic fit over Peter Tolstoy's
mishandling of the investigation of an oldster accused of spreading mutinous rumors (*Kneeb*, p. 124). A Dutch captain warns Peter
of insulting gossip circulating abroad concerning his exaggerated
thrift and Russia's backwardness, and immediately

> a convulsion distorted Peter's cheek. He seized a brass
> candlestick, rose to all his enormous height. Menshikov
> gripped his arm; Apraxin took the candlestick from him,
> put it back on the table. Peter sat down, his face
> covered with sweat. Apraxin's lips trembled; Menshikov
> kept stroking Peter's shoulder, murmuring, "That's all
> right, Peter Alexeevich; wait, Peter Alexeevich. Here,
> have a sip of cold water." (German, *Russia*, I, 348.)

   The haughty General Ogilvie, refusing to attack the fortress
of Noteburg, speaks slightingly of the Russian soldiers, whom he
does not consider adequate for such a task. Peter's reaction is
typical:

> Peter's face was frightening. His neck appeared to have
> stretched to twice its length, fierce veins swelled at the
> sides of his tightly pressed mouth, furies seemed ready
> to leap—God forbid, God preserve us—out of his dilated
> eyes. He was breathing heavily; his large, sinewy hand
> . . . was groping for something, found a quill and broke
> it in two. (*P.F.*, p. 772.)

   Other writers use even stronger colors, depending on their
style and even more on their personal attitude toward the Tsar
Reformer; some indulge in ridiculous exaggerations. For instance,
in Mordovtsev's *Tsar Peter and the Regent Sophia* (1885) several
Streltsy gather in the home of Tsikler, an officer in Sophia's
camp, and discuss the details of a plot to assassinate the Tsar.
Suddenly, "on the threshold, framed by the doorway, appeared a
giant with a powerful staff in his hand. His face was disfigured
by a convulsion; his eyes were bloodshot; his lower jaw was moving

violently from side to side" (p. 212). Or, in Shildkrets' *Our-Savior-on-the-Tallow Church* there is this description of Peter, on receiving the news of a revolt in Astrakhan:

> "Destroy them! Wipe that rebel spirit off the face of
> the earth!" raved the monarch, thrashing about in convul-
> sions. Looking around for someone on whom to vent his
> terrible wrath, distraught, he crushed with a single blow
> the skull of one of the messengers. The courtiers fell
> back and retreated to the anteroom. The Tsar, like one
> possessed, rushed about the room from one corner to an-
> other. Foam spouted from his mouth, the birthmark trem-
> bled in the grey folds of his twitching cheek like a black
> fly caught in a cobweb. (*Our-Savior*, p. 44.)

The two most dangerous cases of mutiny and treason in Peter's reign were, of course, the Streltsy revolts and the affair of Tsarevich Alexis, his son and heir. The treatment in fiction of the latter case merits a separate discussion; Peter's reaction to the Streltsy revolts received comparatively little coverage.

The revolt of 1682, which made Sophia regent, often serves as background for nineteenth-century novels (though never for those of the post-revolutionary period), but Peter was ten years old at the time, and so it is Sophia who is the historical personage surrounded by fictional characters and the center of the usually fantastic plot. Zotov's *The Mysterious Monk* and Vsevolod Solov-iev's *The Tsar Maiden* may serve as examples. In novels featuring the stormy events of 1689, Sophia shares the spotlight with Peter, as in Mordovtsev's *Tsar Peter and the Regent Sophia*, Polezhaev's *The Throne and the Cloister*, and Lazhechnikov's *The Last Recruit*. A. N. Tolstoy provides a vivid scene of Peter's panicky nocturnal flight to the Trinity Monastery, half-dressed, blind with fright, and contorted by convulsions—that flight which some historians and novelists consider to be the origin of his semi-epileptic fits. But the revolt that contributed most to establishing Peter's reputation as a blood-thirsty barbarian was the third, and last, unsuccessful effort by the Streltsy and Sophia to get rid of Peter, in 1698.

It will be remembered that the revolt was crushed while Peter was abroad, so that the bloody reprisals which he instituted on his return had all the markings of a terror meant for and suc-ceeding in complete eradication of open opposition. Descriptions of these reprisals—tortures, mass public executions, headless corpses left for months to rot in the streets of Moscow, severed heads exposed on poles in public squares—were with varying de-grees of éclat and skill described by novelists. But Peter's per-sonal participation in the executions, reported by shocked foreign diplomats and questioned by historians, has been avoided by Rus-sian memoirists, anecdotists, and novelists alike.[33] Still, the fictional image of Peter the Great would not have been complete without the added glimpses of his acting under the influence of overpowering rage, not a momentary one but one lasting over a

period of several weeks and culminating in his beheading a number
of the Streltsy with his own hands and forcing his courtiers to do
likewise.

We see him through the eyes of Àlexis reliving in memory the
moments when

> tipsy, emerging from a drinking bout in the company of
> Menshikov and other guests, the Tsar walks with an axe in
> his hands, sleeves rolled up like an executioner's, along
> a row of kneeling Streltsy and chops off head after head.
> And when he gets tired, guests take turns in receiving
> the axe from him and go on chopping. Everyone is intoxi-
> cated by the sight of blood. (P. & A., II, 96.)

We see him on Red Square beheading the Streltsy with a firm hand
and a happy smile, and watching the execution by his courtiers of
109 Streltsy specially brought to Preobrazhenskoe "for the entertainment of the Sovereign, who was still not satiated with blood."[34]
In A. N. Tolstoy's version of that scene Peter is morose and irritated by the clumsiness of the reluctant amateur executioners, and
has swollen cheeks from a toothache (P.F., p. 337). But he does
not chop off heads himself, though in Peter's Day (1918) he does
(p. 394).

Peter himself is not frequently present in the torture chamber, the usual scene of interrogation of known criminals, sus-
pects, and even informers (these last were customarily required to
prove the truth of their accusations under strict interrogation,
including the use of the knout). And when he is, it is to make
sure that all symptoms of opposition among the populace, all clues
to a possible plot against his life and work, have been thoroughly
investigated. His reactions to the victims' sufferings range from
callousness—"'Have him [the suspect] interrogated,' Peter yawned,
'and tortured'" (Pitirim, p. 339)—to something like the sad,
wise understanding of the reasons behind the fierce popular opposition to him and his reforms he shows in Peter's Day (p. 413).
Peter's role in Alexis's trial is a case apart.

Deceit and dishonesty were the two remaining acts most likely
to incite Peter's frightening fits of wrath. In Mazepa, on an
occasion which involved the use of his famous staff to punish the
culprit, Bulgarin has Peter explain:

> I repeatedly tell everyone—generals, senators, and work-
> men alike—to always tell me the truth, openly and with-
> out fear. I demand nothing except truthfulness and
> diligent performance of duty. I am angered by and punish
> only dishonesty. . . . I demand nothing for myself except
> obedience to my will, which has no other goal than the
> welfare of our Fatherland. (p. 250.)

Indeed, the petite histoire's sources extoll Peter's love of
truth. There is Neplyuev's much quoted story on how he averted
the Tsar's anger at his being late for work by frankly admitting

to having overslept; Golikov's report that once Peter pronounced the words "May God forgive you," no punishment ever followed and the matter was closed once and for all; Nartov's reports of Peter's leniency toward confessed culprits, whom he admonished, "Don't do it again. Confession earns forgiveness; for conceal-ment there is no mercy. A secret sin is worse than one which is brought into the open." Nartov also quotes Peter's praise of Prince Yakov Dolgoruky: "Prince Yakov is my true helper in the Senate; he is sensible in his judgments, does not fawn on me, and always tells the unadorned truth to everyone, whatever his rank."[35] There are many anecdotes on Dolgoruky's being rewarded by Peter for such hazardous truthfulndss and plain talk. One of these was made into a novella, *The Tale of the Blue and the Green Cloth* (1844), by Kukolnik, who specialized in these literary animations of anecdotic materials; and there is even a novel by Peter Furman, *Prince Yakov Fedorovich Dolgoruky* (1901), consisting largely of a patchwork of the honest Prince's pronouncements.

Anecdotes about Peter's own truthfulness are less popular and are not used by fiction writers. (There is, for instance, the one quoted by Galizin about the Tsar's promising marriage to a German pastor's daughter who would not reciprocate his affection on any other terms and later returning her to her father with a gift of 1,000 ducats,[36] a generous gesture, since Peter was notoriously stingy in such cases.) But Pogodin, in *The Trial of Tsarevich Alexis*, and Merezhkovsky relate Peter's luring the fugi-tive Alexis back to Russia with a solemn promise of full pardon and immediately proceeding with the trial for high treason that ended in Alexis's death. Incidentally, Ivanov, who sides with Peter in his *Tsar Peter's Night*, barely mentions such a promise. A. N. Tolstoy does show Peter in a fictional scene assuring Amelia Kniperkron, daughter of the Swedish envoy, that he will never break his promise of permanent peace with Charles XII and, in the middle of his preparations for starting the war, "fixing on her the gaze of his honest, sincere, round eyes" (*P.F.*, p. 498).

At any rate, whether or not Peter would—or could—let truthfulness interfere with his conduct of military, diplomatic, or personal affairs, he demanded it of his subjects and punished disobedience, lies, and dishonesty alike, particularly bribes and theft.

Of course in the eighteenth century bribery was an estab-lished routine in Russian society and a customary tool of Western diplomacy: it was an envoy's duty to know the right persons to be bribed at the foreign courts. In Russia every man of influence, from the lowest clerk (*d'iachok*) to the ruler of a province (*voevoda*), was considered entitled to some token of "gratitude." Integrity consisted in actually rendering the service for which the "gratitude" was paid and in a certain moderation in acquisi-tiveness and greed. Peter's insistence on honesty in handling large sums of money—such as in furnishing Army supplies—fairness and regard for merit in promotions, justice in litigation, and such was an unheard-of severity in a society where trade had been always conducted on the principle "no cheating, no sales" (*ne*

obmanesh' ne prodash') and where bribes were a way of life summed
up in the maxim "An honest man is a sinner, and so is a rogue;
everyone lives by sin" (*greshen chestnyi, greshen plut; iako vse
grekhom zhivut*).

Hence, Peter's efforts to eradicate corruption—faithfully
reflected by fiction—were labors of Sisyphus. To the end of his
days he was surrounded by embezzlers, dishonest officials, venal
generals, and influence-peddling courtiers. Even Menshikov,
Peter's "Herzenskind," was consistently beaten by the Tsar for
embezzlement and bribery, as was also his able financier and
"fledgeling" Shafirov. Fictional characters often do profit by
the new rules of ethical behavior: fair verdicts handed down by
the Senate in several trials are occasions for jubiliation in
Arseniev's *The Tsar's Verdict* (1889) and in a few short stories
by Kukolnik. In *Peter the First* Tolstoy's shrewd peasant Brovkin
owes his wealth and career to his first delivery of good fodder
for the army horses during the Azov campaign, while all other
supplies had proved to be rotten. It should be noted, however,
that these happy endings are due, not to the Senate's probity,
but to Peter's personal intervention. Hence, in Tynyanov's *Waxen
Effigy* Peter's discreet, withdrawn clerk Myakinin prepares, at
his dying master's orders, a comprehensive list of shady deals in
high places. The list compromises the highest dignitiaries in the
land and reaches up to the Empress Catherine herself; Myakinin
destroys it at the latter's orders just as she is about to succeed Peter on the throne.

In short, in fact as in fiction, nothing succeeded, whether
Peter's almost homicidal attacks of anger—such as against voevoda
Shein, accused of selling commissions in the army, shown by A. N.
Tolstoy—nor beatings personally administered by the Tsar with his
staff, nor various punishments ranging from exile to hanging. In
To India in Peter's Time Danilevsky made an impressive use of the
historically documented execution of Prince Gagarin, and Yury
German in *Youthful Russia*, of the downfall of voevoda Rzhevsky,
in both cases for embezzlement and bribes. Stählin tells of
Yaguzhinsky's reaction to Peter's desperate proposal to issue a
ukase providing the death penalty for thieving. The favorite had
to point out that *everyone* in Russia was stealing, some more frequently than others, some more openly than others. Was Peter
prepared to become a master without servants, he asked, a monarch
without subjects? (no. 48).

Finally, Peter had sudden outbursts of anger which, though
not aggravated by convulsions, would petrify with fear those who
had the misfortune of provoking them. Stählin reports that the
architect LeBlond, having incurred the redoubtable Tsar's wrath
and been threatened with his staff, was so frightened that he took
to bed and died shortly afterwards (no. 96); and that an apprentice who had pulled Peter's hair while putting on his famous working cap fled in terror when the Tsar drew a dagger and brandished
it over the culprit's head. The man spent many years wandering
about and living from hand to mouth before he dared to return at
the news of the Emperor's death, even though the latter regretted

his rashness and announced the man's free pardon all over Russia
(no. 83). Peter is known to have regretted his lack of self-
control and to have on occasion tried to make up for it to the
victims, but the motif of his irascibility and of the fear it inspired have had a lasting effect on his image.

Peter's giant physique and the gargantuan quality of his
work and pleasures are matched by the grandeur of his vision as a
statesman, the colossal scope of his reforms, and his inexorable
pursuit of the goal which he insisted he did not seek for selfish
reasons but for the future welfare of Russia. If that goal had
to be achieved against the wishes and at the cost of untold sufferings of the Russian people—"Our people are like children [he
explained] who never tackle the alphabet unless forced by the
master to do so, and consider themselves wronged at first, but
when educated, are grateful. . . . As for Peter himself, you must
know his life is of small value to him, provided Russia lives in
wealth and glory.[37]

Serious writers like Merezhkovsky and A. N. Tolstoy succeed
in conveying the sincerity of these sentiments through the general
atmosphere of their novels and their rendition of the Tsar's personality. Writers of lesser caliber are satisfied with letting
Peter declaim pseudo-quotations of himself: "'Yes, dear Franz,'"
Peter exclaims passionately in Masalsky's *The Streltsy*, "I promise
you on my word of honor to dedicate my whole life to the enlightenment of my people!'" (p. 468). Mordovtsev, in *The Tsar and the
Hetman*, has him address soldiers at Poltava thus:

> My chilren! Russia's sons!" said Peter in a voice so
> powerful that neither the roar of the cannons nor the
> crackling of the rifles could drown it, "Remember that
> you are fighting not for Peter, but for the realm which
> has been entrusted to him from above. You are fighting
> for your children, for your homes, and for Russia. And
> as for Peter, let it be known that he does not value his
> life so long as Russia lives, being dedicated to her
> glory, her honor, and her welfare! (p. 270.)

Of course, for Russian fiction he is the acknowledged "man
at the helm," "he who cut out a window into Europe," and "the
warrior." Yet Peter's statesmanship, which is, after all, what
justifies his claim to greatness, finds its expression in fiction
almost exclusively in such grandiloquent utterances which the
authors use liberally to dramatize the highlights of the plot.
His appearances on the battlefield are few. His reforms are seen
by fictional characters as they were by his contemporaries:
piecemeal, at short range, as innovations affecting their lives,
usually adversely, not as part of the process whereby Russia
joined the family of European nations. They see details but not
the overall picture, the trees but not the forest. They experience the results of a war sapping the vitality of the nation;
they witness the rise of St. Petersburg, the phantom city built
on marshes and its builders' graves; they are bewildered by a

flow of often contradictory ukases; they sometimes dimly perceive an emerging society split into mediaeval peasantry and modern upper classes. And, at all times, they feel the presence of the perpetrator of that change, the colossal, lonely figure carrying Atlas-like the burden of unshared responsibility for millions of lives present and future, the burden of Russia and of history. In the words of Pososhkov, endlessly quoted, "though he pulls up-hill with the strength of ten, millions pull downwards."[38]

Peter accepts the burden of his awesome responsibility in the same spirit that he accepts the means of shouldering it, his autocratic power. His right of acting as he pleased had been never questioned by anyone, his own vision of "Russia living in wealth and glory" stayed forever undimmed, and his certainty of a tsar's absolute immunity from criticism remained unshakable. If he had yet to learn the Western theory of the divine rights of monarchs, he and his subjects had inherited a faith in autocracy that had originated in Byzantium centuries before. Peter's simple credo was "His Majesty is the autocratic monarch who need never give account of his actions to anyone." And he never did.

Fiction writers accept this attitude, in fact promote it in Peter's image. They do so subtly, through small details of the characterization of Peter the statesman, as does A. N. Tolstoy; with exaggeration, as does Shildkret; and flamboyantly, as do Mordovtsev and Lazhechnikov. The foundation of St. Petersburg, the future capital of the ideal state of Peter's dreams, is a favorite occasion. A. N. Tolstoy remarks casually: "When the first foundations were laid during a mighty drinking session in Peter's dugout amidst toasts and cannon salutes, it was decided to call the future fortress Piterburg" (*P.F.*, p. 622). For Shildkret this style would be much too tame; his Peter is not just an autocrat but hysterical and even childish:

> May 16, 1703, on Whitsunday . . . on the marshy wasteland of one of the Neva's shores . . . was founded the fortress named after St. Peter—Sankt-Petersburgh. The monarch seemed to have gone crazy. He reeled all over the island, roared like a beast escaped from confinement, fell and rolled on the muddy soil, breathless with laughter. Sud-denly quiet, he jumped up, stretching to his full, enor-mous height, and, arms proudly crossed, fixed the horizon with his burning gaze. It was as if he earnestly be-lieved himself to be the only master of all the seas on earth:
>   "The sea!" he exclaimed, "My darling! My love!" Having thus laid the cornerstone of Russia's future capi-tal, Peter violently tore off his hat, knelt down, and tried to say something, but his voice broke. Suddenly, leaning on Menshikov's shoulder, he burst into tears, as children do, unable to control his feelings. (*Mamura*, p. 357).

Lazhechnikov's admiration for the statesman's power knows no bounds:

> Why does ecstasy burn in his eyes? The genius forgets
> reality while creating a new country around him. . . .
> The great one plans—and it *is* reality. What is a dream
> with others is a magnificent deed with him. Peter rises,
> he seizes Sheremetev excitedly by the arm and says, "Sankt-
> Petersburg will be here!" . . . With the eloquence of the
> creative, all-powerful genius, he imparts his gigantic
> plans to those around him. . . . Steel flashes over the
> grove, centuries-old trees fall with a groan, and within
> a few hours the whole island is cleared.[39]

Accompanied by Yaguzhinsky and Menshikov, Mordovtsev's Peter
chooses a suitable site for his new capital:

> The Tsar's intent gaze took in everything; it was weighed
> by his creative thought and penetrated by his all-embracing
> genius. . . .
>   "Sire! An eagle is circling over you" exclaimed
> Yaguzhinsky; "A lucky omen!"
>   The Sovereign thoughtfully looked at the smooth
> glide of the kingly bird's gigantic wings. "What a
> flight!" he said softly.
>   "Your flight, Sire," said Menshikov. . . .
>   "Tomorrow," replied Peter, "my axe will fell the
> trees here . . . and my mighty edifice will stand here as
> long as the earth stands and the sun moves in the skies!"
> (*The Crowned Carpenter*, pp. 184-84.)

Yet, at the end of a long day full of intense activity symbolizing the Tsar's whole life telescoped in A. N. Tolstoy's
novella *Peter's Day*,

> . . . sated and drunk with all that is enjoyable to a
> human being, the Tsar appears to listen. In all this
> satiety, as always at a wrong time, the time when one
> should simply go to bed and rest, his perverse, greedy,
> unquiet, and hungry soul is stirring anew. No wine can
> numb it, nor food, nor amusement; it gives him no rest,
> no respite. What, if not that unrest, makes Peter travel
> winter and summer, in cart and carriage, on horseback
> . . . from Azov to Arkhangelsk, from the Demidov found-
> ries to Vyborg, to Berlin? . . . He builds, gives orders,
> sits in judgment, sends people to the scaffold, commands
> regiments, and sees: the days are too short, one life is
> not enough. (p. 411.)

This is a noble restlessness, the kind that positive Soviet
characters are also endowed with under Socialist Realism: it is
the urge to help promote the lawful historical process of progress,
never sparing one's own energies or those of others. Fiction
notes and admires this characteristic in Peter, and he seems to
wear it just as routinely as his green uniform. But there are

other forms of that restlessness—Peter's impatience; his feverish, insatiable curiosity; his chaotic activity, his jerky, uncontrollable movements—all of which remain less used in fiction, certainly never explored. And yet, these are important aspects of Peter's personality, and it is their understatement that is largely responsible for the stiff, "waxen effigy" quality of his image in Russian fiction.

Fiction indeed sees him as indefatigable, ever in motion, traveling from one end of his vast realm to the other, taking personal part in everything from shipbuilding to diplomacy, from composing military regulations to issuing ukases on the proper manufacture of shoe-leather. What is left out is the tension, the vehemence of contradictory emotions lurking behind and prompting that ceaseless activity. As Leo Tolstoy remarks on Peter's restlessness, "Feverish, hurried activity is the usual companion of dissatisfaction with one's self and especially with others. Not everyone realizes that."[40] Yet, Peter's restlessness was revealing.

To repeat: Peter's image is not created by an abundance of historical facts bodily transplanted into the world of fiction; the authors use considerable selectivity and do so for various reasons. They may be influenced by literary and cultural trends, by tsarist censorship, in the case of Soviet writers by political considerations, by fastidiousness, by a reluctance to mar the grandeur of the Reformer's memory. But the main determinants in their choices of recorded facts, apocryphal anecdotes, and malicious gossip seem to be whatever might emphasize the hugeness, coarseness, and mysterious dichotomy of good and evil in everything Peter did and was. Peter's characterization, therefore, is based on his inherent contradictions and oddities, the result being a larger-than-life image of a person somehow not altogether human.

8. "Le Czar s'amuse"

His virtues were his own, while his shortcomings belonged
to his upbringing as well as to his country.
                    Scheltema, 1742

Leo Tolstoy, irritated by his failure to capture Peter's elusive
personality in his novel, exclaimed: "He was nothing but a drunk-
en fool!"[1]—"fool" not in the sense of "imbecile," of course, but
in that of "clown," "jester," or "buffoon." And, indeed, the most
shocking of the Tsar's grotesque amusements was his favorite mock-
religious institution, the notorious "most-crazy, most-drunken
council" composed of Peter's chosen court jesters and drinking
companions. Bergholz politely calls them "the restless brethren"
(*Diary*, III, 148).

They were a motley crowd consisting of nobles from the Tsar's
entourage, most of them reluctant participants, at least in the
beginning, and of all-too-willing commoners, ranging from the
brilliant favorite Menshikov to sundry riffraff recruited among
sailors and shipyard workers. Nikita Zotov, Peter's erstwhile
teacher and governor who was created count, says Korb, in 1710
during one of the "sessions"[2] by a very drunk Tsar, presided as
the "Patriarch" and "Prince-Pope." Old Prince Fedor Romodanovsky,
the sinister head of the secret chamber of political investigations, bore the title of "Prince-Caesar"; and everyone, including
Peter himself, had to pay him homage. Court jesters—all nobles,
from the able young engineer Balakirev to the senile Prince Shakhovskoy—somersaulted and engaged in mock fights (Shildkret, in
one of his novels, has them do that stark naked, but this is
poetic license unsupported by historical evidence). Peter, as
usual, was in the center of everything, personally composing the
profane and obscene ceremonial, a parody of the Church hierarchy
and services.

The council was apparently founded in October 1691, when a
book on Church hierarchy was ordered and "brought for the Great

95

Lord into His Royal chambers, the receipt being made out by the chamberlain, Garvilo Golovkin"[3]—evidently as a guide in establishing the council's hierarchy.   A. N. Tolstoy, the only chronicler of this event in Russian fiction, chooses an earlier date, before Peter's marriage (which took place in January 1689), when Peter was barely sixteen years old and had only the Foreign Quarter as the site for his amusements.   Tolstoy has Peter, annoyed by the visit of an old and venerable boyar who had come to admonish the young Tsar about his unseemly behavior, take the old man to Lefort's house.

> At the table, on a high chair, sat Nikita Zotov, wearing a paper crown and holding a pipe and a goose egg.   Peter unsmilingly bowed to him and asked for his blessing, and the archpriest blessed him with the pipe and the egg so that he could lead the company in drinking.   Those present, about twenty in all, intoned church hymns in nasal voices. The Prince, not daring to offend the Tsar, stealthily spat and made the sign of the cross under his greatcoat. But when a naked man [Menshikov] climbed a wine barrel holding a cup and the Tsar and Grand Duke of All the Russias pointed him out with his finger and announced sonorously, "This is Bacchus our god; let us worship him," the Prince turned deadly pale and swayed.   The oldster was carried to his sledge in a swoon.
>   From this day on, at Peter's orders, Zotov was called "the all-drunken pope, archpriest of the god Bacchus," and the meetings at Lefort's, "the all-crazy, all-drunken council."   (*P.F.*, 109-10.)

Shildkret contributes a scene showing the initiation of a new member of the council: an orgy about 1690, in which Zotov climbs on the dinner table to excommunicate "all nondrinking heretics" while the chorus chants the ritual ecclesiastic responses, the monarch's "velvety baritone" soaring above all other voices (*Mamura*, p. 50).   In *Tsarevich Alexis Petrovich* Polezhaev describes an orgy at a council meeting at Menshikov's while the host's young son is dying in another part of the house.   Kostylyov relates (though without going into details: Soviet writers are not wont to shock their readers) the "unspeakably obscene ceremony" of the election in 1717 of the new "patriarch," old Peter Buturlin, scion of one of the noblest families, in place of the deceased Zotov.   The Tsar, bearing as usual the modest rank of protodeacon, is shown chanting: "In the name of all the drunks, in the name of all the beer mugs, in the name of all the fools, in the name of all the clowns . . ."—a parody of the church ritual prescribed for such occasions (*Pitirim*, p. 427).   The longest, strangest, and most disgusting scene is the portrayal of the same "election" in Merezhovsky's *Peter and Alexis*, though Peter, for a change, is not drunk, does not sing, and in the midst of the orgy broods on problems of state and on that of unfortunate Alexis's disposition and behavior (*P. & A.*, II, 131-35).

The scandalous feasts of the "most-crazy, most-drunken council" continued throughout Peter's lifetime. Assuming that they satisfied the need for relaxation in a man so hugely active and of such very coarse tastes, there still seems to have been no need for the Tsar to display his drunken and profligate companions to an increasingly shocked and restive populace, except perhaps because of a despot's insistence on having his whims accepted as law.

Some of the anecdotists, creators of the Reformer's image, explain the public appearances of the council by Peter's desire to disassociate the populace from old religious customs through ridicule—something between a huge practical joke (Villebois says "fêtes comiques et burlesques") and shock treatment.[4] Soloviev considers it "just a playful game at kings, popes, and patriarchs, a game understandable at the [cultural] level of the youthful society of those times." Unquestionably, the cultural level of Russian society was not high in the seventeenth century. Even the profane ceremonial of the "most-crazy, most-drunken council" was not completely Peter's invention: *The Feast of the Pothouse Drunkards* (*Prazdnik kabatskikh jaryzhek*) contains a drunken parody of church rites strikingly similar to and possibly serving as prototype for that used at the council meetings. A copy of that blasphemous parody, dated 1666, is known to have circulated among the populace during the reign of Tsar Alexis, Peter's pious father. So the blow dealt to the populace by Peter's pageants was not only one to their religious feelings but also to their sense of propriety. Their tsar, beating the drum and walking at the head of a clownish procession, was a far cry from the tsar of old, resplendent in goldcloth and jewels, surrounded by his nobles, proceeding from the Kremlin to attend services in the cathedral on Red Square.

In fiction, the favorite occasions for the public appearances of the "council" are those most notorious historically: the wedding of the court jester Yakov Turgenev in 1694 and that of "patriarch" Zotov in 1715. The details strictly follow the descriptions supplied by eyewitnesses, Zhelabuzhsky and Prince Kurakin, in their memoirs, which are fantastic enough not to require any fictional embellishments. The following is the 1694 wedding as portrayed by Shildkret in *Mamura*; Shildkret makes Turgenev senile, though he was only forty-four at the time:

> Turgenev was dragged out, sobbing and protesting, and seated in the Tsar's best coach, upholstered in velvet. The bride, a sexton's widow, moved contemptuously away but upon a warning look from Prince Boris Golitsyn immediately became friendlier and even embraced the groom. Crowds came running from everywhere, eager to see Peter's fun. Into the wedding procession came carts drawn by oxen, pigs, goats, and dogs; boyars and servicemen of all ranks, dressed in matting sacks, grey and colored patchwork coats trimmed with cats' paws, and squirrels' tails, straw boots, mouseskin gloves, and bast

hats. Behind the coach, marching smartly as if on parade,
hurried the noblest courtiers and the generals freshly
appointed to head the Azov campaign. All wore new velvet
coats and were holding batons in their hands. The monarch
himself walked in front of the coach beating the drum with
the zeal of a true musician. On each side of him ran
Menshikov and Shafirov, purple with strain, blowing with
all their might into trumpets that glittered blindingly
in the sun. In the rear twelve bald corporals carried a
throne occupied by the Prince-Patriarch Nikita [Zotov].
He was already quite drunk and singing some obscene ditty,
while rhythmically beating on the bald heads of his retinue with a small hammer. The wedding ceremony was performed in a tent pitched in a field between the villages
of Preobrazhensk and Semenovsk [seats of Peter's famous
regiments] by a bald little priest, so old he had long
lost count of his years. (*Mamura*, pp. 108-9.)

    Alexey Tolstoy, describing the same scene in *Peter the First*,
draws attention to the Tsar's stubbornly pushed-out lower jaw and
his rolling eyes observing the terrified crowd as he marches in
the procession steadily beating the drum. (Peter, incidentally,
was good at drum-beating, though otherwise he disliked music.)
Zotov is wearing a tin miter and a red mantle and is holding a
cross fashioned out of two pipes (*P.F.*, pp. 223-4). Kukolnik's
version of the wedding in "The Sentinel" (1843) is decorous and
suitably merry. The bride (a fictional German Fräulein) and the
curly-headed groom are young and in love and owe their happy union
to the intervention of the kind monarch. The latter's presence
is assumed but not described, and there is certainly no question
of his drum-beating. The wedding procession of preposterously
costumed nobles is faithfully related—but as a huge, riotously
funny joke.[5]
    We know from Bruce, a participant in "Prince-Patriarch"
Zotov's wedding, and from Golikov's lengthy and carefully documented description of it that all the arrangements for the wedding
cortege and for the costumes of the participants, all of whom were
carrying musical instruments or sundry noisemakers, were worked
out in minute detail by Peter. It was a full-fledged masquerade.
To mention only a few items: the groom came as a cardinal; the
redoubtable Prince Romodanovsky (aged 73) as King David, complete
with a lyre; foreign diplomats as German shepherds playing flutes;
court doctors in red mantles, carrying books; Tsaritsa Catherine
and her daughters, old Dowager Tsaritsas Martha and Praskovya,
and their respective retinues in Spanish, Polish, and even Chinese
national costumes. Female members of the "most-crazy, most-
drunken council" wore traditional old-fashioned Russian clothes
(meant to prove that these were clothes fit for masquerade costumes only); Peter himself accompanied the newlyweds, dressed as
a sailor. Invitations had been delivered by stutterers; the
cortege was preceded by four runners so fat they could barely
walk, followed by four decrepit oldsters escorting the bridal

couple; the officiating priest was over ninety years old. The
shouts of a huge crowd of onlookers rose above the din made by the
members of the procession and were in turn covered by the sounds
of church bells ringing from all the belfries in Moscow. In spite
of its scenic possibilities, this wedding was utilized only by
Mordovtsev in *The Tsar and the Hetman,* Danilevsky in *To India in
Peter's Time,* and Pilnyak in *His Majesty Kneeb Piter Komodor.*
And even in these novels the festivities, given with few details,
do not figure prominently in the plot and—what is more significant—do not include Peter's participation.

   Other pageants and masquerades which particularly impressed
contemporary foreign memoirists and later minor historians, such
as Waliszewski and Mikhail Semevsky, were little utilized by
nineteenth-century fiction writers inimical to Peter and not at
all by his admirers or by Soviet writers irrespective of their
attitudes. The wedding of the dwarf jester Shansky in 1702, a
colorful enough event, is one example. The wedding feast, which
took place at Lefort's house, was attended by the Tsar, by most
of the members of his entourage, and by the entire "most-crazy,
most-drunken council" arrayed in their clownish "priestly vest-
ments." Moreover, it was immortalized in a crude gravure made
and distributed by Peter's orders among the populace[6]—yet the
occasion went unrecorded by fiction.

   Again, the historical pageant celebrating the success of the
second Azov Campaign in 1696 is barely noticed. A. N. Tolstoy
does present the event as part of the two briefly chronicled Azov
campaigns, complete with triumphal arches, the "Prince-Pope" rid-
ing with sword and shield on a chariot, Lefort in a suit of armor
being driven in the Tsar's gilded sledge, and Peter in sailor's
garb and a felt tricorne with an ostrich feather walking in the
procession (*P.F.*, p. 285-6). Mordovtsev is lavish with commentary
ridiculing "the childish naiveté, coarseness, and gaudiness" of
the pageant, and the participation of Peter walking behind Lefort's
sledge as "a simple captain, Peter Alexeev" (*Tsar Peter*, p. 190).
Finally, Merezhkovsky glimpses the scene briefly through the eyes
of six-year-old Alexis perched on the shoulder of his giant father,
who is marching in a green bombardier uniform—and thus it is seen
as a magnificent spectacle (*P. & A.*, I, 229).

   The atmosphere is understandably very different in Merezhkovsky's portrayal of the funeral of Peter's favorite dwarf in
1717.

   > First thirty young choirboys came by two's, next a tiny
   > priest selected from among all the St. Petersburg clergy
   > because of his diminutive size. Six small raven-hued
   > horses in black coverlets reaching to the ground pulled a
   > child-size casket on a miniscule hearse. Next, led by a
   > tiny marshal carrying a huge baton, marched solemnly,
   > hand-in-hand, twelve pairs each of male and female dwarfs
   > in long mourning mantles. All were arranged by size like
   > organpipes—hunchbacked, bigbellied, pigeon-toed, snout-
   > faced, knock-kneed, and dog-headed—all sorts of monsters,

frightening rather than funny. On both sides of the
dwarfs along the procession walked giants, the Tsar's
grenadiers and messengers, carrying lighted torches and
candles. One of the giants, wearing a baby shirt and har-
ness, was led by two of the smallest dwarfs with long grey
beards. Another, swaddled like a baby, followed in a cart
drawn by six tame bears. At the end of the cortege came
the Tsar with all his generals and senators. Dressed as
a Dutch ship drummer, he walked with the mien of one absorbed in an important task, beating a drum. . . . The
time was past four in the afternoon, and darkness was
coming fast. It was snowing big wet snowflakes. (*P. &
A.*, II, 90.)

This was a somber period in Peter's life. There were several
funerals in the Tsar's family: those of crown princess Charlotte,
Peter's daughter-in-law, and of his two small daughters, Natalya
and Margarita, in 1715; of Martha, Tsar Fedor's widow, and of
Peter's favorite sister Natalya in 1716; of Peter's infant son,
Paul, in 1717; finally, in 1718, of Tsarevich Alexis. (The funeral of Alexis was preceded on its eve by festivities celebrating
the launching of a new ship and was followed on the next day by
a garden party at the palace; it being made known that since
Alexis had been found a traitor at his trial, his death did not
rate court mourning.)[7] Neither these funerals nor several other
magnificent pageants of Peter's later years, like the celebration
of the treaty of Nystadt in 1721 and Catherine's coronation in
1724, found their reflection in fiction. Writers generally avoided
dealing with periods later than the Battle of Poltava, possibly
because they were less colorful and offered fewer possibilities
for the plot. Even the dwarf's funeral appears only in Merezhkovsky's novel, which is dedicated primarily to Alexis's flight
and death. Taking place in the midst of the gathering storm of
Peter's political confrontation with Old Russia and Alexis, the
scene sheds an interesting light on the outlets Peter sought for
his suppressed emotions, on the grotesque forms these outlets
were apt to assume, and on their adverse effect on Peter's image
in fiction. It was the vision of the Tsar with his entourage
participating in ludicrous pageants and drunken orgies that caused
Leo Tolstoy to sum him up as "the drunken syphilitic Peter with
his buffoons."[8]
  Jesters, the standard accessories of any mediaeval court,
were extremely popular at that of the Russian tsars well into the
eighteenth century. They were primarily buffoons, male and female,
whose role was dissipating the fog of boredom hanging over the
palace, especially in the women's quarters. They were usually
deformed—dwarfs, hunchbacks, half-idiots—lisping, stuttering,
jabbering. They somersaulted, slapped each other's faces, pulled
out their tongues, and cracked inane jokes; they carried bits of
gossip and collected rumors from the outside world. Peter hated
this "collection of lazybones and freeloaders," and fiction
usually has them scatter like rats at his approach to hide in the

nooks of the old Kremlin. His own jesters were different, and
their deformities were seldom physical, though he did have several
dwarfs and an imported giant, the already mentioned Bourgeois.

Peter's jesters—most of them nobles and often holding this
degrading position as punishment—fell into two categories. Some
were bona fide fools, like Peter's former tutor, Zotov; the stolid
Prince Buynosov, a fictional character in *Peter the First* who owed
the job to a diplomatic faux pas; and Yakov Turgenev, described
by Kurakin as "an old man, harmless but funny in his ways and
weak of mind." Others were shrewd, unscrupulous men, capable of
serving Peter as informers by eavesdropping at feasts on drunken,
malcontent guests, and of tactfully choosing the right moments
for making intelligent political remarks or for clowning. Such
were Buturlin, Shakhovskoy, and, of course, the notorious Balakirev, who, after returning from abroad with a diploma in engineering, chose the career of the Tsar's jester as the more influential, lucrative, and interesting of the two.

All these men were almost *ex officio* members of the "most-
crazy council" and usually figured prominently in sundry grotesque
pageants, such as the dwarf's funeral. They were the bridegrooms
at the weddings of Shansky, Turgenev, and Zotov, as well as prin-
cipals in the inaugurations of the council's "Patriarchs" (Zotov,
and his successor Buturlin).

Since pageants and jesters were popular in Russian historical fiction, Peter's historical jesters have been familiar figures
to its readers, but as fictional characters they are few. Besides
Prince Buynosov only two deserve to be mentioned: the old dwarf
Ekimovna in *The Blackamoor of Peter the Great*, the fool (*dura*)
who amused the guests of her master, Prince Rzhevsky, by ridiculing Peter's innovations in dress and manners. She was, however,
smart enough to keep quiet when the Tsar unexpectedly joined the
company. The other is Lazhechnikov's dwarf, Goliath, son of
Samson.

While jesters were often victims of Peter's practical jokes
and his malicious enjoyment of inflicting humiliating situations,
they were, in a way, meant to be treated in such wise. The fun
derived by the Tsar from his own version of *riazhenye*, the traditional Yuletide masquerade, was another, more serious matter.
"It is an old custom of the Russians," says Kurakin, "to celebrate
the Yuletide season by friends' gathering in the evenings in each
other's homes, those of low condition dressing up as mummers
themselves, nobles watching sundry funny plays performed by their
servants. According to that custom His Majesty with his attend-
ants also had such Yuletide festivities at his court" (pp. 73-74).
Kurakin adds that a detailed account of these in some cases obscene and sadistic amusements would fill a large book and that
"people prepared for them as for the hour of their death." The
material the memoirist did provide was extensively used in Petrine
novels dealing with different periods of the Tsar's life, though
in reality the *riazhenye* were discontinued after his return from
his first journey abroad in 1698. Cases of such "fun" were also
recorded at later dates, as, for example, that of old Golovin,

who was, in December 1724, seated naked on the frozen Neva and
smeared with soot "to represent a demon." He died of pneumonia
shortly afterwards, surviving Peter by two days.

The practice of deflating the importance of staid nobles by
wounding their pride and ridiculing old Russian customs continued
to the end of Peter's life, but "fun" was not necessarily the only
goal pursued. Besides appealing to Peter's coarse sense of humor,
the grotesque pageants, the practical jokes, and the mandatory
"new look" in clothes and manners were part of his reforms and a
radical way of stamping out the opposition to them. Peter was
not, it is generally agreed, wantonly cruel by nature. The famous
anecdote about his kindness in sparing the life of a bird used in
an experiment with a pneumatic bell (Nartov, no. 101) is significant. The bird's death would have made no political sense nor
would the sight of its sufferings have been amusing: once his
scientific curiosity was satisfied, Peter released the victim.
But the compulsory shaving of the boyar's beards and the forced
attendance of their wives and daughters at the assemblies were
part of the great change Peter was imposing on Russia. Ivan the
Terrible imposed his will on the boyars by fire and the execu-
tioner's axe, Peter (at least in their understanding), by making
them look like fools and act like clowns. Their feelings are
best expressed in a capsulated survey of Peter's early reforms
within one morning in the life of Prince Buynosov in *Peter the
First*:

> Upon awakening, the Prince is faced with a general feel-
> ing of malaise—which he expresses by the untranslatable
> Russian term *skuchno*. He reluctantly dons unfamiliar,
> uncomfortable clothes and a wig, feels with distaste the
> stubble on his face where his stately, silken beard used
> to be. A grinning servant presents him with a saucerful
> of powdered chalk and a little rag, with a reminder of
> the Tsar's ukase on cleaning teeth in the morning. [This
> ukase is a poetic license of the author.] During the
> customary reading of religious services, the prince's
> mind wanders to the difficulties of his present situation.
> Men, grain, and money had to be given to the army. This
> meant diminished income from his already impoverished
> estates and the threat of still heavier taxation was loom-
> ing in the future. Great noble families, besides being
> ruined financially, were constantly being insulted by the
> Tsar's treatment of them, a forced participation in his
> disgraceful amusements and shocking orgies. . . . After
> the prayers and an inspection of his deteriorating house-
> hold, he joins his wife and daughters who, dressed in
> foreign finery, drink coffee in the dining room when, the
> prince muses, they should be embroidering quietly in the
> women's quarters upstairs, these disrespectful wenches
> whom the Tsar has personally ordered to be taught dancing
> and the newfangled *politesse*. His dignity suffers further
> during the visit of *boyarynia* Volkova, neé Sanka Brovkina,

daughter of a poor peasant turned wealthy merchant and married by Peter to his former squire. "Prince Buynosov forced to make a monkey of himself and before whom?" he thinks as he bows and scrapes in the new courtly manner before the elegant guest, who, moreover, is putting ruinous ideas about the latest ladies' fashions into his daughters' heads. Hence to the Kremlin, once the seat of dignity and propriety presided over by the august person of the Orthodox tsar, now full of impudent upstarts officers, lowly clerks scribbling endlessly useless ukases, and boyars sitting around engaged in desultory quarreling and fruitless complaining. The Tsar is away at the Voronezh shipyards busily building ships in preparation for a war with Turkey. "What for?" the boyars query; "didn't we just lose two campaigns against the Sultan?" (*P.F.*, pp. 349-63.)

Identical complaints are voiced by Kukolnik's old-fashioned boyars in 1700, Zagoskin's in 1711, Masalsky's in 1721 and by Pushkin's Prince Rzhevsky in 1723, the year of the Blackamoor Ibrahim's return from Paris—no Petrine novel is without its enemies of the New, usually cast as villains or at least ridiculed by the author. The crux of the opposition was over the shaving of beards (*borodobritie*) and the social gatherings (*asambleia*). The reorganization of the army, the creation of the fleet, the centralization of the administrative system—nothing impressed contemporaries and appealed to writers of Petrine fiction so much as these two novelties, which reached to the core of the Russian way of life. They upset homes, made women "disobedient and frivolous," deprived men of their God-given adornment and source of masculine pride. They did, however, help novelists create the feeling of the era, that indispensable attribute of any work of historical fiction. A whole cast of *commedia dell'arte* characters—old-fashioned parents, foppish or backward suitors, enlightened heroes and heroines—act within the two camps of Peter's supporters and his more or less loyal opponents. The main test is the new look and, of course, Peter's encouragement of the use of tobacco. The characters of the nineteenth-century authors, like Salias and Zagoskin, bow to the Tsar's will, though not without considerable soul-searching:

"A man's beard . . . which is worn even by the Saints—does one dare shave it, even at the Tsar's order?"—[Salias's] Kiselnikov pondered, feeling, of course, that this was a problem a thousand times more important than a ukase concerning new taxes![9]

Zagoskin's hero says: "As God is in Heaven, our father Peter Alexeevich never orders anything just at a whim or for his amusement . . . even though I do not know why our most wise Sovereign wants us all to dress in a foreign manner, there must be a good reason! . . . So I ordered a

suit of German clothes, sent for my barber, and had my
beard shaved." (*Russians*, pp. 340-41.)

On the other hand, Akinfy Demidov, a Soviet author's hero,
simply follows the leader's example unquestioningly:

The mother shook her head in disapproval.
"Why did you bare your face given to you by God?   It
is a sin!"
"I approve of shaving!" the son answered, looking
straight into his mother's eyes.   "Peter Alexeevich himself, the tsar of the Russian land, has his face shaven
in the same way!" (*The Demidovs*, p. 246).

In *Peter the First*, the Tsar, "incomprehensible, totally
alien, a changeling whose smile froze the hearts," with his jesters snips off the beards of Old Russia's most respected boyars.
Mockingly, he advises the stunned, outraged men to keep the beards
and have them put in their coffins to show at the Last Judgement
(p. 331).   In *Mamura*, they do that without Peter's advice.   After
leaving the scene of their humiliation, performed by the Tsar
"screaming with laughter" in an atmosphere of "paralyzing fear,"
the boyars take their "shamed faces" to church and pray God to be
allowed eventually to present their beards to Him as proof of
their having kept His Law as long as it was possible (pp. 293-94).
The compulsory shaving of beards and the use of tobacco were
more significant to Orthodox Russians than the new look in clothes
and manners because these acts directly offended their religious
feelings.   The removal of beards was viewed as an attempt to change
the look given to man by God, who had created him in His own
image; the words of the Bible "Not that which goeth into the mouth
defileth a man but that which cometh out of the mouth, this defileth a man" (Matthew 15:11) were understood to apply to tobacco
smoke; and the branding of recruits was, of course, considered—
especially by the Old Believers—to be the sign of the Antichrist.
Harsh measures were used during the reigns of the pious tsars
Alexis and Michael in order to instill proper respect for the com-
mands of the Bible.   Men were excommunicated for wearing short
hair and no beard; short hair and foreign dress were forbidden in
1675; the use of tobacco, forbidden by Michael, was punished with
the knout and by cutting off the nose by Alexis, though he relented
in the last years of his life and legalized the use of "the devil's
weed" (Soloviev, VII, p. 569).   The sect of Old Believers, whom
Peter treated with amused tolerance[10] and whom Alexis had severely
persecuted, came into being after the latter had the Patriarch
Nikon revise the translation of service books and so created a
schism among the faithful.   Yet, fiction writers chose to ignore
the harsh measures of Peter's predecessors in favor of portraying
those he used to reverse their policies.   Of course, though the
measures were much the same, the Tsar and his aims were very different and, among other things, presented infinitely more colorful
material.

The tsars of old were the anointed representatives of God on earth, distant and powerful as He. They lived behind the walls of the Kremlin, surrounded by the noblest boyars, seen, resplendent in cloth of gold and precious stones, only during their ceremonial and religious appearances. To the populace, their lifestyle, bearing, and actions were models of propriety, the essence of the national spirit in Holy Russia, and the symbol of her greatness and glory. Their people were proud of them.

But Tsar Peter, while still the anointed autocrat, was always in a hurry, dashing from one end of Russia to the other in a land where slow, deliberate manners denoted wisdom. He was a monarch whose motto was hard work for everyone—including himself—and whose amusements were gross and clownish in a land where leisure was synonymous with bliss and propriety with virtue. Ruler of a nation deeply suspicious of any change, especially one originating beyond its borders, he kept lowly company, favored foreigners, and spent his whole reign changing Russia into a European country. Pressed by a flurry of peremptory ukases, Russians underwent the surgery of Peter's Change, transforming their homes, their social system, the education and careers of their sons, the status of their wives and daughters, the site of their capital, and, with the introduction of the new calendar, time itself.

Fiction writers are fond of showing the "incomprehensible, totally alien, changeling" Tsar as a benevolent giant relaxing in what he considered to be the friendly cultural atmosphere of a modern social event, enjoyable to him and so unquestionably enjoyable to everyone else. Pushkin's Korsakov, recently returned from Paris, asks Ibrahim in a low voice: "Que diable est-ce que tout cela?" It was an *asambleia*, the scene that would henceforth appear in practically every Petrine novel. What Korsakov saw in *The Blackamoor of Peter the Great*, were

> ladies sitting along the walls, the younger ones sparkling with all the luxury of their fashionable attire. Gold and silver shone on their dresses; their slim waists rose like flower stems from their hooped skirts; diamonds glittered in their ears, in their long curls, around their necks. . . . At the sound of the most inferior music imaginable, ladies and gentlemen stood facing each other in two long rows. The gentlemen bowed low; the ladies curtsied even lower, first straight, then to the right, next to the left, straight again—and so on and on.
> (*Works*, I, 16-17.)

In *Peter's Day*,

> four sweating musicians sawed on and blew into their instruments: a violin, a flute, trumpets, and a bassoon. . . . Boyars' wives and daughters, decked out in dresses German in design but weighing a Russian *pud* [36 lbs.] and wearing no jewels (which were at that time forbidden), apple-pink with rouge, brows painted to form a thick

black line, were clinging clumsily to their partners,
hopping and jumping about on the waxed floor. Smoke
drifted into the hall from the next low-ceilinged room,
where, seated at long tables, Peter's "fledgelings" were
playing chess, smoking pipes, drinking wine, and slapping
each other's broad, sturdy backs. (p. 407.)

In *Peter and Alexis*,

ladies, when not dancing, sat silently, bored and moody.
When dancing, they leaped about like wound-up dolls,
answering compliments with wild stares. Daughters seemed
to be permanently stitched to their mammas' skirts, and
on mammas' faces was written plainly: "We would much
rather have drowned our girls than brought them to an
'*asambleia*.'" (I, 270.)

And in Kukolnik's "The New Year,"

the old house was full of older women relatives [of the
prospective bride] who resembled . . . glazed and gilt
gingerbread rather than human beings. Motionless, they
sat crowded on benches along the walls [while] . . . the
young girls, bejewelled and painted, concentrated on trying to keep their feet from showing from under their
skirts. In the adjoining room men were busy discussing
the sudden disappearance of a respected merchant's beard.
(p. 178.)

Peter, in his green military coat, is almost invariably present, smoking his pipe, playing draughts with some broadshouldered
foreign sailor, drinking the "flinn" (warm beer with brandy and
lemon juice) or "triple-pepper-brandy" (*P. & A.*, I, 270), or
watching the dancing and sometimes joining in it himself. Apple-
cheeked wives of Dutch sailors or of German burghers from the
Foreign Quarter, chatting merrily and knitting, are meant to give
a pleasing cachet to Peter's social event.

It might be noted that women liberated from their special
quarters in the pre-Petrine homes were those whose husbands and
fathers—nobles and rich merchants—had been able to afford to
keep them there. Town housewives and especially peasant women
had been always free to go wherever their work or duties took
them, and their lives were not much affected by Peter's reforms
at that period or, indeed, later.

If proof were needed that Peter's interest in Westernizing
his subjects did not blind him to the dangers involved in the
process, his treatment of the newly bred Russian *petits maîtres*
can serve as such. Not all of the young noblemen sent abroad to
study returned to Russia as expert engineers or diplomats. In
Petrine novels, among Peter's historical fledgelings—the Ibrahim
Hannibals or Nepluyevs—and the fictional Brothers Brovkin, Sim-
skys, and Ivlyovs, there are dandies like Yury German's "shematon

galant" Spafariev, Pushkin's Korsakov, and Kukolnik's Blekly, the
last so frenchified in his speech that he could not make his
country-bred Varenka understand that he was proposing to her.[11]
All three are historical personages, as is also a smart Kalmuck
serf whom Peter discovered helping his oafish "navigator" master
during an examination; the serf was given his freedom and the
surname of Kalmykov, and he eventually made a career in the navy,
with his former master serving under him as a shiphand. The Peter
who reproves Korsakov for extravagance in wearing velvet pants
"such as I myself don't wear," who makes Blekly and Spafariev ruin
their elegant attire by splashing in the mud alongside his buggy,
and who promotes Kalmykov is the historical Peter as well as the
fictionalized one.[12] The anecdotists Feoktistov and Golikov, as
much as the authors who used their anecdotes, helped to contribute to Peter's image his dislike of extravagance and sloth and
his appreciation of real value in a man irrespective of his social
origins.

By the same token, he disliked the "possessed" men (*besnova-
tyi*) and women (*klikusha*) and the "fools of God" (*iurodivyi*); he
considered them useless cheats who staged their epileptic seizures
in public places to escape work, and favored "exorcising them
with a knout, the knout's tail being longer than the devil's."[13]
There was another consideration; like the boyars, they too represented the opposition, whether raving about the coming of the
Antichrist and the approaching end of the world, or predicting,
among other things, the annihilation of St. Petersburg. The "fools
of God" who, protected in fact and in fiction by their established
status of holiness, upbraided Boris Godunov and Ivan the Terrible
continue this literary tradition in Petrine novels, with the difference that they never dare face Peter himself. No novel is
without its Ivanushka, Fomushka, Agapushka, Fedya, Vasya, or just
nameless prophet of impending disaster, voicing popular dissatisfaction:

> Barefoot, stinking, half-naked, his hair full of last
> summer's burrs, the *iurodivyi* scampered towards the
> church. There was a general groan on the porch: the
> "man of God" was holding a piece of raw meat in his
> hand. This meant he again was about to say something
> which would start the whole of Moscow whispering. Right
> in front of the church he sat down, his pockmarked nose
> buried in his lap, waiting for more people to gather.
> . . . Beggars gathered at the church entrance said
> cautiously: "War is coming and the plague." (*P.F.*,
> pp. 341-42.)

The "possessed" often were caught and knouted for their
prophecies; the "men of God" seldom were, usually being hidden in
time by pious people.

Peter's aversion, then, was not esthetic; in fact, he liked
monsters and freaks of nature, living or dead—anything unusual
and grotesque. After all, his Kunstkamera, a shrine to his

insatiable curiosity, recognized as scientific by petite histoire and as morbidity by most fiction writers, plays an important role in his image. If the populace revered the "men of God" and considered monsters the work of the devil, this to their Tsar was a matter of supreme indifference.

9.   Grotesque and Uncanny Features

> The grotesque is, in almost all cases, composed of two
> elements, one ludicrous, the other fearful.
>   Ruskin, 1884

> See, you can learn by my example what a wretched animal
> man still is.
>   Peter the Great, dying, 1725

As was shown, the most popular among the Petrine anecdotes are
those involving strange behavior: acts which were unseemly in
the eyes of the populace, shocking in those of foreigners, and
grotesque in the rendition of fiction. Peter's fictional image
has all the recognizable elements of the grotesque, beginning
with physical deformities—supernatural height, pigeon-toed gait,
abnormally thin legs, huge hands and feet, at times a deathly,
expressionless, mask-like face.

Next, there are moved by invisible strings the sudden, uncon-
trolled gestures like those of a puppet. Peter's extravagant, eccentric actions seem to belong to the same category of compulsive, mechanical movements. Shildkret shows the monarch not only rolling on
the ground out of excitement during the founding of St. Petersburg,
but also hopping about on one foot for joy at the suppression of the
Bulavin rebellion. Both scenes are fictional but not too outrageously
implausible in a novel if one considers that Peter actually did
publicly dance for joy on the tables at the celebration of the signing
of the treaty of Nystadt in 1721.[1] There is a folk tale about how
Peter whipped "the dumb Lake of Ladoga" with a knout as punishment
for its having given him a rough crossing. Surely, no such story
had ever been told about any other Russian tsar? Perhaps this er-
rant echo of Kings Canute's or Xerxes's legend reflected the widespread image of Peter as a *foreign* autocrat of whom any such unusual and unproper behavior could be expected.[2]

Detail of the Waxen Effigy of Peter the Great: The Death Mask.

Peter the Great Taking a Walk. *Painting by Serov, 1907.*

There is a quality of dehumanization apparent in Peter's external characterization as well as in some aspects of his behavior; animal comparisons are frequent. Peter yells at a clumsy soldier in a piercing voice, like a crowing rooster (*P.F.*, p. 63). Terrified courtiers, listening at the door behind which Alexis confronts the enraged Peter, hear sounds resembling those made by a beast attacking a human being (*P. & A.*, II, 204). The motif of an enormous cat runs through his characterization in fiction and in folklore. It has its source as much in Peter's appearance—he has "a face of a cat or a tiger," says Merezhkovsky; and at his death the populace composed a song about mice joyfully burying a huge, fiercely moustachioed cat—as in his reputation for cunning and cruelty. In *Peter the First* he snorts like a spitting cat: with fear, as a child facing the Streltsy mob (pp. 52-53); with laughter, as a matchmaker in Sanka Brovkina's marriage (p. 620); with embarrassment, writing a summons for Catherine to join him in the camp at Narva in 1703 (p. 750; he felt he was ridiculous for missing her so much). His snorting guffaws at being called the Antichrist by the half-crazy Dowager Tsaritsa Martha helped to persuade her that her visitor was indeed no other than the Evil One assuming the features of a changeling cat (*P. & A.*, I, 88-89).

The element of nonhumanness is even more apparent in Peter's bizarre, often sinister acts committed seemingly in cold blood but actually prompted by insensate rages, stemming in turn from irrational impulses and complexes unexplored by modern psychiatrists, let alone by Peter's contemporaries, by historians, or by writers of fiction. Peter's participation in the executions of the Streltsy in 1698, of his would-be assassins Tsikler and companions in 1697, and of Catherine's maid of honor, Marya Hamilton, in 1719, are among the most notorious of these acts.

The figure of a giant chopping off the heads of the rebellious Streltsy with almost supernatural force and apparent relish visits Alexis in nightmares years later. Peter is ghoulish in all these scenes in *Peter's Day* and in Polezhaev's *The Throne and the Cloister*; and the Streltsy widow's wail, "The day he does not shed blood is the day he eats no bread."[3] He looks uncanny mounting the scaffold on which Marya Hamilton is to die for having killed her newborn child, the punishment for that crime having been established by one of his ukases several years earlier. Mordovtsev's rendition of this scene in *Idealists and Realists* is typical:

> On the scaffold appeared the gigantic figure of Peter. He looked thoughtful, but a nervous tic never left his energetic face. The executioners recoiled before that colossal frame . . . the girl mounted the scaffold in her white silk dress trimmed in black ribbons . . . the Tsar turned away from that lovely head bent in prayer. . . . Something sparkled—the axe! Something fell with a thump on the boards of the scaffold—the severed head! . . . A shout of horror rose from the crowd and froze in the air.

The Tsar stooped down, picked up the dead head by the hair, looked attentively for a long while into the face as if trying to fix it in his memory and kissed the dead girl.   Next, turning to those standing nearest the scaffold, he pointed the head with his finger and said: "These are veins; along them flows the venous blood; and those are the arteries conveying the arterial blood, which is quite different from the first one.   These are the muscles of the neck, they contract and relax, like little mice." . . . And he kissed the dead head again and gave it to Dr. Blumentrost, saying: "Take this head and, having prepared a proper kind of alcohol, put it in a jar in our Museum of Arts (*Kunstkamera*) with the other rarities, there to remain forever for the edification of our subjects and their issue.   Let them know that in our realm vice is punished and virtue rewarded."   And he retired majestically.   No sound came from the crowd.   Their Tsar's calmness and his brand of justice weighed too heavily . . . on their souls.[4]

The scene is repeated, practically unchanged, in Shildkret's *The Eagle Cup* (p. 388).   Stählin mentions Peter's presence at the execution but says "he turned away" from it; d'Escherny tells of the Tsar's kissing the dead head and making the sign of the cross but omits his lecture on anatomy; Nartov skips the story altogether; and, of course, Galizin, Semevsky, and Waliszewski tell it in full with embellishments, as does Mordovtsev again in his novel *The Crowned Carpenter* and in his popular history *Russian Women of Modern Times*.   The story is overgrown with barnacles of gossip, and novelists made extensive use both of the historical fact and the rich anecdotic lore.

The execution of Tsikler and his accomplices is perhaps the most macabre and repulsive of the three.   Tsikler had participated in the 1682 Streltsy revolt organized by Sophia with the help of Ivan Miloslavsky, in which two of Peter's uncles were murdered and Peter's own life was in danger.   After the fall of Sophia's regency in 1689, Tsikler, like many other Streltsy, continued to serve, like them became part of the growing popular dissatisfaction with Peter, and finally headed a plot to assassinate the Tsar and return Sophia to power.   The plot was discovered; and Peter, enraged, not only had the culprits hanged, drawn, and quartered, but also ordered the corpse of Miloslavsky, dead for thirteen years, exhumed, and the coffin dragged by six pigs to the scaffold to "witness" the traitors' death.

The story, told by Andrey Matveev, whose own father had also been murdered in that early revolt,[5] is avoided by earlier—and thus of necessity more discreet—fiction writers, such as Masalsky, Lazhechnikov, Kornilovich, and Zagoskin.   Zotov does tell it in *The Mysterious Monk*, but with suitable condemnation of the plotters and without mentioning the scene of their execution.   But later novelists such as Polezhaev, Merezhkovsky, Shildkret, and A. N. Tolstoy miss none of Matveev's gory details: blood pouring

through the boards of the scaffold into the open coffin, the
sight of the decomposed corpse, the shocked, terrified crowd.[6]
And, as Tolstoy sees him, there is the Tsar on horseback, surrounded by his generals, racked by convulsions as if by some invisible force (*P.F.*, p. 289). The term "dance of death"—a series
of strange, mechanic movements performed by a grotesquely misshapen
figure—seems singularly appropriate here.

There is in Peter another attribute of the grotesque, something that made him different not only from what the other tsars
before him had been or what an anointed monarch was supposed to
be, but different from other human beings as well. "Sometimes it
seems that the two elements he loves best—water and fire—have
merged in him creating a strange being, good or evil, belonging
to God or to Satan, I cannot tell, but in any case not a human
being" (*P. & A.*, I, 116), says Merezhkovsky's Fräulein Juliana,
and as will be shown later, she is not alone in having such doubts.
And while she dismisses as unbecoming childishness some of Peter's
eccentricities, others evoke in her that mystical fear that sensitive people sometimes feel at the sight of a grotesque abnor-
mality. On the other hand, Peter's loyal admirers—historians,
anecdotists, and fiction writers alike—prefer to treat his manifold bizarre characteristics as innocent and occasionally even
endearing, though admittedly hard to explain.

For Peter has strange whims and phobias and even stranger
likings. Anecdotists and fiction writers were most impressed with
his love of surgery—a scientific interest according to Stählin,
morbid inquisitiveness according to Leo Tolstoy. The operation
he performed on the wife of the Dutch merchant Borst against her
wishes and resulting in her death received little attention in
fiction, as also did the unnecessary autopsies of his daughter-
in-law Charlotte, who died in childbirth, and his sister-in-law
Tsaritsa Martha, who died of natural causes.[7] But the anecdote
about his pulling out a healthy tooth of the wife of his aide
Poluboyarov at the latter's instigation is extremely popular and
seems to be considered by many a good joke and deserved punishment for an unfaithful wife.[8] He also had a predilection for
kissing which served to express a variety of emotions. Scheltema
recorded that the Tsar, out of admiration for the wonders of the
science of anatomy, kissed the smiling lips of an embalmed child
in a Dutch museum (and perhaps—who knows?—the lips of the
severed head of Marya Hamilton?) and, out of respect for his
statesmanship, the statue of Richelieu (pp. 127, 300). Bergholz
reports on the manner in which Peter demonstrated his friendship
for the Duke of Holstein, fiancé of his daughter Anne:

> The monarch kissed [the Duke] repeatedly, caressed him,
> patted him on the shoulder, several times tore the wig
> off his head and kissed him on the top and the back of
> his head, his brow, even pushed down his lower lip and
> kissed him on the gums between the lip and the teeth,
> insisting the whole while that he loved His Highness
> like his own soul and with all his heart. (*Diary*, III, 127.)

Novelists' use of this eccentric feature is limited to an entry
in Fräulein Juliana's diary, though Peter is often shown kissing
fictional merchants and carpenters in appreciation of their patriotic generosity or skill and, of course, saluting buxom hostesses
and pretty brides.

Fräulein Juliana showed perspicacity in noticing the elemental
character of Peter's love for water and fire. It is known that he
had a fear of water in childhood—one of his earliest phobias.
The sudden interest in sailing he showed as an adolescent, which
soon developed into a permanent obsession, has never been explained. D'Escherny attributes the metamorphosis to the Tsar's
overcoming his fear for reasons of state (*Mélanges*, no. 24). Voltaire maintains that Peter "dompta la nature" by jumping into
water in spite of his aversion for it, causing his aversion to
change in time into a "goût dominant."[9] And fiction makes occasional use of the story how the boy-tsar discovered "the grandfather of the Russian Navy." The fact is that Peter's delight in
sailing in any weather, his keen interest in shipbuilding, the
proficiency he acquired in manning a ship, and his overpowering
love of the sea are a built-in part of this fictional image, a
symbol of his statesmanship.

Yet, somehow, this by no means uncommon or unnatural inclina-
tion has in Peter's case a tinge of morbidity, perhaps because of
the hardships it imposed on his contemporaries. The building of
St. Petersburg had nothing to recommend itself to Peter's subjects except as Russia's access to the Baltic Sea—Peter's cher-
ished dream but a meaningless advantage in their eyes. The terrible, unwholesome climate; the cost in human lives and taxes; the
abandonment of Moscow in favor of the new capital, unsettling and
insulting to the populace—all this contributed to the aura of
mysterious evil which, in Russian literature, had always surrounded
this foggy, alien city and its creator. But to Peter no sacrifice
was too great if it served to raise his "paradise" on the sea or
to build the navy destined to defeat the mistress of that sea,
Sweden.

Fiction likes to see Peter as the "man at the helm," figur-
atively and literally. "It *is* a Paradise, eh, Alexashka?" (or
Yaguzhinsky, or some other courtier) he says, inhaling with relish
the cold, wet wind from the sea. "Don't be afraid," he tells the
panicked sailors on a boat tossed by the stormy waves; "your Tsar
is with you!" (Nartov, no. 130; *Mamura*, p. 356). Courtiers,
foreign diplomats, ladies of his own family, including the two
old dowager tsaritsas—everyone, seasick or not, had to get used
to seafaring and learn to like it. He forbade building bridges
to connect the islands in the Neva on which St. Petersburg was
built so as to force the inhabitants to use boats as means of
transportation. He himself used his small rowboat (*vereika*), and
it is mostly in it or in his one-horse buggy (*odnokolka*) that he
travels in all seasons along the paths of Russian historical fiction, a familiar yet awesome figure.

Peter's other obsession is fire, the element he loved like a
salamander. He never missed an opportunity to act as a fireman—

there were plenty of fires in wooden Moscow—and he was known on
several occasions to have left a party to do just that (Korb, I,
219).   Nevertheless, Peter's appearances in the role of fireman
are rare in fiction.

He liked fireworks even more; thrifty as he was, he spent
money lavishly on elaborate pyrotechnics, illuminations, and cannon salutes as part of feasts and pageants, deriving double satisfaction from a combination of his two favorite entertainments.
The reactions of the crowds to their monarch's appearances against
these flaming backdrops differ.   In works such as Kukolnik's *The
Sentinel* (p. 244) and "The New Year" (p. 198), and in Fedorov's
The Demidovs (p. 275), they show a childish delight in the fireworks, grateful for what the memoirist Kurakin called "the fiery
fun" (*History*, p. 71).   In *Peter the First* crowds are mostly
silent, fascinated by the strangeness of it all and by the sight
of "the Tsar, like some fiery spirit," dashing about and directing
the show (p. 335).   But in Pilnyak's *His Majesty Kneeb Piter
Komondor*, people cower on the ground at the sight of fiery animals
erupting in the sky (pp. 109-10), and in Kostylyov's *Pitirim*
frightened crowds talk of the devil's flames, of frozen stars, and
of the coming of the Antichrist (p. 423).   And an eerie aura of
petrified acquiescence prevails at a garden party in *Peter and
Alexis* featuring ornate fireworks and a procession of the "most-
crazy, most-drunken council."   The party is given in honor of the
unveiling of the marble statue of Venus, the "white she-devil" to
whom the summoned court is paying ceremonial homage.   The presence
of mysterious evil forces is suggested by a violent thunderstorm;
lightning extinguishes the fireworks, while the guests flee in
panic.   (I, 27-29.)

Peter's flights from curious crowds, his sudden attacks of
paralyzing shyness at court receptions, and his escaping from
palatial apartments to sleep in servants' closets were mentioned
by A. N. Tolstoy and Danilevsky; but such things happened only
outside Russia, when Peter was, one might say, taken out of his
natural habitat.   Pilnyak, Tynyanov, and A. N. Tolstoy did note
the canvas ceilings stretched low in Peter's rooms,[10] and it is
generally accepted as part of the Tsar's taste for simplicity that
he preferred small rooms—in fact, disliked large, high-ceilinged
ones.   But no author elaborates on these symptoms of mild agora-
phobia and an insecurity complex; apparently, as in the case of
his stinginess, these details seem too petty to suit Peter's
magnificent, towering figure.   Peter's fear of death by assassination, which could bring on convulsions and outbursts of maniacal
rage and cruelty, is evident in *Peter the First* in scenes such as
the flight to the Trinity Monastery in 1689; the macabre revenge
taken on the corpse of Ivan Miloslavsky, that "terrible specter rising again out of memories of Peter's childhood" (p. 283); and the
berserk suppression of the Streltsy revolt for the "terrible deeds
which [Peter believed] were prepared" (p. 332).   Foreign envoys and
memoirists reporting on the rumors circulating on the sudden death of
Tsarevich Alexis and the savage persecutions of his supporters suggest the same reason: Peter's fear of a coup and assassination.

Unsurprisingly, though, in Petrine novels by authors such as
Żotov, Masalsky, Lazhechnikov, and Kukolnik, Peter knows no fear
and pardons his fictional would-be assassins. This magnanimity
may have its source in an anecdote by Stählin (no. 26) about how
the Tsar once spared the life of a plotter, changing his punishment to "exile in far-off provinces"—presumably Siberia. This
group of writers shunned any reference to the affair of Alexis,
while Merezhkovsky and Ivanov prefer to attribute it to Peter's
concern about the fate of his reforms rather than about his own
survival.

For, his escape from Narva notwithstanding, Peter was no
coward, though not a born warrior like Charles XII of Sweden, to
whom war was not a means of achieving fame or territorial con-
quests, but an end in itself. The wars Peter waged for thirty
years were to gain access to the seas and to permit Russia to join
the family of European nations. Historical fiction, in spite of
the genre's preference for glorious warriors and their deeds of
arms, recognizes Peter's uniqueness in this respect by casting
his image primarily as that of a Reformer, as the "Crowned Carpenter," and as the "Man at the helm" leading the ship of state
to power. In him the fear of death was not faint-heartedness but
a deep-seated complex traceable to the shock received in 1682.
This fear was human and understandable, but it added to his personality touches of estrangement and of incongruity which were
camouflaged by historical fiction, a genre not given to psychological insight and explanation of subconscious phenomena.

At the very bottom of Peter's phobias lay a pathological
fear of cockroaches. D'Escherny insists that, like the Tsar's
early aversion to water, it was inborn—and it persisted throughout his life. Stählin says that "though nobody could be less
subject to petty, childish squeamishness than was this great
monarch, the sight of one of these insects sufficed to drive him
out of the room" (no. 25); Golikov acknowledges an early inborn
fear of water but draws the line at cockroaches (pp. 1–8), as do
Nartov and all of Peter's admirers among the fiction writers.
But, acutely sensitive to the grotesque in Peter, Tynyanov and
Merezhkovsky bring this particular phobia into focus. Fräulein
Juliana writes in her diary:

> I saw him once turn pale and tremble with fright, his
> features convulsed, at the sight of a cockroach. It was
> as if he had seen a ghost or an unnatural monster; it
> seemed that in a moment he would faint or become hysteri-
> cal like a timorous woman. If one were to play on him
> one of those jokes he is so fond of playing on others,
> and placed on his naked body half a dozen spiders or
> cockroaches, he probably would die on the spot, and
> surely historians would not believe that the conqueror of
> Charles XII died from the touch of a cockroach's feet.
> There is something striking in this fear shown by the
> giant Tsar, before whom everything trembles, at the sight
> of tiny, harmless vermin. I remembered Leibnitz's theory

of monads: it is as if the nature of insects—not the
physical nature but the metaphysical one—is hostile to
the Tsar's nature. I felt his fear was not just ridiculous but frightening as well: it was as if I suddenly
glimpsed some ancient mystery. (*P. & A.*, I, 120-21.)

Tynyanov appears to think that one can identify the nature
of the mysterious fright: for some reason, a cockroach sym-
bolizes death for Peter—his own death:

Onto a blue tile of the stove [in the room where Peter
lies dying] crawled a cockroach. It stopped. And looked.
He had had three fears in his life, all big ones: water,
blood . . . and vermin, the fragile cockroaches. The
last fear had stayed with him always. And what was there
in the cockroach to make one afraid? Nothing . . . except
that no one was capable of destroying a cockroach or pro-
tecting oneself against it.
    And now he, Peter, was weeping, and he could not see
the cockroach through his tears. And when he wiped his
eyes with the bedcovers, then he saw it.
    The cockroach stood there, and moved its whiskers,
and looked. Where would its feet carry it now, those
innumerable feet? [Peter tried to reach a boot to throw
at the roach but failed.] His teeth began to chatter because in the meantime the cockroach was standing there
unwatched, and waited, and perhaps it had already fallen
off? Suddenly, it did, with a thump, and was gone. They
both were gone: Peter Alexeevich lay devoid of all
consciousness, empty, as if in a drunken stupor. All
strength had left his body. . . . And when he looked at
the stove there was no cockroach on it and he managed to
convince himself that there never had been one at all,
that he had just imagined it. Actually, it could not
have happened; where could the cockroach have come from?
He lay for a while overwhelmed with weakness and so,
forgot it. (*Effigy*, no. 1, pp. 17-18.)

If Peter is not subject to fears (his fear of cockroaches
could be, and was, termed dislike), he certainly inspired fear in
others. In fact, his image radiates an atmosphere of fear, ranging from the physical dread of his unlimited power and his ready
use of it, including that of his staff; to awe at the grandeur of
his personality and deeds, which caused Pushkin in writing Peter's
biography, to "approach the task with fear and trepidation";[11] to
the mystical "unearthly fear" (*nezdeshnii uzhas*) experienced by
Merezhkovsky and by the populace, who believed their tsar to be
the Antichrist. A blend of all these sensations of alarm, reverence, and mystical ambiance has surrounded Peter's image with the
halo of a superhuman being, a deity.
    Indeed, making use of the premise familiar to the Russian
Orthodox readers that the anointed monarch is God's substitute on

earth (*Bog zemnoi*), fiction writers have their characters routinely
consider and sometimes address Peter as such. "Thou art our earthly God," says Zotov's Menshikov (*Monk*, p. 265), Streshnev in
Kornilovich's *Tatyana Boltova* (p. 51), and the author Kukolnik
himself in his "The New Year" (p. 157)—all the while appealing
for mercy for a criminal. As such, Peter also possesses God's
attributes. He "sanctifies labor with his august hands" when
wielding a hammer in Arseniev's *Arisha the Ducky* (p. 8); he works
a miracle by building St. Petersburg while being, as Prince Yakov
Dolgoruky explains in Kukolnik's *Tale of the Blue and the Green
Cloth* (p. 179), "himself a miracle created by God"; "Our Father
Peter the Great, thou hast created us who did not exist before
thee!" (intones Krekshin.[12] Merezhkovsky's Archbishop "Fedos"
(Feodosy) explains to Peter why he should adopt the title of Emperor: "You are God on earth; this is what *Divus Caesar* means;
August Caesar—Emperor—God" (*P. & A.*, I, 126). Peter himself
seems to perceive the validity of this reasoning when, according
to Nartov, he proposes at a party a toast to "those who love God,
myself, and the Fatherland," in that order (no. 42).

Nor are poets missing from this laudatory chorus. "He was
your God, your God, O Russia!" exclaims Lomonosov. "Has God
descended to earth in his shape?" queries Derzhavin, adding elsewhere: "God creating His miracles seldom creates such men. Having created Peter the Great, He has been resting ever since."
And Sumarokov apostrophizes Peter's birthplace, the village
Kolomenskoe, as "Russia's Bethlehem." Even writers of the petite
histoire contributed to the deification of Peter's image with a
story reported by Golikov. According to him, an old retired
veteran living on charity in a diocesan hostel in Nizhny Novgorod
was discovered burning candles and praying before Peter's portrait
which he had hung among the icons. And he refused to discontinue
the practice in spite of the remonstrations of the bishop himself
(no. 132).

If not always acknowledged as God, Peter still invariably is
something of a superman and still inspires fear bordering on awe.
People are "afraid even to bow to him—who knows, perhaps it is
forbidden?", afraid to speak to him: "just the sight of him makes
your tongue stick to your throat"; afraid to meet him face to
face: "Tsarevich Alexis scuttled like a rabbit into the bushes
bordering the garden path"; afraid to think of him even: "'Why
did the Antichrist close down my church?' thought Stroganov—and,
so thinking, looked over his shoulder."[13] The feeling is so
powerful that it survives Peter himself: a threatening gesture
from the mechanized mannequin of Peter in Tynyanov's *The Waxen
Effigy* makes the cynical, hard-boiled courtier Yaguzhinsky flee
in panic from the invisible Presence, the still-awesome "It."

Yet fear is mixed with a strange fascination. Peter, as was
shown, is unnaturally strong, omnipotent, almost palpably acti-
vated by an outside invisible factor, like the mechanism which
frightened Yaguzhinsky. Waliszewski, while acknowledging the
presence of such a factor, identifies it simply as Peter's violent
temper, his lack of self-control, and hence the dangerous

unpredictability of his reactions (*Petr Velikii*, p. 172). But
Merezhkovsky sees him steering the ship of state with a steady
hand towards a goal he alone could perceive with a clarity derived
from divine inspiration.

> "The giant man at the helm looked at the flooded city.
> In his face—calm, firm, as if carved in stone—there was
> no uncertainty, no fear, no pity, as if there was indeed
> something nonhuman in him, something that gave him sway
> over people and the elements, something powerful and im-
> perious like Fate." (*P. & A.*, I, 187.)

This sway held over people, if not over the elements, is of
course a familiar attribute of an autocrat, a tsar's birthright,
but Peter's will in the fictional world is a juggernaut, ready to
crush the slightest sign of opposition, a force accepted with
tremulous, reverent acquiescence. "The Tsar's will is the mother
of the Law, for it brings the law into the world," says Mordovtsev's Prince Dolgoruky; "As You will, Sire," says Kornilovich's
Romodanovsky, "You are above the Law, and therefore your acts cannot break it!" And Lazhechnikov comments in an author's aside:
"Peter's will bowed to no earthly power, while everything and
everyone bowed to that will."[14]
    A supreme being then, for some; for others a pagan god,
descended from the clouds to lead Russia to glory—as seen by
Kheraskov in his poem *Rossiada* (1778) or as hailed by Merezhkovsky's crowd of sycophantic courtiers: "Mars, the worthy mate of
the marble goddess Venus" (*P. & A.*, I, 25). He is Arseniev's
stylized giant out of Russian folklore with "a voice like an
archangel's trumpet, eyes like lightning, and hands like iron
vises" (*The Tsar's Verdict*, p. 11). For Pilnyak he is a monster
with

> an enormous body, unclean, sweaty, ungainly, pigeon-toed,
> spindle-legged, corroded by alcohol, tobacco, and syphilis.
> With the passing of years his round, red, old woman's face
> grew flabby; his cheeks and red lips hung loosely; the
> red, syphilitic eyelids did not meet; and insane, drunken,
> savage, childish eyes peered out of them. (*Kneeb*, pp.
> 107-8.)

He is a boor, skipping about on one foot and clapping his hands
for joy in Shildkret's *Our-Savior-on-the-Tallow Church* (p. 91)
and thumbing his nose at a merchant in *Mamura* (p. 47).
    God, monster, noble statue, clown—Peter's image is built on
contrasts inherent in his personality and in the impression he
creates on the inhabitants of the world of fiction.
    There are no indifferent, middle-of-the-road, or simply ob-
jective creators of Peter's image; there are only admirers and
detractors. It is as if Peter's own feelings were so intense
that he could not inspire lukewarm feelings in others. The adulation felt by Lazhechnikov, Kornilovich, and Kukolnik is evident

even in their style and in every detail of Peter's characterization. Shildkret, Leo Tolstoy, and of course Pilnyak are emphatic in their personal hostility and consequently artistic disparagement. Soviet writers as a group reflect the current Party policy in the interpretation of history and thus of Peter's role in it, and any feelings that can be detected in their works on the subject are not theirs alone. Alexey Tolstoy avoids showing his feelings by making Peter a mirror in which is reflected the changing Russia.

The attitudes of Pushkin, Merezhkovsky, and young Alexey Tolstoy (Mordovtsev's seem to change in each novel) are ambivalent. Pushkin's fragments of his unfinished *Materials for a History of Peter the Great* abound in critical remarks, but his poems breathe pride at the grandeur of Peter the Great of Russia, and his Ibrahim in *The Blackamoor of Peter the Great* is full of admiration for his august protector. Merezkovsky in *Peter and Alexis* is torn between the call of the New and the nostalgic appeal of the Old, represented by the conflict between the Tsar reformer and his heir. Merezhkovsky's characters, however, firmly take sides, successfully passing their creator's own ambivalent feelings on to the reader.

And finally, everyone—Peter's contemporaries, historians, writers, and fictional characters alike—recognizes the elusive element of strangeness which is impossible to capture or explain, but unmistakably present. Pushkin and both Tolstoys keenly felt the artistic challenge of creating a genuine image of the Tsar, one true to his inner self. None of them succeeded, all being in some way prevented from finishing their respective novels—A. N. Tolstoy by death, Pushkin and Leo Tolstoy by an unexplained inner resistance which they never experienced in any of their other works.

A little-known nineteenth-century play by R. Zotov is worth quoting, as it conveys the near-deification of Petrine fiction of that period. In *The Shipbuilder of Zaandam; or, His Name Is Ineffable* (1841) Peter does not appear at all, nor do the two young Russians accompanying the Tsar on his first journey abroad, who serve as Peter's intermediates in the accepted benevolent deux ex machina plot resolution common to plays of that period. This is the final scene of the last act, as Peter is leaving Zaandam. A bust covered by taffeta is brought in, a gift to a Dutch shipbuilder:

> *The Shipbuilder*: Who is he? *Voice of a Russian Apprentice*: His name is not to be spoken. He is our father, our benefactor, our idol, our all in all! Let others call him First and Great, but with us Russians, it is He! His name is ineffable!
>
> (Everyone kneels. Gun salutes and shouts of "Hurrah!" backstage. The orchestra plays "God Save the Tsar." The curtain falls.)[15]

Thus, for Zotov's fictional characters Peter assumes the

status of the Biblical and ineffable Jehovah (Yahweh). He is also
omnipotent and invisible—i.e., faceless—to the mortals, his
subjects. These characteristics, however, do not belong exclusively to the supreme Good; they also are among the signs of the
Antichrist. The scene in A. N. Tolstoy's *Peter's Day* illustrates
this point:

> A scream resounded throughout the dark building [of the
> workers' barracks at St. Petersburg]: "Our Tsar has been
> replaced by a changeling in the foreign land! This one
> is not our Tsar at all: I saw him yesterday myself. He
> has no face; his is not a human countenance, and his head
> twists and he rolls his eyes, and earth will not bear
> him, it is caving in under him. Woe, woe to the Russian
> land! We have been betrayed, Orthodox people!" (p.
> 401.)

The screaming voice belongs to Varlaam, a historical personage, a monk turned Old Believer, who first appeared in fiction
as the protagonist of Mordovtsev's novel *Idealists and Realists*.
Before taking vows he was Captain Vasily Levin, long suffering
from fits of melancholy and epilepsy. In 1722 he was arrested and
later executed for announcing to gathered crowds the end of the
world to be preceded by the reign of a tsar Antichrist—Peter.
Levin-Varlaam was not the first to begin spreading this news
among the populace; in 1702 another Old Believer, Grigory Talitsky,
composed and distributed pamphlets explaining that, according to
the Scriptures, the Antichrist was to come as the eighth Russian
tsar—which Peter was, counting from Ivan the Terrible. Talitsky
was also arrested, tortured, and executed; but the rumor of the
Antichrist persisted, and many an unfortunate who was caught
spreading the sinister news in the marketplace or in a tavern
died on the rack. Their testimony, found in the protocols of the
Secret Chancellery Archives, which were made available to historical researchers in the 1880's, was revealed to the public by
Soloviev in his *History* and by Semevsky in his sensational *High
Treason!*—the title refers to the dreaded formula used in the ar-
rests and all their consequences.

These materials, in spite of their picturesque possibilities,
had to be handled by fiction writers with caution. Popular dissatisfaction with government was not a topic readily acceptable
to tsarist or Soviet regimes, though the names of Varlaam and
Talitsky could be and often were mentioned in scenes of torture
and investigations as part of the historical background. The no-
tion of a tsar Antichrist would have been incongruous in a realis-
tic novel of any period: even Merezhkovsky could not use its
mystical aspect except in plausible circumstances, such as the
half-dream or vision of the insane Tsaritsa Martha. Still, there
are numerous episodes conveying the atmosphere of fear and despair which was created by such rumors and in turn caused them to
spread—and they could not fail to affect Peter's image.

There are scenes such as the one in *Peter and Alexis* in which a group of tramps camping by the Neva comments on the sights and sounds—fireworks, shouts, and music—of Peter's garden party across the river in honor of the statue of Venus. The reaction of these people to the thunderstorm that puts an end to the party is typical: it is an omen, they say, that doomsday is near. There are scenes, such as the one in *Peter the First*, of a whole settlement of Old Believers burning themselves, their wives, and their children alive rather than face being drafted and marked with the seal of the Antichrist—a cross with which the army branded the right hand of the new recruits to prevent desertions. And numerous scenes are scattered throughout historical fiction of Old Believer priests explaining to Peter's unsophisticated subjects the apocalyptic meaning of the word *emperor* and of the "number of the beast, 666,"[16] and the sinful nature of the hardships suffered under him. These included the never-ending war, the back-breaking taxation, the godless pageants, the use of tobacco, the shaving of beards, and the building of St. Petersburg. In his *Our-Savior-on-the-Tallow Church* Shildkret even has Evdokia, Peter's rejected wife, repeat confidently that the "Tsar is the Antichrist born of the impure maiden" (p. 32), one of the many strange rumors concerning Peter's birth.

These rumors ranged from the fantastic to the hagiographic to the scandalous. The fantastic rumors were the masses' nonreligious interpretations of Peter's strange behavior and striking physique. As already mentioned, the aureole of holiness, power, and prestige traditionally surrounding the person of the anointed, lawful monarch did not allow for an assumption of his wrongdoing or for criticism of his person. Hence, the explanation of Peter's reforms and himself as his simply *not being* in reality the tsar.

He had been, it was said, either turned into a changeling by witchcraft during his travels in foreign, heretic countries or sealed in a barrel and flung into the sea, where he had perished, while a false tsar returned home in his stead. For those who had less faith in witchcraft there was the story that Tsaritsa Natalya had borne a girl and that a boy had been substituted, probably Lefort's son; hence, Peter's incomprehensible love for foreigners and their heretic ways. Natalya's virtue was not questioned, and her deception was explained as a fear of disappointing her husband, who wanted a son.[17] Fiction writers who wished to utilize these popular tales found them in the same protocols of the Secret Chancellery which provided the tales of Peter the Antichrist. They were told on the rack by the unfortunates arrested for "words offensive to the Lord" (*bogoprotivnye slova*), that is, for *lèse majesté*. These rumors are used in fiction as examples of the masses' ignorance or else of their dissatisfaction with Peter's reforms, depending on the period and the author's stand in these matters. While not affecting Peter's image directly, they add to its quality of alienation and loneliness.

Only somewhat less fantastic than the folk tales is the hagiographic story about Peter's conception and birth. According to the editor of Krekshin's *History*, Sakharov, it is based on popular folk tales; Stählin included it in his collection of anecdotes (no. 114) as typical of the Russians' devotion to Peter's memory. But Krekshin does not treat the story as an anecdote, still less as a fairy tale. According to him, Simeon Polotsky, a learned monk of great repute and influence at the court of Tsar Alexis, became aware on a certain night on the basis of the constellation of the stars that a great tsar to be named Peter had been conceived. The next morning Polotsky announced the news to the tsar, supplementing it with a prediction of the future monarch's greatness and of the exact number of years he would live. The tsar was overjoyed, though for his own reasons he had the astrologer monk followed by four policemen (*uriadnik*) for the next twelve weeks. Polotsky's prophecy, Krekshin continues, was conformed and enlarged by a certain nameless but very holy "God's fool" (*blazhennyi*), a frequent visitor in the Kremlin.[18] The story, though well known to those partial to the petite histoire, has not been used in historical fiction.

Scandalous gossip was used, however, though it was presented as such and with caution. Tsarevna Sophia in *Peter the First* speaks venomously of the good times Tsaritsa Natalya was known to have had with Patriarch Nikon in her youth—and isn't it funny how "little brother Peter" has no resemblance whatsoever to Tsar Alexis? (*P.F.*, p. 43.) Years later, the tsaritsa's own daughter, Tsarevna Natalya, repeats with gentle sadness and envy the gossip about her mother's love for a courtier, Musin-Pushkin, "of angelic or, rather, diabolic beauty," and about how he was suddenly sent away to be a voevoda in Siberia (*P.F.*, p. 739). The Streltsys in Mordovtsev's *Idealists and Realists* (p. 146) talk of Peter's resemblance to Prince Prozorovsky. Shildkret and Pilnyak point to another boyar, Tikhon Streshnev: Shildkret, in *Mamura* (p. 60), in passages showing intimacy between Streshnev and Natalya, allegedly still young and beautiful in 1694; and Pilnyak, when he has Peter order Tolstoy to find out immediately whether Streshnev was indeed his, Peter's father (*Kneeb*, pp. 122-3). In the *Beginnings of the Novel on Peter's Reign* Leo Tolstoy states that

> in less than a year after the death of his wife, Tsar Alexis began a love affair with an unmarried girl, Natalya, and two years later, so as to conceal his sin, married her. The wedding took place on January 22, and in May she bore an illegitimate son. Nobody knew whether the child was the tsar's or some other man's. (p. 152.)

Tolstoy not only questions Natalya's virtue, but goes on to accuse her of poisoning her four stepsons. He points out that two of them died young; that the future Tsar Fedor's health was ruined, and that Ivan, who later shared the throne with Peter, became a half-idiot. But all six stepdaughters, who presented no obstacle to Peter's succession, remained in excellent health. In the second draft of the novel, Tolstoy corrects his mistake on the date of Peter's birth—he was, of course, born in May 1672, in the year following the first anniversary of his parents' marriage in

January 1671—but lets stand the other accusation against Natalya,
that of her poisoning Fedor and Ivan. To justify this license of
imagination, Tolstoy could have quoted historical analogy, since
poison had been used many times in the Kremlin's political intrigues, and also a historical source, the *Mémoires* of Prince
Peter Dolgorukov (p. 102). These had also given Pilnyak the inspiration for his scene alleging Peter's doubts about his legitimacy and had provided many a spicy item of gossip to some of
Peter's detractors.

There are no legends connected with Peter's death, unless
one counts the folk talk reported by Barsov. "God's fool" Faddey,
the story goes, told the Tsar during his inspection of the Petro-
zavodsk foundries in 1724 that he would die within a year and was
duly arrested for such wanton talk. On his deathbed Peter recalled
the prophecy and ordered the man to be released and given a pension (pp. 12-13). Otherwise, there is little in petite histoire
concerning Peter's death except opinions and anecdotes on its
causes. The best known is the popular story of the severe cold
the Tsar caught rescuing some drowning sailors; others are malicious gossip, including one story about death from excessive
drinking at a meeting of the "most-crazy, most-drunken council"
and one about death from infection aggravated by an old case of
neglected venereal disease.[19] According to Stählin, a famous
German doctor insisted that the great man had been allowed to die
of a simple urinary tract ailment that could easily have been
cured (nos. 110 and 111). The populace marked the Tsar's demise
with a rhyme on how the mice buried the cat which had died from
its gluttony while devouring them, though Golikov describes the
popular "sobbing, howling, screaming, and fainting" at Derbent
upon the news of Peter's death (*Anecdotes*, p. 525), and Neplyuev
vows he fainted and lay senseless for twenty-four hours (*Notes*,
p. 652).

Fiction's portrayal of such grief is scant and dignified.
The following is a fair sample: "The old smith from Tula realized
that an irretrievable loss had been suffered by the nation. On
that grey morning, a few minutes after five o'clock, the monarch,
having suffered untold anguish, passed away in the arms of the
Empress Catherine." (*The Demidovs*, p. 313.)

There is an anecdote concerning Peter's last words, repeated
by Belyaev and Stählin, which was used in its entirety by Shklovsky as one of his quaint *Novellas on Peter*:

> He was dying in atrocious pain, in the throes of desola-
> tion. He squeezed his doctor's hand, leaving a dark
> bruise that took a long time to disappear.
>   Suppressing his moans, Peter said: "See, you can
> learn by my example what a wretched animal man still is."
> (p. 29.)

Peter's feeling of utter futility is conveyed in a death scene in
Tynyanov's *The Waxen Effigy*:

Farewell, Russia, the big ship! In whose care am I leaving you? Sons and small daughters, my guts, my little
innards died, every one of them! And as to the eldest
villain, I did him in myself! All will be reduced to
nothingness. . . . His time is up, he has been sold, betrayed [by Fate?], the soldier's son Peter Mikhaylov (no.
1, p. 16.)

On the whole, authors did not extend to Peter's death the mysterious, awesome ambience he radiated in life, which may serve to
explain the limited appeal of the topic in general. He lived
like a god but died like a mortal—and this did not fit the lofty
image that had been created for him.

Part III

Part III

10. The Entourage

A great man died, a man impatiently desiring the new as
supreme good. He died, drowned in hate, having done much
old-fashioned evil. But his great will lived on.
Shklovsky, 1970

Much of Peter's image is revealed through his relationships with
other people, fictional characters as well as historical personages. Peter's treatment of those around him—his wives, mistresses, members of his large family, courtiers (including the
"fledgelings of Peter's nest"), generals, and workmen at the
shipyard—gives the reader a close-up of Peter the man. Glimpses
of Peter the statesman can best be found in his treatment of the
populace—the faceless millions, the suppliers of manpower and
money, for whose future power and glory he had, he insisted, been
toiling all his life.

The most striking feature revealed by these human relationships, a feature of which many artists were keenly aware, is the
duality of Peter's personality. He is basically kind, perhaps
even capable of tenderness and love, but at the same time, he is
capable of intense, grotesque cruelty. He is not a sadist—even
his detractors, like Waliszewski, recognize that—but can be provoked to revolting deeds by anything thwarting his despotic will,
by sudden fear, rooted in an insecurity complex, and by jealousy,
which was, in fact, a combination of the first two. Many of his
amusements and hobbies, and even certain details of his reforms,
bear the mark of cruelty, which again, in spite of appearances,
is not sadism but an unhappy combination of coarseness and insensitivity. It is the latter trait which Pilnyak seems to have
in mind when he describes Peter's eyes as "those with which a
child looks at a cat when sticking a needle in it, or when apply-
ing a red-hot iron to the snout of a sleeping pig (*Kneeb*, p. 108).
In *The Waxen Effigy*, Tynyanov's Peter, delirious and racked by
the unbearable pain of his mortal illness, decides to issue a

ukase on the use of torture similar to that which he is suffering
now: it is not to be applied during any investigation more than
once because under it "a man is liable to change into something
different from his self" (no. 1, p. 14).   He had never realized
that before.

He is insecure and hence suspicious—whether by nature or by
circumstance, it is impossible to say.   Living in the thick of
events, involved in incessant activity, and facing popular unrest,
he is a desperately lonely man.   The loneliness of monarchs and
the burden of power they carry have long and often been acknowledged by them—witness Shakespeare's King Henry IV or Pushkin's
Tsar Boris Godunov—but in Russian fiction Peter's loneliness is
magnified by the enormous scale of his goal and of the activities
it entails, by the inadequacy to their tasks of his would-be
helpers, and finally by the peculiarities of his own personality.
He is lonely because there is nobody to share, or even to glimpse,
his lofty vision of a new Russia, lonely because he is feared and
misunderstood by everyone—friend and foe, subjects and family,
Russians and foreigners, none of whom he could wholly trust.

Considering the protracted controversy between Westerners
and Slavophiles over Peter's Europeanization of Russia, foreigners
in Petrine novels are surprisingly few.   The Foreign Quarter
figures prominently as a setting, of course, and as an alleged influence, but except for Lefort and the Mons family, of whom more
later, its inhabitants are nameless theatrical extras.   Pastor
Glück is sometimes mentioned as the future Empress Catherine's
guardian, but he has no speaking lines anywhere except in Lazhechnikov's *The Last Recruit*.   All three Doctors Blumentrost, father
and two sons (their identities much confused in the minds of fiction writers), appear whenever medical help is needed.   Foreign
doctors attend the deathbeds of Tsar Fedor, Tsaritsa Natalya, and
Peter himself, and are present in the torture chamber of Tsarevich
Alexis.[1]   The faithful mercenary old General Gordon acquires a
personality in *Peter the First* and in German's *Youthful Russia*;
the Saxon envoy Koenigseck plays a historically unjustified role
in the fall of Anna Mons; Merezhkovsky shows glimpses of the
scholarly James Bruce.   There is also Devier, Petersburg's chief
of police, unrecognizable in Kukolnik's and Merezhkovsky's respective characterizations; and a few foreign officers, fictionalized
in all but their names, appear in the early stages of the Swedish
War in several Petrine novels.   Other foreigners as fictional
characters are usually cast in secondary roles, are often brutal
or dishonest, and serve to show Peter's attitude toward foreign
influences as well as the moral superiority of Russians.   The last
tendency was particularly evident during the height of the Soviet
patriotism trend in works such as Yury German's *Youthful Russia*
and Selvinsky's *From Poltava to Gangut*.   It is, however, also
present in such recent works as Lebedev's *The Doomed Freedom*
(1975).

Lefort, according to Zotov "the extraordinary man whose name
will forever be dear to every Russian," is a foreigner whose role
in Peter's life was historically too considerable to be disregarded

by fiction. He is, however, variously presented as an adventurous bonvivant, as Peter's evil genius, and as the inspirer of the Tsar's greatest deeds. The authors of the petite histoire saw him only as the last; in fact, according to Helbig, Bruce, and Scheltema, there would have been no reforms, and hardly any greatness shown by Peter, if it had not been for Lefort. Zotov, Vsevolod Soloviev, and Masalsky, in *The Mysterious Monk*, *The Tsar-Maiden,* and *The Streltsy*, respectively, endow him with nobility of character and charm. A. N. Tolstoy does not commit himself as to Lefort's character but stresses his charm and its influence on the inquisitive boy Peter. Shildkret, in *Mamura*, makes Lefort a homosexual and insinuates that he corrupted both Peter and Menshikov. A. N. Tolstoy gives a moving account of Peter's grief at Lefort's death, and so does Danilevsky, who, moreover, bases the fictional plot of *To India in Peter's Time* on Peter's generosity toward Lefort's imaginary illegitimate daughter to whom the Tsar transfers the affection he had felt for his mentor and friend. Since Lefort died in 1699, he does not participate in Petrine novels featuring Peter in his mature years. Anna and Willim Mons belong to Peter's personal life, which will be discussed later.

What, then, do foreigners contribute to Peter's image? Far from being their dupe or victim, as folklore and the fictional villainous boyars alleged, the Tsar uses foreigners to serve his own goals, much as he does the Russians, without any consideration of rank, birth, or moral value. While Peter's historical remark that he would need Europe for a few decades and then would turn his back on her did not find its way into fiction, he confirms it with his whole attitude. Zagoskin lets a loyal foreigner, Weide, assure a group of other mercenaries that the Tsar eventually will have no more use for them than for a lemon he had squeezed the juice out of. (*Russians*, p. 439). Peter consistently appoints Russians to positions of leadership, as figureheads at first— "to shut the boyars' mouth," says A. N. Tolstoy (*P.F.*, p. 285) of Shein's promotion to generalissimus in the Campaign of Azov—but then in earnest, as Russians gradually rally around him. These are the old guard, like Sheremetev and Golovin, and the upstart "fledgelings of Peter's nest," like Menshikov and Yaguzhinsky, Ivlyov and the brothers Brovkin, historical personages and fictional characters alike. His unseemly behavior—ranging from pipe-smoking to the profane rituals of the "most-crazy council"— was blamed on the bad example of his friends from the Foreign Quarter, even though the council's permanent members were all Russians, and the inhabitants of the Foreign Quarter were—except for a few mercenaries in Russian service, like Lefort—sedate middle-class burghers. Had he associated with the right kind of foreigners—nobles and diplomats—he would have found them as deeply concerned with court etiquette and dignified behavior as were Peter's critics among the Russian aristocrats. But Peter had no regard for either of them and was impatient with etiquette and courtly manners whether at home or abroad. He wanted helpers —efficient, reliable people—about him, and he did not care where they came from.

Helpers, as is often shown in fiction, could be recruited from among the old guard. Streshnev, Yakov Dolgoruky, and Voznitsyn are treated by Peter, even though grudgingly, with a certain respect, sometimes with affection, and with impatient condescension. They are stolid and slow to accept change, but their very old-fashionedness guarantees their loyalty to the monarch. If they are too stupid or dissolute, they still can be employed as court jesters, as are Prince Shakhovskoy, a historical personage in *Peter's Day*, and Prince Buynosov, a fictional character in *Peter the First*. If unfit for any kind of service, they are relegated by Peter and by fiction writers to the ranks of nameless, disgruntled boyars or merchants—ridiculous in the works of Zagoskin, Kukolnik, and Masalsky, malevolent in the works of Kostylyov and Yury German. Representatives of serious opposition, potentially dangerous to Peter's reforms, constitute a separate group.

The really valuable, efficient helpers are found among younger people. Again, rank does not count for much in their choice, only ability. Of the young noblemen sent abroad to acquire Western know-how, such as Neplyuev and Konon Zotov (joined in fiction by their doubles, such as Danilevsky's Kasatkin and Mordovtsev's Lykov), some were found deserving of pursuing a strenuous career at Peter's side. Others were not, like Ivan Golovin—according to Nartov (no. 123), consistently ridiculed by Peter—and became the prototypes of foppish, comic characters occasionally bested by their own servants (in German's *Youthful Russia* a Kalmuck), who had accompanied them abroad and studied while their masters wasted time and money carousing.

The "navigators" (so called because they were mostly meant to serve as officers in the future Russian navy) are favorites with the writers of historical fiction. They present convenient opportunities for Peter to display his calloused hands and his simple clothes and to express his contempt for frivolities and for people who take them seriously. Modest, dedicated, hardworking young men—whether a historical personage like Neplyuev or Mintslov's fictional Tavlin in *During the Storm* (1902)—can count on Peter's showing them the same regal kindness and the same endearing manner he has with simple folk. If he is not lavish in rewarding their services, it is always stressed that he never spends money on personal expenses either. These young men love their Tsar as much as they fear him and are his faithful servants, though they would not dare treat him with the familiarity shown by fictional sailors or smiths. Nor do they make the Tsar appear overly human and vulnerable: these qualities, in the works of Merezhkovsky, A. N. Tolstoy, and Ivanov, are revealed only in personal relationships, with Anna Mons, Catherine, Alexis, and Menshikov.

Peter's personal aides (*denshchik*) are usually Russians of noble birth, though mostly impecunious and lacking influential protectors at the court, so that they owe their careers to Peter alone. He has few illusions about their integrity or morals (and does not bother to conceal the fact), but they are presentable, capable, efficient young men, employed by the Tsar as needed, in

any capacity—officers, foreign envoys, valets—and always ready
to execute his orders, whatever they may be.   In fiction they fare
better than do the international adventurers like Weide, Devier,
and Villebois.   Yet, Rumyantsev was no less involved in the mysterious death of Tsarevich Alexis than was Weide; Yaguzhinsky was
no less zealous than was Devier in organizing the enormous net of
domestic spies that Peter called "the soul of the nation"; and
the services of Villebois, who, in the words of Dolgorukov,
"n'avait ni foi ni loi," were so valued by Peter that—as the man
boasts in his memoirs—he was let off with only a few months of
imprisonment for drunkenly assaulting Catherine in her bedchamber.
Neither the story (which, incidentally, is denied even by Dolgorukov [*Mémoires*, p. 211]), nor, for that matter, Villebois himself is ever mentioned in fiction.

The aides are presented, above all, as Peter's trusted companions, and whenever their personal shortcomings threaten to cast
a shadow on their august master, they are treated by fiction with
a caution not necessarily shown by petite histoire.   Mordovtsev,
for instance, repeatedly refers to Yaguzhinsky as "pretty,"
"feminine," and even "lascivious"; Merezhkovsky and even Kukolnik
extoll Rumyantsev's unusual good looks; Yury German shows Menshikov sulking at Peter, lips primly folded, smelling a flower, but
this is a far cry from Dolgorukov's and Villebois's bluntly calling them the Tsar's "minions," though Tynyanov does call Menshikov
that.[2]   Orlov's unsavory role in the trial and death of Marya
Hamilton is mentioned only by Semevsky and Mordovtsev in their
semihistorical works: *High Treason!* and *Russian Women of Modern
Times*, respectively.   In general, authors of Petrine novels have
found it safer to surround Peter with fictional navigators or with
aides carefully purged of the undesirable characteristics of the
prototypes on which they are modelled.

What matters, apparently, is that all Peter's helpers are in
fact part of his image, human tools serviceable in the same way
as an axe, a gun, a boat.   He uses them all.   Shafirov—a half-
Jewish salesman with a talent for business, foreign languages,
and diplomacy—is (gainfully!) employed by Peter as private secretary and as secretary of foreign affairs; he is the first man to
be granted the title of baron in Russia.   The turncoat nobles
Prince Romodanovsky and Peter Tolstoy, former supporters of Sophia,
once they cast their lot with Peter are invaluable in his service;
they are cruel, cynical, intelligent, and unscrupulous.   Both men
were at one time in charge of political investigations and, consequently, of the torture chamber and they hold established positions in these capacities in fiction.

Prince Romodanovsky—Mordovtsev calls him "our native Torquemada" (*Crowned Carpenter*, p. 11)—radiates an atmosphere of fear
which resembles, and influences, Peter's own, with the difference
that the fear the prince inspires is purely physical, a recoiling
of human flesh before the threatening fierceness of a beast.   In
fiction he is usually compared to a beast: the trained bear he
kept to guard his home becomes his badge, a symbol of his personality.   He is obese and clumsy; his eyes protrude like a

crab's; his drooping mustache resembles a cockroach's whiskers;
he has an ape's face and gnashing fangs. Peter himself, prompted
by Yury German, tells him, "You've come to resemble a beast completely, my amiable prince; are you perhaps swilling too much
wine? Your mug is all swollen and is turning blue." (*Russia*, II,
317.)

In fact and in fiction, however, he is a pillar of strength
for Peter. Tireless and ruthless in persecuting the Tsar's enemies, he thus removes from Peter's fictional image the stigma of
excessive bloodshedding. He is incorruptible (a rare virtue in
Peter's Russia) and reliable. Kornilovich, Shildkret, and A. N.
Tolstoy have the "native Torquemada" come to Peter's help after
the defeat at Narva by delivering to him the secret treasury which
Tsar Alexis had left for use in national emergency. According to
Golikov (no. 28), the honest courtier was actually Prince Prozorovsky, but Prozorovsky was unknown in the world of fiction,
while Romodanovsky, Peter's constant companion, could give Peter's
image a needed human touch by supplying him the opportunity of
being grateful to an old, trusted friend. Romodanovsky is thus
important to Peter's characterization and, whether beast or human,
is not cast as a conventional villain.

Tolstoy the Judas—Merezhkovsky (*P. & A.*, 213) and Shildkret
(*Mamura*, p. 237) openly call him that—is something else again.
There is nothing beast-like in his appearance; on the contrary,
he is suave, soft-spoken, well travelled, and educated. He carries out the most difficult of Peter's assignments: bringing
Alexis back to Russia and to his death, a feat of diplomacy rewarded by the title of count, decorations, and vast lands.
Merezhkovsky and Ivanov stress Tolstoy's urbane and respectful
manner with Alexis, the shrewd mixture of cajoleries and threats
he used in persuading the unfortunate Tsarevich to throw himself
on the Tsar's mercy, and his promises of complete pardon. In
Peter and Alexis he is shown getting his victim, exhausted by
torture, to sign his own death warrant in the shape of a confession of high treason. In Polezhaev's *Tsarevich Alexis Petrovich*
and Ivanov's *Tsar Peter's Night* he is shown actually participating
in Alexis's murder by strangulation. According to Dolgorukov, he
was "a man of immense intelligence, . . . false, capable of anything, completely lacking in conscience and pity." Peter himself
is said to have told Tolstoy that were it not for his head being
so clever it would have rolled long ago—a popular anecdote in
Russian fiction. But Peter used Tolstoy as he would use a sophisticated and valuable, if dangerous, tool.

These helpers bring out Peter's skill in handling people,
his lucid appraisal of character, his ever-ready suspiciousness,
and his pathetic desire for loyalty and love. It is this desire
that sometimes causes him to question his own unfavorable judgment
in order to avoid the painful realization of its soundness, for
he trusts but a few and even those few do not always deserve his
trust.

He did not trust the clergy: the best among them opposed
Peter's innovations and censured his behavior, as did Bishop

Mitrofan (whose refusal to enter a palace decorated with statues of pagan gods was dramatically described by Golikov, Merezhkovsky, and Mordovtsev) and Metropolitan Stefan Yavorsky, who faithfully loved Alexis in fact and fiction.   And as for those who, like Arkhimandrites Feodosy Yanovsky and Feofan Prokopovich, aided and abetted in the subjugation of the Orthodox Church to the Tsar or, like Bishop Pitirim, persecuted their erstwhile brethren, the Old Believers, Peter never mistook their cynical opportunism for a genuine attachment to his reforms or to himself.   Moreover, they did nothing to dispel the shadow of godlessness cast on Peter's image by the activities of the "most-crazy, most-drunken council."

Nineteenth-century writers avoid introducing clergy, whether as historical personages or as fictional characters, and take Peter's personal religiosity, proper in an Orthodox tsar whatever his eccentricities, for granted.   After all, memoirists remind us, he established fines for talking in church, denounced atheists, and participated in services by singing and reading the Gospels. Yet if these anecdotes were not directly incorporated in plots, they had their influence on Peter's image through his fictitious pious pronouncements and his frequent appearances in church.   The image is blurred in this respect, however, because of differing interpretations of Peter's pious actions and behavior by post-revolutionary writers.   In Kostylyov's *Pitirim* (pp. 426-7) cour-tiers, recalling the meetings of the "most-crazy council," marvel at the convincing hypocrisy of the Tsar's decorous prayers in church among the admiring populace.   Whole monasteries of greedy, sanctimonious clergy oppress and exploit the common people with Peter's approval, so long as they pay heavy taxes to support his wars; Shildkret's *Our-Savior-on-the-Tallow Church*, Kostylyov's *Pitirim*, and Yury German's *Youthful Russia* provide illustrations. On the rare occasions that a priest appears in a positive role, as in Pilnyak's *His Majesty Kneeb Piter Komondor*, he is invariably opposed to Peter's reforms or at least to his servants' imple-menting them.

The anecdotes involving religion which do get interwoven with fictional plots are interpreted by both nineteenth-century and postrevolutionary writers as examples of Peter's contempt for superstitions.   Such are the two variants of his uncovering the fraudulent source of the tears shed by the miraculous effigies of the Mother of God (an icon in Russia, a statue in Poland) while denouncing the clergy for deceiving simple, pious folks, and his explaining for the same purpose the "miraculous" fireproof quality of an asbestos cloth bought from devious monks by Evdokia or, in some versions, by Catherine.[3]   But whatever the truth about his personal piety—and historians are as unsure of it as are fiction writers—Peter does not trust the clergy any more than he does anyone else, checking even on the sobriety of the ascetic Metropolitan Yavorsky *and* the bonvivant Arkhimandrite Prokopovich, who had falsely denounced this his rival.

Dishonest, venal bureaucrats fill the pages of memoirs and collected anecdotes and crowd Petrine novels.   Their misdeeds con-tribute considerably to the creation of Peter's image by bringing

out his persistence in carrying out his reforms practically single-
handedly and his determination to develop a workable administrative apparatus and train men in its service. He rewarded good
performance with land and titles and punished bribery and embezzlement with everything from hanging, to confiscation of property
and exile to Siberia, to thrashings he personally administered
with his staff. Thrashings, incidentally, were often applied in
private so as not to impair the culprits' efficiency by discrediting them in the eyes of their subordinates. A thrashing was not,
however, considered a dishonor; rather, in the words of one
"fledgeling," Tatishchev, it was "an act of kindness conveying
the monarch's favor." Belyaev relates how Peter, driving with St.
Petersburg Police Chief Devier, came upon a poorly kept street,
thrashed Devier for neglect of duty, and then continued the drive
conversing in a friendly manner. He comments characteristically:
"It was indeed flattering to be punished by a monarch who would
beat you and reward you within the same minute" (*Cabinet*, p. 68).
Accordingly, remarks Merezhkovsky, Devier slapped in the face by
Peter at an assembly "experienced no sensation other than physical pain" (*P. & A.*, I, 178).

Naturally, no one representing the opposition was to be
trusted, and opposition was everywhere. There was the nobility—
old men like Prokudin in Zagoskin's *Russians at the Beginning of
the XVIIth Century*, Rzhevsky in *The Blackamoor of Peter the Great*,
or Sleptsov in Kukolnik's *Two Ivans, Two Stepanychs, Two Kostylkovs*, to mention just a few. They had all been ruined by domestic reforms and were nursing their hurt at being replaced with
sundry riffraff at the side of their monarch. And there were also
such among their sons, who like fictitious Styopka Odoevsky and
Mishka Tyrtov in *Peter the First*, became highway robbers. The
populace was restive. There were reports from the Secret Chancellery of ominous confessions forced by torture during interrogations. Open rebellion, ruthlessly suppressed, flared up all
over Russia: the Moscow Streltsy plot of 1698 was followed between 1705 and 1709 by the Astrakhan, Bakshir, and Bulavin rebellions and the Ukrainian Hetman Mazepa's treason. Moreover,
Peter could not help but hear the lament of the populace provoked
by his incomprehensible innovations and shocking personal behavior, as well as by heavy taxation and the never-ending war.

A. N. Tolstoy, Mordovtsev, and Merezhkovsky tirelessly introduce pious oldsters and gossipers of both sexes who foretell
the end of the world preceded by the arrival of the Antichrist
and distribute subversive literature. These faceless malcontents
are shown creeping like insects into every crack of a disturbed,
apprehensive Russian society: into Evdokia's chambers, Sophia's
cell, peasants' huts, and merchants' stalls. And, like a powerful beast surrounded by attacking hounds, Peter sullenly refused
to retreat: he keeps imposing his will on a reluctant nation,
fighting wars, swinging his legendary axe in "cutting Russia's
window into Europe"—and growing more lonely and distrustful as
time goes on. No wonder a large part of his image is the element
of fear: his own, born of suspicions he knew to be well-founded,

and that of the guilty as well as the innocent within the reach
of his unpredictable outbursts of anger.

Yet—and this is part of his historic reputation, as well—
he can be kind and friendly toward insignificant people and enjoy
a supper in a sailor's home as heartily as any of his notorious
parties and pageants. In fact, in Russian historical novels,
Peter, when dealing individually with simple folk, is overflowing
with kindness and benevolent almost to excess. Even Pushkin allowed him, against any plausibility, to go some thirty miles outside St. Petersburg to greet his favorite, Ibrahim Hannibal, on
the latter's return from Paris: "'I was informed of your arrival';
said Peter, 'and went to meet you. I have been waiting here for
you since yesterday.'" (*Blackamoor*, p. 10.)

In his "New Year" Kukolnik, whose admiration for Peter
borders on servility, has him listen patiently to some remarks by
his new aide Rumyantsev (a highly fictionalized historical personage) which would not have been tolerated by the humblest of
officers:

> "Why don't you go watch the fireworks, Alexander" asked
> the Sovereign.
> "What is there to watch? Lights, that's all . . .
> A poor kind of fun, Sire; you'll start a fire some day
> with it!"
> "Nonsense, Alexander. When order reigns in the city,
> the fireworks are not dangerous."
> "Make some order in the city first, and then start
> wasting fuel just for your amusement."
> "I will, I will; just you wait a while."
> "Oh, it takes a long time for you to make good on
> your promises!"

To complete the ridiculous tenor of such scenes in that story,
Peter personally teaches Rumyantsev the correct steps of the
minuet; the court jester had taught him all wrong (pp. 171-75).
There is a somewhat similar scene in *The Demidovs*, a novel by a
Soviet writer. Peter does not teach anyone to dance, but at the
sight of the spouses Menshikov performing "our own Russian national
dance" with the young master of the forge, Demidov, he "roars with
friendly laughter" and, throwing aside his tricorne, shouts:
"'Well, you crazy folks, what are you up to?' delighting everyone
present with these signs of benevolence" (p. 302).

Peter is even more benevolent toward the Brovkin family,
whose loyalty to him has helped them on the road from rags to
riches:

> One evening, Ivan Artemich [Brovkin] was sitting down-
> stairs in the basement kitchen playing cards with some
> peasant visitors by a tallow candle. Suddenly, in the
> low door appeared a head in a tricorne . . . everyone
> was petrified with fear . . . Peter Alexeevich asked for
> some kvas . . . sat down on a kitchen bench. [After

arranging for a marriage between Brovkin's son and Princess Buynosova, Peter] ordered the cook to get supper
ready. Ivan Artemich pleaded that they should go upstairs . . . it was unseemly to stay here! Peter
Alexeevich only laughed: "I won't go upstairs. It's
warmer here. Cook, fetch everything you've got in the
oven!" . . . he joked, treating the peasants with wine.
Ordered them to sing. (*P.F.*, pp. 451-52.)

He enjoys making people happy, and readers of Russian historical novels cannot help but notice the regularity with which
Peter engages in matchmaking, usually achieving in this way a
happy ending for the fictional plot. In real life he was considerably less lucky in this respect, since the marriages he arranged for his son Tsarevich Alexis, his daughter Tsarevna Anne,
and his two nieces all turned out to be unhappy, or short-lived,
or both. Fictional marriages, however, are another matter, and
after a false start in Pushkin's *The Blackamoor of Peter the
Great* (since the marriage of Ibrahim and Natalya is sure to prove
an unhappy one), Peter busily marries fictional characters and
historical personages—indiscriminately and, as will be shown
later, without much regard for historical accuracy. Thus, to
cite some examples, he marries Rumyantsev to Marya Matveeva in
Kukolnik's "New Year," his jester Turgenev to Charlotte Blomberg
in the same author's *Sentinel*, Turbin to Anna Gurov in Arseniev's
The Tsar's Verdict, Volkov to Sanka and Artamoshka Brovkin to
Natalya Buynosova in *Peter the First*, Menshikov to Darya Arsenieva
in Sokolov's *Menshikov*, and Burmistrov to Natalya in Masalsky's
The Streltsy. There are many more. He also promises in Mordovtsev's *The Tsar and the Hetman* to marry his favorite, Yaguzhinsky,
to Matryona Kochubey, and would have kept his promise but for
history's making this fictional match impossible: she eloped
with Hetman Mazepa.

Dunya, in Danilevsky's *To India in Peter's Time*, marries
Kasatkin without Peter's help or permission, but he stands sponsor
to their son, as well as to Menshikov's in Sokolov's novel of that
name, the smith's daughter in Arseniev's *Arisha the Ducky*, the
first child of Gustav Traufetter and Louise Segevold, whom he had
united in Lazhechnikov's *The Last Recruit*, and many others. In a
way, he also arranges the marriage of Barchukov and Varyusha, the
protagonists in *The Wedding Rebellion* (1886) by Salias de Turnemir,
along with the hundred historical weddings of the Astrakhan Rebellion in 1705.

The lower the origins of his godchildren or the hosts of the
homes he visits, the more informal and benevolent that "Tsar-
muzhik" as a Soviet writer calls him,[4] shows himself to be.
Neplyuev's story about a ruble and a kiss Peter bestowed at a new
mother, a sailor's wife, and a piece of carrot pie and a glass of
aniseed vodka he consumed on that occasion in their humble home
reappears with slight variations in most of the Petrine novels
irrespective of the period. Two excerpts from works dated, respectively, 1889 and 1946 may serve as illustration:

"Our dear Father Tsar! Our heavenly light!" exclaimed the buxom Ustinya, falling to Peter's knees. . . . "Why such kindness to us, humble people?"
Peter raised her graciously and kissed her on the lips. The aide brought in a bottle of aniseed vodka and the Tsar's silver tumbler. . . . Ustinya put a pot of cabbage soup and all the simple fare she had on the table. (Arseniev, *Arisha*, pp. 10-13).

In Nikita's house . . . on the table stood simple fare: cabbage soup with mutton, a mincemeat pie. . . . Nikita brought some vodka, the guest drank it . . . with satisfaction. "Where is the missus?" asked Peter. A woman, rosy-cheeked and buxom, entered. . . . Peter drank the mead she offered him and kissed her heartily. (*The Demidovs*, p. 18.)

It is before these humble subjects that he likes to show off his physical strength and his skill by forging a piece of iron, felling a tree, and taking over the steering wheel of a ship. In at least one poem he repairs an old fisherman's boat incognito, in at least one novel replaces an axle on a cart wheel.[5] He is known to accept in good humor many a rebuke from the laborers and sailors whose place he is, in such cases, taking. Golikov (*Anecdotes*, no. 2) tells the story about Akim, the pilot seaman who during a storm off the shores of Arkhangelsk in 1694 saved the Tsar and all his retinue by wrenching the boat's steering wheel from Peter's hands, and how on landing safely he was not only graciously forgiven by the Tsar but also rewarded with money. The anecdote was used by Zotov in 1842 in his *Mysterious Monk* and by Yury German in his *The Youthful Russia* in 1952 as well as by others.
The picture is not always idyllic, of course; as we have seen, Peter's image is permanently enveloped in an atmosphere of fear, even when he is in a kindly mood, and certainly when he is morose, which is often. In *Peter's Day* A. N. Tolstoy shows him on a gray, rainy St. Petersburg morning driving a dogcart along the rutty, muddy streets. He ignores the snappy salute of a company of soldiers shivering in their drenched coats, ignores the clerks hurrying by with low bows, and the simple folk clad in sheepskins and mostly barefoot who kneel in puddles, too fearful to remember that, according to the monarch's ukase, they are, at his passage, "to stand decorously, with hats off." Only the fat German baker standing outside his shop greets the Tsar with a smile, a wave of his pipe, and a merry "Gut Morgen, Herr Piter!" and is answered with a hoarse "Gut Morgen, Herr Müller!" (*Peter's Day*), p. 395). For, it was whispered resentfully, Peter was always nice to foreigners. No, simple folk could not be trusted either.
Thus, he distrusts them all—bureaucrats, generals, senators, clergy and laymen, peasants, foreigners, his own flesh and blood, his fledgelings. He thought he could trust Catherine and, of course, Menshikov.

The place Alexander Menshikov held in Peter's life was comparable to that of Lefort's, but since Lefort died in 1699, it was longer lasting and more complex. Fiction recognizes him as a major influence upon Peter's image, and no Petrine novel fails to introduce Menshikov at Peter's side. Some novels even bear his name, an honor which he shares only with that paragon of virtue Prince Yakov Dolgoruky.

The facts of Menshikov's life are well established, except for those of his origin. Some memoirists report him to be an impoverished nobleman's son who was forced as a boy to earn his living by selling pies in the streets; others insist that his father was a stable-man in the Kremlin. Both versions may be correct in that a position in the Tsar's stables could have been prestigious enough to have been filled by an obscure nobleman. The pie-selling is a fact supported by numerous anecdotes and is part of Menshikov's characterization in fiction, something in the nature of Peter's staff, a prop without which the traditional costume for the role would be incomplete. Introduced by Lefort, Menshikov entered Peter's life early and remained powerful to its end as the Tsar's factotum, and beyond it as kingmaker, putting on the throne Catherine and then little Peter II, son of the unfortunate Alexis. His fall came in 1727, two years after the death of his master and creator and two years before his own—in Siberia, a penniless exile. Peter is reported by Nartov (no. 138) and Stählin (no. 95), among others, to have said to Menshikov: "Remember who you are, Alexashka. I made you, and I can break you too." But it was that child emperor who, at the instigation of Menshikov's enemies, broke him, because for Peter to have done so would have been like breaking his own arm—"the only arm left to me now," he said after Lefort died, "a thieving one but faithful."

Menshikov's road led from pies to riches, favors, and power. Fiction writers enjoy telling of the titles Peter bestowed on his favorite, including that of a duke (although this title, unlike count and baron, did not "take" in Russia); of the positions he held (governor of St. Petersburg and later of all the northern provinces, senator); and of his military ranks (field marshal, admiral). The orgies of the "most-crazy council," the first "assemblies," and, in later years, luxurious balls took place in Menshikov's palaces. His enormous riches—vast lands, thousands of serfs—are endlessly stressed in fiction. The millions he kept in foreign banks, however, were not the result of Peter's bounty; to his benefactor's sorrow, Menshikov acquired them illegally, through shady business deals, bribes, and embezzlement.

Tynyanov shows him musing during his deathwatch for Peter:

> He liked everything to be done fast and well, everything
> to be plentiful, of the best quality, administered
> thriftily and with care . . . he felt a certain secret
> sweetness on his lips, the sweetness of owning so many
> riches, of owning more than did anyone else . . . and at
> times he marvelled to himself, "The more I own, the more
> I covet still other things." (*Effigy*, no. 1, p. 6.)

He was venal, daring on the battlefield, handsome, vain as a peacock, enamored of costly clothes, and illiterate (though German makes him write a long love letter to his wife Darya, whom he is known to have betrayed with, among others, her own sister). He is Peter's shadow, his *Herzenskind*, indispensable, alert to every change of mood (according to A. N. Tolstoy, bribing the Tsar's valets to be informed if Peter has spent a restless night), ever ready with a timely suggestion, flattery, a word of comfort. It was he who removed Anna Mons; guided Catherine, his own mistress, into Peter's bed; and years later—if one is to believe Helbig—persuaded Peter to crown her empress in hopes of seeing her children on the throne and himself as regent. It was he, historians and gossipers claim, who mismanaged the education of Tsarevich Alexis, taught him to drink, and generally helped to alienate him from his father.[6] *Peter the First* shows Menshikov in action, cautiously probing to see whether Peter has dismissed faithless Anna Mons from his memory and is ready for a suggestion for her replacement. He boasts of his new mistress, won over from old Marshal Sheremetev, who had just captured the fortress Marienburg and Catherine with it. "It was difficult to find out whether Peter was listening at all. When the story was finished, he cleared his throat. Alexashka knew the meaning of all his coughs by heart; he understood: Peter Alexeevich had been listening very attentively." (*P.F.*, p. 617.)

Does, then, fiction represent Menshikov as an archvillain and Peter as putty in his skillful, unscrupulous hands? Hardly. He was genuinely attached to his master and eager in promoting his successes—and so his own. It takes Helbig to suggest that Menshikov poisoned not only Catherine (though there was some such talk on the cause of her death in 1727), but also Peter himself.[7] Moreover, Peter was not an easy man to influence and had no illusions about his favorite. He liked to remind Menshikov of the pies (no Petrine novel misses that reminder) and humiliate him by public beatings (every author, from Merezhkovsky to A. N. Tolstoy to Fedorov, remembers that). Yet he loved his constant ally and companion, feeling that he was not alone, that he need not fear betrayal, while "Alexashka" was around. Astute and pragmatic though he was, Peter could be vulnerable in relationships with the few people he loved.

Besides, Menshikov was, in the words of Dolgorukov (a memoirist little given to compliments), "unquestionably a man of genius. Practically illiterate, he won battles and was an able administrator and a consummate diplomat."[8] So Peter refused to act on the Senate's numerous presentations of the muddy sources of Menshikov's wealth and shielded him from the punishment he freely meted out to other corrupt officials because, as he bluntly stated on one occasion, "Alexashka's services are indispensable to the conduct of government affairs" (Stählin, *Anecdotes*, no. 95).

It was not until 1723, after a particularly scandalous trial, that Peter allowed the Senate to fine Menshikov one million rubles —a stupendous sum, but a lenient verdict, considering that anyone

else would have forfeited everything, including his life. But,
Nartov says, Menshikov lost something more precious than money:
"He lost the Sovereign's favor and love. . . . His Majesty with-
drew his trust from him, harboring henceforth suspicions also in
other various and important matters." It was on this occasion
that Peter answered Catherine's usual plea of forgiveness for the
culprit with the statement that has since become as much a part of
Menshikov's fictional characterization as his humble beginnings
selling pies: "Truly, Menshikov was conceived in lawlessness,
his mother bore him in sin, and he'll end his life in thievery.
Unless he mends his ways, I promise you, Katenka, he'll forfeit
his life; it is not the first time that I spare him today" (Nartov's Notes, no. 148).

Peter's loss was at least as great as Menshikov's and could
not have occurred at a worse time. The trauma of Alexis's flight,
subsequent return, and trial had revealed the continuing depth of
opposition to Peter's reforms; while Alexis's death, followed two
years later by that of little Peter's, left the Reformer without
heirs who would have continued his work. Peter knew better than
anyone else that his two living daughters were as Dolgorukov
bluntly states, "doubly illegitimate, having been born while the
spouses of both their parents were living" (Mémoires, p. 29).
Villebois and Waliszewski raise this question too.

And, says Danilevsky, "already Peter's eye was balefully
discerning the approach of the impending affair with Mons" (To
India, p. 113). The Tsar was beginning to suspect that Catherine
—his companion of over twenty years, the baseborn, illiterate
Livonian peasant whom he had just crowned empress of All the
Russias—was unfaithful to him with a pretty, foppish youth of
the (apparently fateful for Peter) Mons family.

His health was failing. Peter's image in works of fiction
whose plots deal with the later period of his reign reflects the
gradual change in him. There are references to his sporadic attempts to diet at the insistence of his doctors and to his taking
"Martsian waters" in European and Russian resorts. His looks de-
teriorate, he ages considerably, and he begins to wear glasses—
a detail always meant to be pathetic. Kostylyov notes that "the
Tsar's face was deeply lined; he had grey, puffy bags under his
eyes. Pitirim had heard that the death of Tsarevich Alexis had
left its mark on the monarch, and he could now see that it was
indeed so" (p. 332). Ivanov describes Peter asleep after a night
of anxious thoughts, "his aging, yellow, tired head resting on a
pillow bathed in the first rays of dawn" (Tsar's Night, p. 150).
The head resembles "the Emperor's head on the pillow in a coffin,
a head on which suffering had etched an indelible mark" (Fedorov,
The Demidovs, p. 313). And Merezhkovsky glimpses "a yellowish
face, so puffy it appeared swollen, with something heavy, rigid
in it, like in a death mask" (P. & A., I, 214). Merezhkovsky
goes even further:

> And now, when his life was nearing its end, [driving in
> his inevitable dogcart] on that mournful autumn morning,

he thought of the years that had been [so lovingly] spent together with Katenka, who now had proved unfaithful, had traded her "old man" for a nobody, a good-looking German kid of low origin. His feelings were not those of jealousy, anger, or indignation, but of the helplessness felt by a child abandoned by its mother. He handed the reins over to his aide, slumped in his seat, and his head bent low like a feeble old man's, nodded at the jolts of the dogcart on the uneven, cobbled pavement. He looked very old and drained of all strength. (*P. & A.*, II, 73.)

Works dealing with the last years of Peter's life convey a deepening atmosphere of tragedy. There emerges in his image a sense of futility, of loneliness, and of receiving too small a personal dividend on a life spent in the tremendous effort at statesmanship. Events conspire to accentuate this feeling: there is the case of Alexis in (1717 and 1718); the death in 1719 of the Tsar's now only son and heir, Peter, aged three; *Herzenskind* Menshikov's scandalous affair in the Senate in 1723; finally, in November 1724, the certainty of Catherine's infidelity, already suspected for some time, and the execution of Willim Mons. Peter died two months later, in January 1725.

11.   Women

He was of an amorous disposition, disinclined to be faithful, suspicious, prompt at taking a dislike, violent in
his decisions, and implacable in vengeance.
        D'Allainval, 1745

The great Monarch never showed himself to be dominated by
carnal lusts.
        Feodozi, 1772

Nothing perhaps enhances the characteristic dichotomy in Peter's
personality more than his attitude towards sex and women. He was
capable of a lasting attachment to one woman: in fact, he seemed
always to need a permanent, faithful mate, one who was simultaneously lover, companion, friend, and mother—a wife. He accepted, patiently for him, several years of lukewarm marriage to
Evdokia, exquisitely portrayed in *Peter the First*; maintained a
long liaison with Anna Mons; and for twenty-three years, to the
day of his death, there was Catherine. But being Peter's mate
was not easy—or safe.
        It was not so much a matter of his notorious thrift (stingi-
ness, his cook Velten could have said). Peter did indeed boast to
the king of Denmark about his never wasting money on women; and
the complaints of Miss Cross, the English actress whom he rewarded
with 500 guineas at the end of his stay in London in 1698, are
well known. Also, Villebois reports that the Tsar's *prix fixe*
for chance encounters was a ducat (two rubles), adding, however,
that the expense added up to a sizable sum annually (*Mémoires*,
p. 86). Yet, Anna Mons was adequately supported and received
valuable gifts. If the gifts were eventually taken away, it was
in punishment for her boldness in considering marriage before
Peter himself had decided to end their liaison. Also, if Tsaritsa
Evdokia was conveyed in a mean sledge from the palace to the

convent, if no provision was made for her maintenance there, and
if for the next twenty-six years she subsisted on charity from
her unwilling relatives, this too was in punishment for her disobedience. She had refused to retire to the convent when Peter
expressed his wish to terminate their marriage. Catherine and
her children were always taken care of; and after she was proclaimed Peter's wife and tsaritsa (the actual marriage, Dolgorukov,
Galizin, and Semevsky suggest, was never performed),[1] she had her
court, diamonds, and palaces and could, says Semevsky (*Treason!*
p. 202), even make it illegal for anyone but her to wear ermine
in Russia. But she began with the famous ducat for the first
night with Peter at Menshikov's house.

When his women were submissive and did not interfere with
his work or amusements, Peter could be kind and devoted and enjoy
a stable relationship. When he was absent, whether on the war
fronts or travelling all over Russia checking on the performance
of the bureaucrats, supervising work in the shipyards, or over-
seeing the building of St. Petersburg, there were letters. History
preserved, and fiction made ample use of, sentimental and rather
prim letters from and to Anna, and an intimate and warm, occasionally jocular, exchange of letters with Catherine. In both
cases the letters were often accompanied by small gifts: a few
lemons, oysters, wine and vodka, and even flowers. There are no
known answers to Evdokia's pathetic letters complaining of her
young husband's prolonged absences and reporting on little
Alexis's health.

But Peter demanded to be everything to his mate and exacted
complete subservience and an incessant catering to his eccentricities and moods. Evdokia's undoing was her insistence on her
marital rights, her insufficient desire to please, and her belief
in other laws besides Peter's will—to mention only Russian tradi-
tions and court etiquette. Anna Mons had no talent, perhaps no
taste, for the life of a courtesan and could not—or would not
try to—adjust to Peter's violent temper and barbaric ways; perhaps, as A. N. Tolstoy shows in *Peter the First*, she actually
wanted to get away from him. Catherine lasted so long because
she was infinitely pliable: a merry, buxom "missus" (*khoziaika*)
to Bombardier Peter Mikhaylov; a stately, ornate empress to Peter
the Great, emperor, Father of the Fatherland (Lazhechnikov even
makes one of his fictional characters address her as "Mother of
the Fatherland"); and a mate always ready to adjust to Peter's
every whim, including his infidelities.

Peter demanded absolute fidelity from his wives and mistresses, present *and* past, and when his jealousy was aroused
could become violent and cruel. Writers of fiction and of petite
histoire disagree on whether Marya Hamilton was executed because
the child she had killed at birth was, as Helbig insists, Peter's
(*Günstlinge*, p. 115), or rather because it was another lover's—
either way she would have hurt Peter's pride. Glebov was impaled
as the alleged lover of Evdokia and she herself flogged and sent
to a Siberian convent twenty years after she had been abandoned
by Peter; Willim Mons was beheaded because Peter had received an

anonymous letter involving the handsome courtier and Catherine.
The contents of the letter were never revealed, nor does any proof
of the affair exist, but Peter personally took Catherine to look
at Mons's head exhibited on a pole and, smashing a mirror in her
presence, threatened to destroy her in the same way.[2] Had he not
died several weeks later, he might have carried out the threat:
Andreev reports that Tolstoy and Osterman implored the Tsar on
their knees to avoid such a scandal for the sake of his daughters' future. Yet, he expected tolerance for his own numerous
infidelities, being—in the words of his personal doctor, Robert
Erskine (Areskin in Russian version)—"possessed by a legion of
demons of lust." The phrase was much quoted by foreign memoirists or anecdotists who could safely afford to do so—such as
Villebois or Waliszewski—but in fiction only by Fräulein Juliana
in *Peter and Alexis* and, of all people, by Menshikov in A. N.
Tolstoy's "Martha Rabe" (1931). Peter's first meeting with
Catherine, in "Martha Rabe" is considerably less romantic than it
is in *Peter the First*.

Peter apparently saw no inconsistency in his treatment of
his permanent mates. They had his favor and his love; they were
in a position to return that love and to please him: what else
could they desire? Certainly not to be allowed to interfere with
the serious business of his work, war, and reforms—or to decide
on what amusements he needed for relaxation. Certainly they
could not expect *him* to cater to *their* tastes or to indulge their
whims. Peter the Great would not be dominated by a woman, like
so many of his weak brethren on European thrones. He had no Mmes
de Pompadour or Dubarry, no Countess Cosel, no Nell Gwynn, not
even a Mrs. Keppel. What is more, he has the distinction of being the only monarch in world literature who has had no fictional
mistresses as part of the plot—an important aspect of his image.
In Petrine novels his attitude toward sex and women is delineated
in terms of his relationships with fictionalized Evdokia, Anna
Mons, and Catherine.

It would seem unreasonable to expect that the whole sex life
of a man of Peter's physique, vitality, and coarseness (even if
he were not an autocratic monarch) consisted of an early, love-
less marriage to Evdokia, a youthful infatuation with Anna Mons,
and a long, happy union with Catherine. Yet, a reader of Petrine
novels alone would be led to believe just that. The Crowned Carpenter, the Reformer is shown enjoying domestic bliss in works by
Pushkin, Lazhechnikov, and Fedorov; manfully bearing his disappointment with the flighty Anna Mons in works by A. N. Tolstoy
and Mordovtsev; and enduring Evdokia's stolid backwardness in
Kukolnik's short stories and in *Peter the First*.

True, Pilnyak, describing Peter kissing Marya Hamilton's
severed head, adds, "Yet, he had once kissed that girl's living
lips differently." Shildkret has Peter angrily thinking in that
moment: "She killed my son, the Tsar's own flesh!" (*Eagle Cup*,
p. 377). And Tynyanov, mentioning the same scene, states bluntly:
"Yet he used to sleep with Marya at one time, and she had many
dresses and sables and drove in an English-made carriage" (*Effigy*,

no. 1, p. 34); the latter part, incidentally, is poetic licence:
Marya, like most of Catherine's maids of honor, was largely impecunious). Still, descriptions of the orgies of the "most-crazy
council" do not include the participation of its female members,
and most authors concentrate on creating a different sort of
image for Peter. Ivanov and Yury German, for example, present
him as statesman. Kostylyov, in *Pitirim*, and Mordovtsev, in
Idealists and Realists, stress his despotism and cruelty; Kukolnik,
Kornilovich, and Lazhechnikov present the benevolent Tsar-Reformer.
On the whole, fiction uses only those aspects of Peter's sex life
recognized by and used in textbooks of Russian history.

Not so in petite histoire, which was well known to the reading public and could not but have influenced the kind of image
fiction was creating for Peter, even though the two portraits
often seemed to represent different persons. Writers contribut-
ing to petite histoire, in fact, show considerable interest in
the subject; there is even a consensus of opinion in such otherwise differing anecdotists as the Chevalier d'Eon and Golikov,
Dolgorukov, and Stählin. Stählin (no. 105) states simply: "The
Tsar shared the foible of almost all great men: he was very fond
of women." "He used to have several mistresses at the same time,"
says Dolgorukov (p. 172), and Galizin (p. 127) adds: "He was
not overly fastidious in his choices; his love affairs were only
casual and never harmed his work." D'Escherny (no. 34) agrees:
"His finest trait was that he never kept mistresses of favorites.
He was content with what he could obtain without any difficulty
at the court from some of the prettiest and least demure among
the waiting women or maids of honor, none of whom ever possessed
any influence over him or drew him into considerable expense."
Says d'Eon (no. 15): "Peter knew no other passion than the love
of glory. He indulged in occasional debauches but never for long,
and never became involved in anything that could influence his
judgment." Golikov (no. 98) cites a case of Peter's goodhumored
acceptance of being refused by the beautiful wife of a merchant,
and comments admiringly: "What a rare virtue in a man and
[especially] in an autocrat is such complete control of his pas-
sions!" Nartov sums it all up and is worth, therefore, quoting
in extenso:

> Amidst the many labors and cares of his government, the
> Sovereign liked occasionally to converse with a beauty,
> not longer, however, than for half an hour. True, His
> Majesty liked the fair sex, yet never did he become bound
> by passion to any woman and was prompt in extinguishing
> the flames of love, saying: "A soldier may not wallow in
> lust. It is unforgivable to neglect service for a woman.
> Being prisoner of a mistress is worse than being prisoner
> of war because you can regain your freedom at the hands
> of the enemy within a short time but female fetters last
> long." He made use of any woman he liked when he met her,
> but always with her consent and without any compulsion.
> Besides, he had such a gallant manner and such pleasant

ways with the fair sex that very few could refuse him.
This we observed to be the case not only at home but also
in foreign countries, especially in Poland, when he would
set out on that kind of hunting with [King] August.
(*Notes*, no. 145.)

Except for the episode in Shildkret's *Our-Savior-on-the-
Tallow Church* (pp. 54-55) where Peter, with Catherine's connivance,
rapes her servant girl, and perhaps the episodes in Pilnyak's
His Majesty Kneeb Piter, Komondor (p. 122) and in A. N. Tolstoy's
Peter's Day (p. 410), where sudden outbursts of drunken lust are
used to complete a portrait of Peter the Monster, nowhere else in
fiction does he use force. And except for the episode in *Peter
the First* (pp. 532-34) showing the Tsar's buggy waiting for several
hours outside a Moscow house of ill repute, nowhere else in fiction does Peter similarly risk offending the sensibilities of his
loyal readers.

Bits of malicious gossip about Peter's contracting venereal
disease in the course of his numerous adventures are limited to
petite histoire. Hints of his having homosexual inclinations do
occur in fiction, but their role in the creation of Peter's image
is too insignificant to warrant its discussion in this study. His
mistresses, however, are another matter because their number,
choice, and treatment bears on the Jekyll-Hyde syndrome in Peter's
psychological portrait.

Though novelists do not create for him any fictional mistresses those historically known figure prominently in petite histoire, and several names do find their way into fiction. There
is, of course, Marya Hamilton, who, unsurprisingly, has the sympathy of all the authors and is usually cast in fictional plots as
an innocent beauty ruined primarily by Peter's aide Orlov. In
his *Tsar Peter's Night* Ivanov brings in Anna Kramer, though in no
other connection with Peter than her being chosen by him to lay
out Alexis's body for burial (the version used by Ivanov is
Stählin's; according to Helbig and Dolgorukov, Anna also neatly
sewed on the tsarevich's severed head). In *Idealists and Realists* (p. 94) Mordovtsev introduces Avdotya Chernysheva gossiping
at a party about Marya Hamilton's pregnancy, but without any other
reference to her intimacy with Peter than that the Tsar "used
'fondly' to call her Avdotya-the-battle-axe [*boi-baba*]"—with
"fondly" in quotation marks. There is much nastier gossip about
Chernysheva herself by Villebois, Dolgorukov, Galizin, Semevsky,
and Waliszewski concerning the looseness of her morals and their
unfortunate effect on Peter's health,[3] but these stories were not
utilized by fiction writers. Chernysheva allegedly had three
children by the Tsar.

There is also Marya daughter of Count Matveev, who, according to Dolgorukov and Karabanov, was "lovely and charming but
more than flighty in conduct." Peter, having discovered that the
girl (aged seventeen) had other lovers beside him, birched her
soundly in private with his own hand and ordered Matveev to marry
her to Peter's aide Rumyantsev, whom, he said, he trusted to keep

his wife in line.   After this marriage she had by Peter a daughter
and a son, the famous general in the reign of Catherine II, and
after the Tsar's death, three more daughters, presumably by her
husband.[4]   As the heroine of Kukolnik's "The New Year" Marya is a
lovely, innocent girl whom the kindly Tsar happily unites with
his impecunious but deserving aide Rumyantsev, after removing the
father's objections to the marriage with the promise of a great
career for the young man.   Merezhkovsky's Rumyantsev, incidentally, is a handsome oaf helping Tolstoy lure Alexis back to Russia
and trying to seduce his mistress Afrosinya.

Peter also married off his mistress Marya Novosiltseva to a
rich old widower, Stroganov, and, Dolgorukov reports (p. 166),
had three sons from that union.   Stroganova was also renowned
for hard and merry drinking but remained unknown to the readers
of Petrine fiction.

Waliszewski says (p. 365) that the number of Peter's illegitimate offspring was comparable to that of Louis XIV; the
Marchioness of Bareith, who was rivaled only by Waliszewski and
Helbig in her hostility to Peter's memory, claims in her *Mémoires*
(p. 9) to have seen about four hundred servant women with Peter's
babies in their arms accompanying, as Catherine's retinue, the
Tsar and Tsaritsa on their visit to the king of Prussia in 1717.
The marchioness's youthful recollections (she was a child at the
time of that visit) might have been affected by contemporary reports on the three hundred illegitimate children of King August.
Undoubtedly, Peter had numerous illegitimate offspring, and we
can safely leave the matter at that, for not one of them appears
in fiction.

About 1723, however, Peter became increasingly worried about
the state of his succession: his three legitimate sons by Evdokia
were dead, and of the eleven children by Catherine he had no surviving sons and only three daughters[5] of doubtful legitimacy.   It
was then that Peter Tolstoy began to suggest marriage with beautiful Marya Kantemir, Peter's particular favorite and pregnant
by him.   Marya might have become Anne Boleyn to Peter's Catherine
—like Henry VIII he was anxious to have a male heir—but Catherine
and Menshikov approached the girl's physician, and Marya had a
stillborn child.   She survived but would never be able to have
any more children.[6]   Not a hint of that story appeared in historical fiction; not even Marya Kantemir's name was ever mentioned.

As a result of this authorial discretion—commendable and
natural, if possibly influenced by censorship—the Mr. Hyde aspect
of Peter's portrait remains the domain of petite histoire, while
fiction represents the Dr. Jekyll side.   "He was," says Polevoy
in his *History of Peter the Great* (1842), "a dutiful son, tender
brother, loving husband, doting father, thrifty administrator,
master of a peaceful home, and a faithful friend."[7]   And he was
all of that—at least in relation to Catherine and her children.

It is interesting to note how completely Catherine's personality is overshadowed by Peter's in history, petite histoire,
and fiction alike.   After all, she did make a fairy-tale career,

was Russia's first empress and its first female reigning monarch, and succeeded in keeping her place at Peter's side to the end of his life. Yet her only role in fiction—important though that role may be—is that of supplementing Peter's characterization.

Catherine's known biography is a jumble of a few facts, some guesswork, and plentiful gossip (freely used in fiction). In Tynyanov's version, she herself is confused about her identity, waking up frightened from a deep sleep in which she had been the young peasant girl Martha. In her dream she had been lost among her many homes, religions, and nationalities, the several languages she had spoken, the various stations she had had in life, above all, lost among the numerous men whom she had never chosen but had always succeeded in pleasing. At seventeen, she recollects in her dream, "she walked—Martha—along the streets of Marienburg, the old women called after her in Swedish, Latvian, and German that one small, feminine word." But it is as Catherine, empress of All the Russias, that she awakes to recall that the body of her awesome husband is lying in state awaiting burial in one of the rooms of the palace. (*Effigy*, no. 1, pp. 47-49.)

The data on Catherine's life accepted by historians but still mostly based on conjecture are that she was born in 1683 or 1686, one of the numerous children of Samuel, a Livonian peasant, possibly called Skavroshchuk, or Skavoronsky; as a serf he had no surname. Historians prefer to discount several stories that she was the illegitimate daughter of a Livonian squire, either Rosen or von-Alfendel, as well as those of her more respectacle descent from a Swedish quartermaster, Iohann Rabe. (A. N. Tolstoy, however, chose to call her Martha Rabe in a short story of that name.) To use Lazhechnikov's phrase, "The Monarch deigned to give her the [more euphonic] surname of Martha Skovronskaya" when he settled her with Menshikov's two sisters and future wife, Darya, under the tutelage of Anisya Tolstaya in Moscow in 1703. It has been suggested that Peter's letter of January 1708, instructing Menshikov to give, in case of his death, 3,000 rubles to "Katerina Vasilevskaya and her little girl" confirms the version of her having been orphaned in early childhood and living with an aunt, Maria-Anna *Veselevskaya*.

Until 1711 she went by Peter's own favorite incognito name, Mikhaylov(a), living in the palace and known, Helbig insists, as a cook's wife and mother of the said cook's two daughters, Anne (born 1708) and Elizabeth (born 1709) (*Günstlinge*, p. 46). The matter of her alleged secret marriage to Peter in 1711 requires separate discussion, but she was officially declared tsaritsa (and her two daughters tsarevnas) in March 1711 and from then on presumably belonged to the Romanov dynasty.

Baptized a Catholic, Martha (or, according to another version, a Lutheran, Helene-Katharina), the future empress, was brought up in the family of Pastor Glück in Marienburg—as a ward, according to official and officious versions; as a servant, according to others who point to her lifetime illiteracy. She did acquire over the years a fair knowledge of several languages— Latvian, German, Swedish, Dutch, and Russian—but never learned

to read or write in any of them. In 1702 she married a Swedish
dragoon, Iohann, in Marienburg, which was being besieged by the
Russians. After the town's capture, the pretty girl (dressed, the
rumor persisted, in her shift and a uniform coat with which one
of the Russian soldiers had covered her) was noticed by General
Bauer and/or Marshal Sheremetev and was passed on to Menshikov,
who, after a few months, brought her to the attention of Peter
himself. Sometime between 1703 and 1708 she was baptized into
Orthodoxy, named Catherine, and, as was customary in Russia in
cases of unknown parentage, was given as a patronymic the name of
her godfather, Tsarevich Alexis, aged at that time thirteen or
fifteen. This was a strange choice of sponsor, to say the least;
and when Peter's marriage to Catherine was announced several years
later, one of the many reasons for its unpopularity was the
populace's objection to the Tsar's marrying his spiritual grand-
daughter. In a letter sent collectively by Anisya Tolstaya and
her charges to Peter in October 1705, she figures as "Catherine-
with-two-more" (*Katerina sama-tret'ia*) and asks Peter's blessing
for these two—Peter, born in 1704, and Paul, born in 1705.

The matter of Catherine's marriage to the Swedish dragoon
has remained unresolved and controversial, fiction writers each
choosing whatever one of the many versions suited them best, and
the historians and anecdotists, such as Nartov, Stählin, and
Feoktistov, discreetly avoiding its mention. As for the writers
of petite histoire, their stories range from the young husband's
having perished in the fall of Marienburg before the marriage
was consummated—Bruce and d'Eon favor that variant—to Villebois's
report that the dragoon was taken prisoner at Poltava and sent to
Siberia, where he died in 1721, to Dolgorukov's story that the
man was paid a pension to keep silent until his death in about
1747.[8] Finally, Empress Elizabeth, Catherine's daughter, and
Peter III, son of her second daughter Anne, always maintained
that no such marriage ever took place at all—for obvious reasons,
since all the eleven children of Peter and Catherine were born of
double adultery, Iohann allegedly surviving Catherine, and Tsaritsa
Evdokia who died in 1737 certainly surviving Peter. Both tsarevnas
were illegitimate in any case, having been born before their
parents' marriage—if, that is, their parents ever were married.
As was mentioned, several nineteenth-century Russian memoirists
considered that doubtful.

According to Dolgorukov, no trace of a marriage record was
discovered in the course of extensive research conducted, among
others by the erudite Count Rumyantsev, who was Peter's grandson
by Marya Matveeva-Rumyantseva. Yet there must have been some
kind of religious ceremony about the time that Catherine was declared tsaritsa, even though Peter would have been quite capable
of considering that declaration sufficient to the establishment
of her legal status. There were precedents: Marya Miloslavskaya,
a commoner chosen for a spouse by Tsar Alexis, was declared
tsarevna two days before the wedding, which, of course, was to
make her tsaritsa.

Pushkin, who as an archivist had access to unpublished state

documents, states tersely that "in November 1707 (?), in the St.
Trinity Church in St. Petersburg, Peter married Catherine, a
Marienburg wench who had been wife of a Swedish trumpeteer (?)
and later a concubine to Sheremetev and to Menshikov."[9]   Bartenev,
editor of *Russian Archive*, claims to have seen an ancient gravure
showing Peter and Catherine at the altar, each accompanied by a
small girl; these are Anne and Elizabeth, born out of wedlock, becoming, according to an old Russian custom, legitimatized (*pri-
venchannyi*) daughters through their participation in the marriage
ceremony.   Bruce also refers to the presence of the two little
girls, though, as a foreigner, he is unaware of the custom and
assumes their role to be that of bridesmaids.   According to him
the marriage took place privately at "Jaweroff" (?) on May 29,
1711, and was publicly solemnized on February 20, 1712.   Soloviev
in his *History* and Studenkin in his *Genealogy of the House of the
Romanovs* (1878) accept the latter date.   Studenkin even adds that
the ceremony took place in St. Isaac's Church (later Cathedral)
in St. Petersburg.   One has no choice but to leave the matter at
that.   It was never raised in fiction.

In 1721, when Peter assumed the title of emperor, Catherine
became empress.   She was crowned with great pomp and ceremony on
May 7, 1724, although Peter apparently already had his suspicions
in the matter of Willim Mons, but was reluctant to cancel a much
advertised festivity for which the preparations were already completed.   Peter was very fond of festivities.   Upon Peter's death,
on January 28, 1725, Catherine's old friend Menshikov succeeded
in having her proclaimed her husband's successor to the throne of
Russia.   She died of unexplained reasons (several foreign memoirists insist on poisoning and point to Menshikov) two years later,
on May 6, 1727.

Obviously, Catherine cannot fail to influence Peter's fictional image.   She is a telling detail in Pilnyak's grotesque portrait of the Tsar-Monster: "A man enjoying debauchery more than
anything, married to a prostitute, a kept woman of Menshikov"
(*Kneeb*, p. 107).   It is she, "the terrible stepmother with a
viper's forked tongue," who sets Peter against the unfortunate
Tsarevich Alexis, according to Mordovtsev in *Idealists and
Realists* (p. 74).   Conversely, it is to her, his buxom wife nursing their son, that Peter tenderly turns while relaxing between
affairs of state.   The fat, rosy baby mandatory in all happy
families in Soviet literature at the peak of Socialist Realism is
supplied as a stage property by both Fedorov in *The Demidovs* and
Petrov-Biriuk in *Kondrat Bulavin* (1946), but Petrine novels of
all periods characterize Peter as an affectionate father of
Catherine's children.   References to "our little bump" (*shishechka*)
and "our little innards" (*potrokha, potroshonki*)—authentic en-
dearments for their children used by both spouses in their correspondence—are special favorites in fiction and persistently
recur as a means of displaying Peter's yearning for happy domes-
ticity.

It is in the same spirit that Pushkin in *The Blackamoor of
Peter the Great* treats Ibrahim to a dinner *en famille* after

introducing him to "a woman of about thirty-five, beautiful and
dressed according to the latest Parisian fashions" whom the Tsar
greets with a kiss on the lips and addresses as "Kathy" (*Katen'ka*)
and "two youthful beauties, tall, slender, and fresh as roses,
standing behind her, who respectfully approached the Tsar." "No
one," Pushkin remarks in an aside, "could have suspected that the
gracious and hospitable host was no other than the hero of the
Battle of Poltava, the puissant and awesome reformer of Russia"
(pp. 10-11). It is in the same spirit, though in a contrasting
emotional atmosphere, that Merezhkovsky shows an ageing, worried
Peter playing and joking with his two little girls, the quiet Anne
looking on while merry Elizabeth, sitting on her father's knee,
pulls off his glasses "because they make him look like a
grandfather" (*P. & A.*, I, 77). The pretty scene is an oasis
of paternal bliss in the arid desert of loneliness created by
the gnawing suspicion that Peter is losing his "Kathy" to Willim
Mons.

The succession of men Catherine had belonged to before reaching Peter apparently did not bother him: he was not fastidious.
But many writers and readers of Petrine fiction were, and so were
the censors. Hence Lazhechnikov simply informs us that the lady-
like, innocent ward of Pastor Glück, after the capture of Marienburg, "found herself living in Menshikov's home, from which she
went to Peter's" (p. 526). In Mordovtsev's *Tsar Peter and Regent
Sophia*, Catherine, as Martha Skovoronskaya, childlike and shy,
"is employed in Menshikov's house" (p. 19). In *The Crowned Carpenter*, also by Mordovtsev, Peter himself testifies that "Martha
came to love me as an innocent girl-child" (p. 154). So she is
in Petrov's *Kondrat Bulavin*, keeping his house and linen unusually
clean; Peter, impressed by such cleanliness, meets the pretty
homemaker, is attracted to her—and her fate is sealed. A. N.
Tolstoy in "Martha Rabe" reduces Sheremetev's role to capturing
Catherine along with Marienburg and immediately passing her on to
Menshikov (p. 410); while in *Peter the First* Catherine herself explains that "she stayed with Sheremetev only long enough to do his
laundry and cook him a sweet-milk Esthonian soup" (p. 739). Even
in Shildkret's *Our-Savior-on-the-Tallow Church*, Catherine, at her
first meeting with Peter, while loose-mannered, introduces herself as the captive slave of Sheremetev, whom she had left for a
more agreeable lover, Menshikov, without a hint of there having
been other men in her past (pp. 7-8).

So much for her virtue, but her origins—another aspect of
her past which did not exactly qualify her as tsaritsa—could not
be forgotten by fiction writers. Lazhechnikov, in *The Last
Recruit*, hails Catherine enthusiastically as "fantastic in her
fate . . . the inseparable mate of the Father of our Fatherland,
and the rescuer of its greatness on the banks of the River Prut"
(p. 37). The latter title is a reference to Catherine's having
initiated the collection of jewels to ransom the Russian Army
trapped with Peter and herself by the Turks in 1711. Allegedly,
it was on that occasion that Peter promised to marry her if they
survived. Kornilovich in *Andrey the Nameless* rhapsodizes:

> Subjected to hardships early in life by her capricious
> fortunes and barely literate, Catherine left the home of
> a Livonian pastor to ascend the throne as the worthy
> spouse of the Russian Tsar. . . . Her magnificent looks
> still did not measure up to the greatness of her soul.
> An inexhaustible kindness and an angelic gentleness com-
> bined in her with a greatness of mind and spirit rarely
> to be seen, even in a man. Her only care was to preserve
> her husband's love; her permanent endeavor was to protect
> him from any weaknesses and direct him towards every
> noble and lofty goal through understanding, caress, and
> even catering to his whims. (p. 107)

Many writers are less complimentary. Merezhkovsky's Fräulein
Juliana is bitter at witnessing the homage Princess Charlotte has
to pay to "a washerwoman, a common wench, a servant" (*Peter and
Alexis*, I, 99). Danilevsky's Dunya, gazing at Empress Catherine
holding court in her summer palace, reflects on the times when
the former "Martha Skovoroshchenko or Skovorotskaya, Raabe in her
first marriage to a soldier, . . . had lived in the house of a
needy Estonian pastor, cared for his children, swept the floors,
and done the laundry. Having married a captive slave, following
the example of Emperors Basil, Justinian, and Heraclius, the Tsar
had found solace in his new family." (*To India*, p. 78.) There
are other such passages.

Catherine's lowly origins could not have bothered Peter,
who liked to surround himself with lowly companions and had the
lofty indifference of an autocrat toward public reaction to his
acts. Voltaire, who says he does not find it strange that Peter
should have married Catherine, whom no small squire would have
considered making his spouse, explains: "Monarchs like to think
that there is no greatness other than that which they themselves
bestow and consider all stations in life beneath their own to be
equal" (*Histoire*, pp. 537-38). Peter, the consummate autocrat,
certainly did. Nothing perhaps influences this aspect of his
image so strongly as does Catherine's career.

Thus, she, in fact and in fiction, had to be accepted by
everyone early, practically from the very beginning of her relationship with the Tsar. Peter was infatuated with her; reports
(perhaps exaggerated) were that she exercised a tremendous influence on him; above all, she *lasted*, replacing (some say, sup-
planting) Anna Mons, and eventually achieving the status belonging to exiled Evdokia the lawful wife and rightful tsaritsa.
What, then, were the qualities she possessed, to what peculiarities of Peter's own character did these qualities appeal to make
her, quoting Lazhechnikov, "so fantastic in her fate"?

Of course, much of her appeal was sexual but not all of it.
As A. N. Tolstoy's Menshikov knew, "Peter needed not simply a
woman, but a helpmate, a good companion" (*P.F.*, p. 616). Catherine suited him; she was everything he wanted her to be, his
kind of woman spiritually as well as physically. She was his
"missus," who would fuss over his forever neglected diet and

would report in her (dictated) letters on their children (teeth-
ing and baby talk), on the beauty of their garden, even on a new
warship being finished in the shipyards. Fiction makes much of
her darning her "old man's" socks[10] and of her embroidering with
silver sequins that blue silk coat which the Tsar was to wear at
her coronation. She was prolific, and Peter valued that. He
liked to address her as *Muder* in Dutch, "Mother"—actually "mother
genetrix" (*matka*)—in Russian, but she was not a sentimental
parent. All but two of her numerous children died in infancy,
but it was Peter, not Catherine, who became almost distraught
with grief at the death of little Peter in 1719. She was, however, always willing to produce another "little bump" for her
lord, especially a boy, an heir. In *The Tsar and the Hetman*
Mordovtsev portrays Peter on the eve of the Battle of Poltava
overwhelmed with joy at a message from Catherine—a gem in fictionalized Petrine correspondence:

> And, my darling Peterkin [*Petrushen'ka*], though sorely
> ashamed, blushing blood-red with embarrassment, I am go-
> ing, my love, to whisper something close to your ear:
> deep in my womb, under my very heart, your little bump is
> stirring. Maybe I'll give you a son by Christmas. (p.
> 263.)

In the post-World War II period, when prolific mothers were
hailed as heroines in life and in fiction in Soviet Russia, two
Petrine novels introduce Catherine resplendent with the glory of
motherhood. Peter, sick in bed, worried with the rumors of the
Bulavin revolt, summons Catherine:

> She entered, plump, big-boned, rosy, glowing with health.
> The small, darkened room suddenly seemed to fill with a
> peculiar light. She bowed low and hesitantly approached
> the Tsar's bed . . . though she already had three children
> by him, she still could not get used to her exalted posi-
> tion. . . . The Tsar looked at her, smiling. He enjoyed
> knowing that this healthy, sturdy woman was the mother of
> his children.

She is pregnant again and plans to wean the youngest baby.
Peter advises against it:

> "You still have milk, don't you?"
>   Catherine blushed and, looking down, answered: "I
> do, so far." Peter stroked Catherine's broad, soft back
> with his big hand roughened with work, and felt his
> spirit relax and become peaceful. (*Bulavin*, pp. 186-87.)

Fedorov shows the happy royal couple through the admiring
gaze of the famous master of the Siberian foundries, Demidov:

> Next to the Sovereign stood, blooming and plump, the

Tsaritsa Ekaterina Alexeevna. Tall, big-boned, she was
only slightly shorter than the Monarch. Her large eyes
under thick eyelashes radiated warmth and tenderness. She
held in her arms an infant wrapped in silk and lace. The
Tsar, with a happy countanance, kept looking in turn at
his spouse and at their son. (*The Demidovs*, p. 275.)

Whether as concubine or as tsaritsa she remained docile and
submissive, never forgetting she was a former captive dependent
at all times on the Sovereign's favor. Peter remembered that too
—witness the incident of the broken mirror; moreover, the Reformer,
quite conventional in some respects, considered docility a basic
feminine virtue—witness the fate of Evdokia. Thus, though
Catherine would often intervene on behalf of a culprit (Menshikov
more often than most) threatened with the Tsar's wrath and punishment, it was as a supplicant, not as a capricious favorite or as
a confident wife—and the request was usually granted.
    Naturally, Peter would not tolerate jealousy, and Catherine
played the difficult role of a complaisant wife gracefully and
wisely, careful not to incur displeasure by provoking marital
scenes, yet not allowing Peter's casual infidelities to undermine
her own position. Semevsky disdainfully notes that "Catherine
used to befriend her temporary rivals," the latter including her
maid of honor Marya Hamilton and Hamilton's attendant, Anna Kramer
(*Treason!*, pp. 197-98). Pilnyak illustrates that statement with
a cynical episode involving Maria Rumyantseva (*Kneeb*, p. 122);
Shildkret bluntly accuses Catherine of pandering and notes Peter's
appreciation of that (*Our-Savior*, pp. 54-55); Merezhkovsky, quoting Bassevitz (*Diary*, p. 196), says that "the Tsaritsa is not
given to being jealous. He [Peter] relates to her all his adventures, always gallantly stating in the end: 'Still, Katenka, you
are better than any of them.'" (*P. & A.*, I, 118.)
    Such wifely tolerance was met with approval by people who
knew first-hand that Peter could not have been handled in any
other way. Stählin tells an anecdote (no. 105) about a respect-
able girl who, to escape Peter's attentions, spent a year hiding
in a marshy forest. Finally her fiancé and grieving parents appealed to Catherine, and she persuaded the Tsar to reward the
girl's virtue by consenting to her marriage and giving her a good
dowry. Nartov commends the manner in which Catherine caused Peter
to end an affair with a palace seamstress: she promoted the girl
to her own service and introduced her to the Tsar, praising her
beauty and intelligence. "This attitude," Nartov remarks, "so
gentle, tender, and submissive, embarrassed the Sovereign, who
did not fail to understand such subtle diplomacy. . . . He never
summoned the girl to him again and soon married her to a Livonian
nobleman of rank and wealth. He did it in order to prove to his
spouse that this was not a mistress to whom he was deeply attached." (*Notes*, p. 146.)
    Neither was he deeply attached to his other numerous "riff-
raff mistresses [*metresishka*]," as both Peter and Catherine jokingly called them in their correspondence. He birched them,

married them off to complaisant husbands, and considered them beneath his jealousy—or Catherine's. "Katenka" still was the best
of them all. Good-natured and cunning, she preferred to eliminate
harmless rivals by "gentle, tender, and submissive" means. In
the case of Marya Kantemir, she had to act ruthlessly and swiftly
because that youthful beauty represented an immediate danger to
her position at the side of the ageing Tsar. It is fairly certain that Peter never learned of the intrigue behind Marya Kantemir's miscarriage.

Catherine's admirers among historians and authors of Petrine
novels credit her with superior intelligence, some even suggest-
ing that Peter took her advice in affairs of state—a doubtful
proposition, in fact, wholly improbable.[11] It is also variously
suggested that she owed her firm hold on the Tsar to tact,
shrewdness, feminine wiles, even—according to goodwives' gossip
—witchcraft. Whatever her secret, she had indeed mastered the
dangerous skill necessary to handle her redoubtable lord.

Physically too, she was Peter's kind of woman: strong (she
once gained Peter's praise for lifting from its pedestal a statue
weighing 216 pounds), splendidly healthy, with a good head for
drinking. Catherine's earthiness intensifies Peter's own in his
image, just as Nikita Demidov's being such an eminently Russian
blacksmith reminds the reader that Peter is after all a very
Russian tsar. She was not beautiful: her portraits confirm
that. As Helbig says, "lively eyes and colossal breasts are insufficient claims to perfection" (*Günstlinge*, p. 62). But she
radiated vitality, kindliness, and easy good humor—"une brune
magnifique," says Dolgorukov (p. 38). Actually, Ustryalov and
Galizin claim she was a blonde who dyed her hair black, but in
fiction only Merezhkovsky (who sides with Alexis and resents
Catherine) makes use of this information (*P. & A.*, I, 221).
Petrine novels, with few exceptions, show her as a tall brunette,
usually buxom, sometimes stately. A. N. Tolstoy alone endows her
not just with sex appeal but also with naive freshness and great
charm. His Peter longing for the sight of her, happy with
memories of her in a camp at night, is not Pilnyak's coarse "man
who married a prostitute" but a lonely man in love with a truly
feminine woman.

Few authors of Petrine novels fail to introduce a scene
showing Catherine soothing his attacks of rage, which even
respectful Kornilovich describes as coming sometimes all of a
sudden

> during a party or a feast. His hair would stand on end,
> his eyes would become blodshot, and his features would
> become convulsed and distorted. Foaming at the mouth,
> and gnashing his teeth, he would utter screams resembling
> the roar of a wild beast, terrifying to even the bravest.
> In these fearful moments, when no one else dared come
> near the sufferer, Catherine would approach him, rest his
> head on her bosom, stroke it gently and so cause the
> demented man to fall asleep. This seemingly magnetic

> sleep lasted about a quarter of an hour and restored the
> Sovereign to health and gaiety. (*Andrey*, p. 108.)

Authors differ in their interpretations of the source of Catherine's peculiar talent. Merezhkovsky agrees in part with Kornilovich's theory of magnetism and, twice in such circumstances, com-
pares her to a "tamer soothing a wild beast," but also to a
mother tenderly rocking a sick child (*P. & A.*, II, 88, and I,
221). Pilnyak conveys the picture of a child tormented by a
nightmare calming down under the mother's gentle caress:

> Peter stood waving his arms, a spasm pulling his chin
> towards his left shoulder, his eyes wild and helpless like
> a child's. Catherine alone could calm him in such moments.
>   She took Peter's head in both her hands and, leaning
> it against her bosom, softly scratched him behind the
> ears. Next, she sat down by his side, placed his head on
> her ample lap and continued scratching. The Sovereign
> fell asleep helplessly, like a child. (*Kneeb*, pp. 124-
> 25.)

Shildkret, in *The Eagle Cup*, in sharp contrast to Zagoskin's
rendition of Peter's dignified behavior in the Turkish encircle-
ment episode in 1711, also describes him "burying his face in
Catherine's bosom like a frightened child" (p. 264). Tynyanov,
however, unequivocally declares himself for the influence of
Catherine's unusual sex appeal. Peter, near death, is thrashing
about in convulsions, on his bed: "Catherine stooped over him.
Here was what had always attached him to her, fettering his soul
and his flesh—her breasts. And he submitted and gave in. Her
breasts, which barely two months ago had been kissed by His Honor,
the Kammerherr Willim Mons. He quieted down and lay still"
(*Effigy*, no. 1, p. 5). Tynyanov's stance could be supported by
a story told by Peter's favorite aide, Yaguzhinsky. According
to him, *any* pretty woman could calm Peter's attacks, and he would
promptly bring one to Peter at the first symptoms whenever Catherine was not on hand. Golikov and Stählin qualify the phenomenon
as "innocent pleasure which Peter took in the company of Beauty,"
but there are those who disagree, notably Galizin and Dolgorukov.
Authors of Petrine novels, of course, acquainted with the story,
never introduce any woman except Catherine in that role.
     Only three other women have played some role in shaping
Peter's image: Anna Mons, Evdokia, and Tsaritsa Natalya, in that
order. Tsarevna Sophia, Peter's archenemy, has no direct bearing
on his image, though Peter owed many of his complexes, phobias,
and possibly his nervous tics and convulsions to her. Sophia was
a political foe, a plotter, and a potential assassin, locked in
a desperate struggle for power with Peter. Her appearances in
Petrine novels are limited to the period of Peter's childhood and
adolescence, not later than the last Streltsy plot in 1698. She
died in 1707.
     Anna Mons was Peter's first love and mistress; their liaison

lasted ten years. She belongs to the period when Peter, absorbed
in training his "play" regiments and building his first boats,
did not pay much attention to women, including Evdokia, whom he
had married casually to please his mother. He met Anna through
Lefort (some sources make her Lefort's mistress), whose house discreetly provided all the "unseemly" entertainment Peter could afford at the time out of deference to his mother. After Tsaritsa
Natalya's death, the scope of Peter's activities as well as amusements vastly increased, but "Annushka," now openly the monarch's
mistress, firmly held her position in his affections, and when
Peter banished Evdokia to the convent, there was even some talk
of Anna's taking her place.

Anna, however, says Nartov, though "of exceptional beauty
and pleasing manners, was of mediocre intelligence" which she
proved "by preferring marriage to a foreign diplomat, Keyserling,
to continuing as Peter's mistress" (no. 19.) D'Allainval even
asserts that she not only never loved Peter (Mordovtsev and
Shildkret take this for granted in view of her "betrayal") but
that she had "an invincible aversion" for him (*Anecdotes*, p. 13).
A. N. Tolstoy in *Peter the First* shows her afraid of the barbarian
Tsar, tormented by his love, and longing for respectability,
security, and peace. Still, Tolstoy too resents her pedestrian
tastes, her limited horizons, and her inability to perceive the
greatness of the Tsar or to feel his basic emotional vulnera-
bility.

Shildkret, who casts her as a mercenary German adventuress
in *Mamura*, Mordovtsev in *The Tsar and the Hetman*, and A. N.
Tolstoy (few other authors introduce Anna Mons) agree that Anna
never was the right mate for Peter. She was too alien to him in
spirit and habits, though the very fact of her being a foreigner
was undoubtedly a factor in the attraction she held for him in
spite—or perhaps because—of the scandal their liaison caused
among Russians. Perhaps she was too fastidious in her German
bourgeois way; Peter, as we know, could be quite coarse in his
habits. There is no doubt that he felt their parting strongly
(Mordovtsev waxes quite maudlin describing Peter's despair at the
news of Anna's infidelity), and Anna does matter in that she provides the scant element of poetic feeling to be found in Peter's
characterization. Whatever Catherine meant to Peter—the "Muder"
or the "Missus"—Anna at least meant romance, even if he was able,
in the words of A. N. Tolstoy, "to tear this woman out of his
heart like a weed, with roots and with blood" (*P.F.*, p. 616).

Evdokia, though banished from Peter's life earlier than Anna, is,
understandably, more important to Peter's image. They were married
in January 1689. Peter was a restive, lanky boy of sixteen and Evdokia at nineteen, was, according to Mordovtsev, "a real Russian
beauty," blue-eyed, buxom, with a long thick braid," and promising to
grow unbecomingly fat in the future (*Tsar and Regent*, p. 146). Merezhkovsky's Alexis remembers her "round, white, little girl's face
always surprised looking." (*P. & A.*, I, 229). They had three sons
in three years (the youngest two died in infancy), and by that
time Peter was but a rare guest in their home.

Evdokia was a model, traditional Tsaritsa, "modest, gentle, very pious, used to the life of the *terem*. Her time was spent in nursing her babies; reading religious books; talking to the crowd of servants, maids, and matrons of her court; embroidering and sewing; and worrying about and complaining of the ways of her flightly husband."[12] For all that, she is foolosh, tactless, and exasperating to Peter, whom she completely misunderstands. Her characterization by Tolstoy in *Peter the First* illustrates the opinion of Kurakin, a contemporary, according to whom Evdokia was "a princess fair in her person but of mediocre intelligence and of a disposition unsuitable for her husband, which resulted in her wasting her own happiness and destroying her whole family" (*History*, p. 56). Kukolnik introduces her in "The New Year" walking with Peter to church "dressed in a mixture of Asiatic and European fashions" and, seeing some soldiers dressed in the newly introduced foreign uniforms, spitting to the side to ward off the evil spell because "she thought they were German, the main source of discord between the crowned spouses" (p. 161). Shildkret, without a shred of historical evidence, makes her go insane in *Mamura*.

Foreign memoirists such as D'Allainval, D'Eon, and Lady Rondeau, though recognizing Evdokia's inability to deal with Peter, extoll her beauty and even her intelligence[13] and sympathize with her sufferings at Peter's hands, as do, in more cautious terms, the Russians. But, everyone, including, fiction writers, agrees that she had a jealous disposition and that this feeling was not to be indulged by any monarch's spouse, let alone the spouse of Peter the Great. Ustryalov rather naively wonders (III, p. 191) whether there was not after all some indiscretion of Evdokia's that led Peter to treat her so ruthlessly, and Bruce boldly states that there was (p. 106), but there is no need for such conjectures. She bored him, and he wanted to be rid of her —a good enough reason for many a husband and a decisive one for Peter. Had she meekly agreed to retire into a convent when he tried—first through the clergy, then personally—to persuade her to do so, she probably would have received the same living conditions as the other nuns of royal blood: even Tsarevnas Martha and Sophia had fared better under Peter's displeasure than did his wife and the mother of his children. But once irritated by disobedience, Peter did not stop at half measures. Deprived of decent maintenance, forbidden to see Alexis (even letters occasionally smuggled between mother and son presented a grave danger to both, as Alexis's trial showed), Evdokia dragged out a miserable existence for twenty-seven years, foolishly keeping company with Peter's opponents among the dissatisfied clergy and old-fashioned boyars. She is occasionally shown in this role in Petrine fiction, but even Merezhkovsky fails to introduce her personally during Alexis's trial. He only quotes (*in extenso*) her pathetic letters to the Tsar, signed "Your Majesty's former wife, Evdokia," and the protocols of her testimony confessing to her crimes—wearing secular dress after taking the veil, revealing her hopes of again becoming the Tsaritsa under Alexis's reign

after Peter's death, and living in sin with Major Glebov. That
last crime (though Glebov denied the liaison to his last breath)
enraged Peter as much as if it had been committed by a young, beloved wife, not by one he had himself repudiated seventeen years
before.

Tsaritsa Natalya's attitude toward the marriage of her son
and the wife she herself had chosen for him is unclear. Villebois
and Kurakin speak of the mutual hatred between the two women;
Ustryalov maintains that Natalya tried to reconcile the spouses.[14]
Authors, as usual, take their choice, but it is doubtful whether
her attitude really mattered because Natalya's influence on Peter
was insignificant, as are her rare appearances in fiction. He
loved and respected his mother—this is proved by the tender letters he wrote her and the discretion he showed during her lifetime in his amusements at the Foreign Quarter. Her death in 1694
reportedly grieved him deeply, but two days later there was a
feast at Lefort's house in the Foreign Quarter, and in another
several days the Tsar returned to his shipbuilding in Arkhangelsk.

In an authentic letter Peter himself tersely explains his
attitude thus: "Stunned, I inform you of my misfortune and my
utter sorrow, which neither my hand nor my heart is able to express. However, having, like Noah, somewhat recovered from that
grief, setting aside that which is irrevocable, I am now writing
about matters of life."[15] The "matters of life" concerned the
progress of a boat being built in Arkhangelsk.

Peter the First is the only important novel dealing with the
early Petrine period which includes the scene of Natalya's death.
Tolstoy shows Peter feeling his bereavement and loneliness keenly;
crying with his sister Natalya while reminiscing about their
childhood; turning even to Evdokia for comfort and deeply resent-
ing her tactless indifference to his loss (she actually enjoys
the thought of herself succeeding to her mother-in-law's position
at court). Later, at a small, quiet supper at Lefort's, Anna
Mons, acting as Proserpine full of tearful sympathy, presents to
a "subdued, sad Peter" a platter of fruit symbolizing the victory
of life over death. Anna's charm, the champagne, and the sounds
of music drifting from the garden make Peter "shed his sadness"
(*P.F.*, pp. 243-46).

In *Youthful Russia* Yury German makes a different use of this
letter insofar as it affects Peter's fictional image, moving the
background and the time to several years before Natalya's death,
to one of her visits to Peter while he was building his first
ship on Lake Pereyaslavl; "Peter welcomed her with timid tenderness entirely foreign to his usual demeanor. But immediately, as
if putting her out of his mind, he rushed away to supervise the
sailing of his new boat Mars, leaving Ivlyov to wait on his
mother at all times" (I, 57).

Both authors use the spirit of Peter's letter to absolve him
from callousness. Tolstoy shows Peter's grief and then allows it
to be overcome by the vitality which had made Peter always turn
to living matters; German stresses the uncharacteristic tenderness
in the son's behavior towards his mother, as well as the

statesman's priority he gives to the important business of building Russia's fleet.   Nevertheless, in both cases Peter's restlessness is present, as is his way of never letting anything, however important, interfere with the work or amusement that was absorbing his passionate interest at a given time.   There is also the insensitivity which, tinged with cruelty, is always present in Peter's image, side by side with kindness.

12.   The Case of Tsarevich Alexis

> We may not point to his mistakes because we do not know
> whether what we consider a mistake will not prove a
> necessity in that future which still remains closed to
> us, but had already been revealed to him at the time.
>   Polevoy, 1843

In Petrine fiction Alexis is a secondary historical personage,
appearing in lesser episodes as a child or a young boy. Only
four novels deal with his flight abroad, his return and its after-
math, the trial terminating in his death: Polezhaev's *Tsarevich
Alexis Petrovich* (1885), Merezhkovsky's *Peter and Alexis* (1905),
Shildkret's *The Eagle Cup* (1935), and Vsevolod Ivanov's *Tsar
Peter's Night* (1968). No one else attempted to tackle the topic,
not even A. N. Tolstoy, who intended to terminate *Peter the First*
with the Battle at Poltava, in 1709. Mordovtsev's *Idealists and
Realists* (1878) gives a glimpse of Alexis's flight, but not of
subsequent developments, and casts the tsarevich as a secondary
character. Yet the topic offers many fascinating possibilities,
and there are plenty of historically documented materials and
even more of gossip contributed by petite histoire. The reading
public was well aware of both. Apart from prerevolutionary censorship, the reason for authors' reticence seems to be that the
case is extremely involved and unclear: while the sequence of
events is known, their reasons and, above all, Peter's motives
remain a mystery.

Alexis was born on February 18, 1690, when both his parents
were just teenagers. He was nine when Peter exiled Evdokia to a
convent and forbade the boy to communicate with her. Alexis was
brought up by occasional tutors, until at seventeen he was ordered to join the army and the Swedish war, though he never saw
action. At twenty-one he married Charlotte, Princess Braunschweig-
Wolfenbüttel, who died in October 1715, after the birth of a son,
the future Peter II. Two weeks later, a son, Tsarevich Peter,

was born to Tsaritsa Catherine, the Tsar's mistress since 1702
and at the time mother of Anne and Elizabeth, the two daughters
surviving out of five. It is at this point that Peter's motives
become unclear.

Two weeks later, on November 15, 1715, Peter issued a ukase
abolishing the principle of primogeniture. Historians and contemporaries agree that it was then that Peter decided to disin-
herit Alexis in favor of his newborn son by Catherine. There was
an exchange of letters between father and son, unexplained since
both were staying in St. Petersburg, and involving some discrepancy
in dates. Peter charged the Tsarevich with interests and conduct
unfit for a future tsar and threatened him with dire consequences
in language Biblical ("I'll cut you off like a gangrened limb")
and practical ("I'll treat you as I would any other criminal").
Alexis offered to abdicate his rights to the throne and later
agreed to retire to a monastery. Excerpts from this correspondence are freely used in fiction, either *in extenso* or in often
garbled quotes meant to lend historical authenticity to the plot.

Peter was not satisfied. He knew that Alexis's rights of
succession were indisputable and that should he himself die before
his newborn son's majority, Alexis was sure to be welcomed to the
throne by every living soul in Russia except a handful of Peter's
favorites. As to the Tsarevich's becoming a monk, in the historic
phrase, much utilized by fiction, "a monk's cowl is not nailed to
one's head"; he could be released from his vows. So, Alexis was
given six months in which "to improve his habits" and at the end
of this term, in August 1716, was ordered either to withdraw
immediately to a monastery, or to join the Tsar in Copenhagen
to take part in military action there. Alexis replied that he
was coming. Instead, he escaped to Vienna, requested asylum from
Emperor Charles VI, his late wife's brother-in-law, and at first
succeeded in staying abroad incognito. He was soon tracked down
by the Russian envoy in Vienna, Veselovsky (an interesting case
among Peter's "fledgelings," since he eventually chose to stay
abroad permanently) and persuaded by Peter's emissaries, Tolstoy
and Rumyantsev, to return to Russia assured of the Tsar's complete pardon and permission to marry Afronsinya, the adored
mistress who had accompanied him on his flight.

Upon his return on January 31, 1718, he was tried by the
Senate for high treason, was tortured during the interrogation
along with a large number of alleged co-conspirators he had involved, and was sentenced to death. He died two days after the
verdict, on June 26, 1718, thus sparing Peter the public execution of the heir to the throne, which would have caused him intense
embarrassment abroad and could even have proved dangerous at
home: the populace was fond of the last Tsarevich of purely Russian blood they were ever to have.

The cause of Alexis's death has never been established. Officially it was given out as apoplexy, but nobody doubted that
foul play was involved. Diplomats who were incautious in their
speculations were recalled at St. Petersburg's demand: Pleyer,
the Austrian envoy, for reporting that the Tsarevich was

decapitated with a sword or an axe; the Dutch envoy De-Brie, for
alleging that four veins were opened by the Tsar's orders. No information of this kind—in fact, no mention of Alexis's case—is
found in the works of Stählin, Nartov, or Golikov; though a letter
allegedly written by Rumyantsev states that Alexis, in Rumyantsev's
presence, was smothered with a pillow by Tolstoy, Ushakov, and
Buturlin. Ustryalov, while including this letter among other
documents (*History*, VI, 619-26), insists it is a forgery.

   Foreigners, however, are prolific in their conjectures and
gossip. Villebois and d'Allainval declare themselves in favor of
the open veins version; Bruce insists that he personally delivered
poison to Weide in the Tsarevich's prison cell; Helbig accepts
poison *and* decapitation when poison proved ineffectual; d'Eon
charitably suggests "violent grief" and Nestesuranoi, "convulsive
lethargy."[1] Pogodin, in his documentary monograph *The Trial of
Tsarevich Alexis* (1860), asks a sensible question: What does the
manner of death of the unfortunate Tsarevich matter? It is certain that he died, obviously of exhaustion, several hours after
the last torture. The point Pogodin omits to make—understandably,
in 1860—is that Alexis died because Peter had willed it so; that
the last torture took place *after* he has been informed of the
death sentence; and that the Tsar personally participated in that
additional interrogation and dealt some of the blows of the knout
himself.

   With such rich material at their disposal, fiction writers
make their choices. In *Peter and Alexis* (II, 220-22) the Tsarevich dies like a martyr, almost as a saint, serene and happy,
with the vision of Saint John the Baptist administering the Last
Rites to him. Peter is present, inscrutable, almost dazed; it
is he who, in a fit of frenzy, had struck the last several blows
a few hours before. Ivanov accepts and reproduces almost unchanged (as also does Shildkret in *The Eagle Cup*, pp. 382-3) the
death scene in Rumyantsev's letter; thus, in his *Tsar Peter's
Night* Alexis dies a coward, sobbing and struggling with his executioners—Tolstoy, Ushakov, and Buturlin—who finally overpower
him and smother him with pillows (p. 153). In *Tsarevich Alexis
Petrovich* (p. 151), Polezhaev gives his own version: Alexis dies
in the torture chamber under the knout, with Peter present but
not actively participating. Finally, Eustaphieve in his bizarre
work *Reflections, Notes, and Original Anecdotes Illustrating
the Character of Peter the Great, to Which Is Added a Tragedy in
Five Acts, Entitled Alexis the Tsarevich* (1812), uses the official story: Alexis, forgiven and repentant, dies of grief—as
an additional tender touch—in Peter's arms. In the few cases
when Alexis's death is mentioned in works dealing with the last
years of Peter's reign, the Tsar's guilt is assumed to be established. Pilnyak and Kostylyov curtly state that he had personally
strangled his son, and Tynyanov, that Peter "has done the eldest
villain in himself."[2]

   As can be seen, authors take sides and are guided in that by
personal feelings. Pilnyak dislikes Peter as a personality;
Shildkret and Kostylyov, as an autocrat; Polezhaev is primarily

sorry for Alexis; in the eyes of Eustaphieve Peter could do no
wrong; Ivanov believes that Peter saw in Alexis an obstacle on
Russia's path to progress, and as a statesman had to remove him,
whatever the cost to his feelings as a father. Merezhkovsky seems
to justify Peter, but from mystical premises. Now that Alexis
was dead, "Peter knew that his son would plead his case at the
Last Judgment and would explain to him what he could not understand on earth: the meaning of the mystery of the Father sacrificing the Son." (P. & A., II, 226). Moreover, Merezhkovsky
pities Alexis, the Orthodox Church, and the Russian people—and
leaves the impression of not being quite sure that Peter was not
the Antichrist, after all. Actually, nobody was sure; this doubt
is part of Peter's image.

A dark aura surrounds Peter's image in connection with this
affair, mainly because of the persisting opinion that Peter did
not just want to remove Alexis as his successor but deliberately
sought to destroy him. Historians are inclined to think so; the
authors of the petite histoire have no doubts about it; the unfortunates tortured as Alexis's accomplices confirm that such was
the common belief at court as well as among the populace. Finally,
Alexis himself, when asking for asylum, said to Austrian Vice-
Chancellor Schönborn:

> My father is surrounded by evil people; he is exceedingly
> cruel and bloodthirsty, thinks that he is God himself, and
> has the right to take human life. He has shed much inno-
> cent blood, often even killing the unfortunate sufferers
> with his own hand. Moreover, he is inordinately given to
> wrath and vengeance and grants mercy to no man. If the
> Emperor were to surrender me to my father, he would be
> depriving me of my life. (Ustryalov, VI, 583.)

Schönborn's report of this scene was utilized practically unchanged by Ivanov, Polezhaev, and Mordovtsev.

Undoubtedly, there was much truth in Alexis's harsh words.
We saw Peter—being, in the words of d'Eon, of "a defiant and
suspicious disposition" (Loisirs, p. 26)—become insane with rage
when his will was thwarted, and in such cases, he was capable of
extreme cruelty. We know that he could, when it suited his goals,
act with cynical hypocrisy. Did he then, in fact, trap Alexis
into escaping abroad so as to have a pretext for charging him
with high treason, luring him into returning with solemn promises
of forgiveness and then announcing that the pardon was invalid
because the escape was only a screen for a plot against Peter's
life? Merezhkovsky asserts as much and is particularly bitter at
the violation of the confidentiality of the confession during the
trial, an act not only blasphemous but illegal until the ukase
which made it mandatory in cases involving high treason.

Certainly, to Peter, Alexis was a disappointment and, eventually, a menace. A delicate child "with grey eyes like flowers,
small, slight, and pale" (Ivanov, Night, p. 112), "sitting on his
grandmother's lap surrounded by plump pillows and nurses as plump

as the pillows" (*P. & A.*, I, 229), by priests, and, according to
Mordovtsev, by half-crazy "men of God" (*iurodivye*). As a boy he
hates the sea and cries easily, particularly in the presence of
his formidable father (German, *Russia*, I, 451 and II, 477). As a
youth he is effeminate, at least in Selvinsky's play *From Poltava
to Gangut*, where he is shown embroidering (p. 249). Even as a
man, he is sad and shy, and strong emotion makes him faint (Mordovtsev *Idealists*, pp. 6-8, and *Tsar and Hetman*, pp. 116-7). He is
less useful to Peter than any of the "fledgelings," showing no
interest in military exploits, bureaucracy, or diplomacy. He
does not even have a good head for drinking, and Peter despises
him for that too. He obviously leans towards the decorous way of
life proper for an Orthodox tsar, the slow kind of life which
Peter hated and tried so hard to eradicate in Russia and which
Alexis when drunk openly promised to restore after his father's
death. Moreover, he sometimes wishes that death, confesses to it
historically and in Petrine novels—Polezhaev's, Ivanov's, and
Merezhkovsky's—and hears the priests respond, "God will forgive
you. We all wish for it."[3] And this seals his own death warrant,
whether or not it was planned in advance, for, as we have seen,
Peter was apt to panic at the thought of an attempt on his life.

"Now you see," Nartov reports Peter's saying to Tolstoy and
Buturlin after one of Alexis's interrogations, "he is Sophia all
over again" (*Notes*, no. 158). The old nightmare is back and with
it the attacks of rage that prompted the punishment inflicted on
Miloslavsky's corpse at the scene of Tsikler's execution, and the
mass executions of the Streltsy in 1698. The whole scenario is
repeated in the torture and execution of Alexis's friends, relatives, and well-wishers and in the interrogations and imprisonment of Tsarevna Marya and Evdokia. The courageous death scenes
of Kikin, whom Peter had once considered trustworthy, and Glebov,
alleged to have been Evdokia's lover, are reenacted in *Peter and
Alexis* and in Polezhaev's novel.

The pages of all Petrine fiction emanate the atmosphere of
his subjects' hostility toward that which he held dearest: his
vision of a new, changed Russia. This atmosphere is created by
the ragged peasants dying by the thousands as they build St.
Petersburg, by the disgruntled old boyars, by the clergy of all
ranks from village priests to archbishops, by the Old Believers
burning themselves in their forest refuges, by Evdokia in her
convent, and by surviving half-sisters and sisters-in-law in the
Kremlin. At the head of them all stands Alexis, the "hope of the
Russian land," the opposition personified, its spirit and natural
leader, ready to begin demolishing the edifice to whose building
Peter had dedicated the effort of a lifetime. Alexis's death was
the one condition which could make Peter's reforms irreversible;
did he plan that death the way he planned his wars, his bureaucracy, and his police?

Pushkin, in a discussion he had with Pogodin on the murky
events leading to Boris Godunov's accession to the throne, said:

Do you really think that a man possessed with the least

degree of moral sense, not a villain, is capable of calmly
planning a crime? No, he will always shrink from its actual accomplishment, without, however, discarding the idea
as it first occurred to him. He finds it painful to contemplate the deed, so he tries to get it done and over
with as soon as possible, unable to contemplate the details. (Pogodin, *The Trial*, p. 59.)

It might be relevant perhaps to quote the conclusion arrived
at by Pogodin and Waliszewski, since it sums up the attitudes of
fiction writers characterizing Peter in connection with Alexis's
trial and death. Waliszewski is blunt: "Peter was great and
made Russia very great. In this is his only excuse" (*Peter the
Great*, p. 802). Pogodin is almost lyrical: "In the face of his
achievements, still living within the circle of conditions he had
planned and leading the way of life he had determined, we Russians
can only pray that his sins be forgiven and his soul be granted
eternal peace" (*The Trial*, p. 86).

13.   The Backdrop of Environment

His lofty soul no toil could tax
He sailed the seas, he laws appointed,
He wielded sword, and pen, and axe—
This working man, this Tsar anointed.
        Pushkin, *Stanzas*

The environment in Petrine fiction is a backdrop for Peter, acquiring importance only insofar as it serves his characterization.
Naturally, it is meant to re-create the atmosphere of the era,
but the era is above all that of Peter's reforms; they influence
the plot, the dramatis personae, and the environment itself. This
is not the case in traditional historical fiction, whether Russian
or Western. A Scottish mediaeval castle looks much the same,
irrespective of the personality of the monarch who is being enter-
tained in it by the novel's protagonist; a boyar's home has the
same furnishings in Zagoskin's *Jury Miloslavsky* as in A. K. Tolstoy's *Prince Serebryany*, complete with a *terem* and the boyar's
lovely wife, who greets the guests with a low bow, a cup of mead
on a silver platter, and a kiss. The plot—a yarn about the adventures of fictional characters—wholly engages the attention of
the reader, who simply assumes such standard stage sets, whether
"mediaeval" or "Slavic," to be suitable for the given era and so
takes them for granted.

Not so in Petrine fiction. In traditional Petrine novels
the plot is meager; the fictional characters, specifically meant
to typify the Reformer's Russia, are flat; and the psychological
space is filled with Peter's ambiance to the exclusion of any
other element. In Petrine "historical chronicles," such as
Polezhaev's *Tsarevich Alexis Petrovich* and Ivanov's *Tsar Peter's
Night*, the environment is practically nonexistent, the tense
drama of Alexis's trial and death being played on the stage of
Peter's crucial actions and decisions, against a canvas backdrop
labelled "St. Petersburg" or "Moscow." Even in the two great

169

"novels about Peter" by A. N. Tolstoy and Merezhkovsky, the environment is, respectively, Old Russia painfully keeping up with
the pace of Peter's change into a European monarch, and her last,
doomed protest against the "Man at the Wheel" piloting his country into the future over the "iron, bloody waves" of the unknown.

Whenever "Slavic" stage sets are used in Petrine fiction, it
is to create a contrast between the old and the new, to show
changing attitudes and customs. They serve as a background for
old-fashioned weddings: there is Peter's and Evdokia's wedding
in *Peter the First*, a rather undistinguished and joyless affair
with the groom sullen and the bride frightened out of her scanty
wits. There are two weddings of fictional couples described at
length: in *The Crowned Carpenter* by Mordovtsev, who stresses in
a footnote that he still had omitted many immodest details; and
in "Morning's Counsel Is Wiser Than the Night's" (1824) by
Kornilovich, who does not mention his similar omission. Prince
Romodanovsky benevolently participates in both festivities (Mordovtsev makes him jokingly remark about the bride's being led to
"the torture chamber" at the end of the ceremonies), but Peter
does not. There are several detailed descriptions of old-
fashioned boyars' homes by Zagoskin, Pushkin, A. N. Tolstoy, and
Kornilovich—but they represent relics of the past. Up-to-date
characters in Petrine fiction dwell in new, hastily built homes,
such as Lefort's and Menshikov's, blazing with candles reflected
in long mirrors, resounding with dance music and voices of revel-
ing guests.

Even in Peter's absence "Slavic" stage properties serve for
his characterization. The *terem* of the foolish, backward Tsarevnas
Katerina and Marya in Vsevolod Solovyev's *The Tsar Maiden*—Katka
and Mashka in *Peter the First*—is close, gaudy, and crawling with
cripples, dwarfs, and jesters, representing everything Peter
loathed and tried to destroy. In *Peter and Alexis*, the sight of
decaying Kremlin palaces fills the Tsarevich, Peter's son and
antagonist, with infinite sadness. In *Peter the First*, the
crumbling throne hall in the palace of Izmaylovo awakens no other
emotions than impatience at its wasteful dilapidation in Peter's
faithful supporter his sister Tsarevna Natalya. She plans to
adapt the hall for a Western innovation: a theater to perform
her own plays.

Peasant huts are seldom shown in Petrine fiction and then
only as inhabited by fictional characters, which is understandable because foreign envoys failed to describe them for posterity.
Novelists model them on the *izba* of the pre-Revolutionary Russian
village, filling them with smoke from an enormous stove and with
small children as the only discernible characteristics. Nor does
Peter ever appear in these huts, though he is shown occasionally
visiting a soldier's or a blacksmith's home, or the home of an
ambitious merchant who has decided to declare for progress by
giving a new-fangled party called an *asambleia*.

The silver rubles Peter distributes (one of his fictional
godchildren, Arseniev's Arisha the Ducky, wears hers as a talis-
man), the carrot pies he accepts from humble hosts along with the

glasses of aniseed vodka, as well as all the paraphernalia of his
personal belongings are the stage properties of Petrine fiction
and part of his image. The pipe he smokes, the staff he carries,
the dog-cart and the small rowboat he uses for transportation, the
mended socks, the worn military coat, the cotton nightcap and
robe, all serve the same purpose. Against the backdrop of shipyards, his turner's workshop, and military camps (though these are
surprisingly few, considering the wars he waged throughout his
reign), these items are as indispensable to Peter's fictional
portrayal as is the pearl-embroidered headgear in Makovsky's
famous painting of a boyar's daughter. No reader can visualize
Peter outside of his accustomed historical environment, but that,
of course, was primarily St. Petersburg.

The city shares the grandeur and the duality of its creator's
image. Thus St. Petersburg is, in turn, considered to have grown
out of a tyrant's whim, at the cost of untold human suffering, or
out of a vision of greatness for which no price was too exorbitant
to pay.

> That terrible city with its deadly fogs and rotten fevers
> . . . [which] Peter casually founded on the marshes of
> the Neva delta . . . was built as wildly, precipitously,
> and cruelly as was everything he did . . . the working
> folk [*rabotnye liudishki*] starved, rotted alive, and were
> swept away by epidemics. Hardly anyone lasted longer
> than a year; every year more than a hundred thousand died.
> The city was being built on human bones. (Pilnyak, *Kneeb*,
> pp. 53-75.)

Yet,

> The city was covered with scaffoldings and foundation
> pits, filled with the sound of axes and heavy groans of
> logs being hammered into the ground. Skillful, efficient
> hands of peasants, artisans, and soldiers were building
> it; Peter's ukases—confident, brutal, and sweeping—were
> laying the foundations of its presently world-famous,
> severe, and dignified style. These first builders were
> called "working folk" (*rabotnye liudishki*). . . . Their
> life was not easy. In winter howling wolves would attack
> people in the center of the city . . . but even then it
> was already lively and noisy.[1]

Contemporary folklore and historical fiction people St.
Petersburg with apparitions, ill omens, and lugubrious prophecies
of imminent disaster. The top of an alder tree growing on the
banks of the Neva was said to mark the point to which the waters
would rise on the day of the forthcoming Last Judgment and flood
the "accursed city." Reports of a *kikimora*[2] noisily running up
and down the stairs leading to the belfry of Trinity Church were
investigated by the Secret Chancellery in 1722 and were eventually
published by Semevsky and used by A. N. Tolstoy in *Peter's Day*

and by Merezhkovsky in *Peter and Alexis*. According to Merezhkovsky, "An old fishwife from the Okhta Suburb had seen the kikimora
with her own eyes at a spinning wheel: 'stark naked, completely
black, with a tiny head not larger than a thimble, her body skinny,
thin like a blade of straw'" (*P. & A.*, II, 91). All the gossip
and omens—and this was the reason for the Secret Chancellery's
interest in them—led to the same popular prophecy: St. Petersburg, the misty, evil creation of the Tsar Antichrist, would
perish and disappear like a nightmare. A fictional Old Believer
of Mordovtsev's, a "holy elder," asserts that according to the
words of the Bible, "all this will vanish and [moreover] *this
never was*" (*Idealists*, p. 58).

     Other authors do not go so far as to deny the actual exist-
ence of Peter's "paradise," but the prophecy that the city would
return to its former state as a wasteland runs through Petrine
fiction, beginning with the 1880's and continuing to the present
day. "Petersburg will lie waste!" (*Peterburgu byt' pustu!*) repeat fictional and historical characters in works by Merezhkovsky
and Danilevsky, Polezhaev and Mordovtsev, Ivanov and A. N. Tolstoy. The prophecy, widespread among the populace in Peter's
lifetime, was actually repeated by Tsarevna Marya to Alexis, whom
she advised to flee abroad and wait there in safety until his
father's death. That document, revealed, among others pertaining
to Alexis's trial, by Ustryalov in 1859 (*History*, VI, 457), was
not utilized in fiction until the trial itself became a mention-
able subject. But even after writers began to use it, it was not
always connected with the trial and serves mostly as an expression of opposition to Peter, identifying the city with its creator.
Merezhkovsky's Tikhon—mystic, epileptic, disciple of the "elder"
Kornily, and student of James Bruce, who as a child witnessed the
execution of his Strelets father—is struck by the sight of St.
Petersburg:

> Everything was flat, vulgar, tedious. Sometimes, on
> cloudy mornings, veiled by dirty, yellowish fog, it
> would vanish like a dream. In the legendary city of
> Kitezh things that are stay invisible; in Petersburg, on
> the contrary, visible things do not exist, and both cities
> are equally ghostly. . . . [Once he had met Peter and]
> the terrible face seemed to explain to him the terrible
> city: they both were marked with the same seal [of the
> Antichrist]. (*P. & A.*, I, 73-74.)

     It is a phantom city. Its recurrent disastrous floods,
described in prose and verse, are only too true to life and at
the same time symbolic of the elemental nature of Peter's personality. St. Petersburg fascinates Russian writers with its
eerie white summer nights and its curtain of fogs changing rec-
tilinear boulevards into mazes along which fictional characters—
Gogol's, Dostoevsky's, Bely's, and Merezhkovsky's—wander dis-
tracted and spellbound in a half-dream.
     Pushkin's Peter, the Bronze Horseman, gallops along the

city's deserted streets, his hand pointing toward the pale moon
above, the pavement underneath shattered by the heavy thundering
of his steed. The "terrible Tsar" is pursuing a rebel: a
wretched lover ruined by one of the city's floods. Andrey Bely's
Peter, the Bronze Guest, in the persons of a succession of autocrats, keeps on his pursuit of shadowy rebels "through days,
years, minutes along the damp Petersburg boulevards. The metallic,
thundering blows of his ponderous gallop go on crushing lives in
villages and empty fields, in towns and homes. Periods of time
follow each other, forever thundering."[3] Vsevolod Ivanov says,
"All failures and difficulties only succeeded in fueling Peter's
will. His steps thundered like Time itself." (*The Night*, p. 146.)
And finally, another Soviet writer, M. Shurgin, writes, on the
three hundredth anniversary of Peter's birth:

> My soul since childhood has been peopled by Leningrad's
> ghosts. Of a sudden, the present-day, elegant Nevsky
> Boulevard will melt, will vanish before my eyes and be-
> come a forest road full of frightful potholes. What is
> it? Why did the drab, motley crowd suddenly scatter and
> freeze in watchful immobility? Before whom does that
> soldier in a green uniform snap to attention and the
> foreign merchant bow elegantly, his hat sweeping the
> ground? A flat, round, mustachioed face glances from the
> top of a mud-spattered dogcart. Protruding, immobile
> eyes suck in simultaneously the silent crowd, the rigid
> soldier presenting arms, and the servilely bent foreigner.
> It's he "himself," speeding by in a cloud of horse-sweat.
> . . . High above the open spaces of the Neva, above its
> granite banks, proudly rides on Falconet's horse the
> founder of the city, truly the conquering hero in a laurel
> crown and a Roman toga. Yet one of the portraits in the
> Russian Museum shows a different man. The face with its
> small, bristling mustache looks sick and deadly tired.
> Dark-brown eyes seem to plead for something; they hold no
> threat for anyone those eyes, they seem to beg to be al-
> lowed to rest; he—a worker who had mastered fourteen
> crafts.[4]

In a novella by Andrey Platonov, *The Locks of Epifan* (1927),
a fictional English engineer, having made a fortune in Peter's
service, invites his brother to follow his example, adding in his
letter a word of caution: "Tsar Peter is a very powerful man,
though desultory in his pursuits, and unnecessarily vehement. His
mind resembles his country: [it is] full of concealed riches but
startling in its savage wildness."[5]

Envoi

The Bronze Horseman still rides above the city. His waxen effigy
is on exhibit in one of its museums, and his composite image,
lofty and grotesque, floats over innumerable pages of memoirs,
anecdotes, historical documents, and works of fiction.

Yet Peter the Great remains an enigma, not to be explained
by a statue cast in bronze, nor by a museum assemblage of authentic relics, nor by a legend created by fiction. Perhaps this is
so because, as Shklovsky's character visiting the Kunstkamera remarks of Peter's mannequin, "the effigy resembles Peter, but by
reason of its being an effigy, it represents an outward likeness;
yet the true identity is not there."

Reference Matter

Notes

CHAPTER ONE: *On Genre*

1 A. N. Tolstoy, *Stat'i 1910-1941*, in *Polnoe sobranie sochinenii*, 15 vols.
  (Moskva, 1946-53), XIII, 592-93.
2 Yu.N. Tynyanov, in *Sbornik: Kak my pishem* (Leningrad, 1930), pp. 161-64.
3 I experimented by asking my students in a seminar to name the objects which
  first came to their minds when Lucrezia was mentioned and the answer usually
  was: "black velvet, pearls, and cups of poisoned wine."
4 The reader is requested to distinguish between Alexey Nikolaevich (A. N.) Tolstoy (1883-1945), author of *Peter the First* (1929-1945) and "Martha Rabe"
  (1931); Alexey Konstantinovich (A.K.) Tolstoy (1817-75), author of *Prince
  Serebryany* (1862); and Leo (Lev Nikolaevich, L. N.) Tolstoy (1828-1910),
  author of the fragments of the "Novel on the Times of Peter the First" on
  which he worked in 1872-73, and, of course, of *War and Peace*. To complicate
  matters, all three authors were related, as descendents of Peter Ilich Tolstoy (1645-1729) rewarded by Peter the Great with vast lands and the title of
  Count for luring the fugitive Tsarevich Alexis back to Russia in 1717. This
  historical personage often appears in Russian novels and so in this study.
5 L. N. Tolstoy, in *Polnoe sobranie sochinenii*, 90 vols. (Moskva, 1928-58),
  XVII, 640.
6 A. N. Tolstoy, *Polnoe*, XIII, 323; A. Gołubiew, "Budowa modelu," *Tygodnik
  Powszechny*, 13 (252) (1950); L. Feuchtwanger, "Notes on the Historical
  Novel," in *Books Abroad*, 22 (1948), 345.

CHAPTER TWO: *A Biographical Outline*

1 Old Believers (*raskol'niki, starovery*) were schismatics who opposed liturgical
  changes in the Russian Orthodox Church introduced during Tsar Alexis's reign
  by Patriarch Nikon (1605-1681) whom they considered an apostate. The Old Believers steadfastly clung to their dogmas in spite of official church and
  state persecutions which, with varying intensity, continued to the Revolution.
2 For a description of that ludicrous institution, see Chapter 8.
3 For the details of Peter's first nautical experiences see Chapter 9, p. 113.
4 A. S. Pushkin, *Materialy dlia istorii Petra Velikogo*, in *Polnoe sobranie
  sochinenii*, 17 vols. in 21 (Moskva, 1937-59), X, 256.
5 *Polnoe sobranie zakonov Rossiiskoi Imperii s 1649 goda*, 46 vols. (Sankt-
  Peterburg, 1830-1916) IV, no. 2329, p. 643.
6 *PSZ*, V, no. 3006, p. 325.
7 *PSZ*, VI, no. 3708, p. 297.
8 The Astrakhan Rebellion (1705-6), the Cossack Bulavin Rebellion (1707), and
  the Bashkir Rebellion (1705-11)—all, it will be noticed, in the far regions
  of Peter's realm.

CHAPTER THREE: *Sources*

1 *PSZ*, V, no. 3223, p. 385.
2 P. N. Krekshin, *Zapiski*, in *Zapiski russkikh liudei*, ed. I. P. Sakharov

(Sankt-Peterburg, 1841), p. VI.

3 D'Eon de Beaumont, *Les Loisirs*, 12 vols. in 6 (Amsterdam, 1774), VI, 5. Note also that Peter was proclaimed Emperor thirty-two years after his marriage in 1689.

4 François d'Escherny, *Mélanges de littérature* (Paris, 1811), pp. 67, 149-151.

5 François de Villebois (Hallez, Theophile), *Mémoires Secrets* (Paris, 1853), pp. 110-11. The Orthodox Church gives only one name at baptism. Villebois confuses three Tsarevnas: Peter's only sister Natalya (b. 1673), and his half-sisters, Martha (b. 1652), and Marya (b. 1660). He was indeed fond of Natalya but she had not influenced either his break with Evdokia or his marriage with Catherine.

6 Eléazar Mauvillon, *Histoire de Pierre surnommé le Grand* (Amsterdam, Leipzig, 1742), pp. 26, 49, and 159, respectively. Tsar Fedor's first wife, Agafya Grushetskaya, died in childbirth; his second, Martha Apraxina, survived him by thirty-four years; Fedor did not die of poison. Prince Vasily Golitsyn was ambitious, but hardly a timeserver which is what a *vremenshchik* means, it is not a position or title. *Novodevichii monastyr'* (the *New* Convent of the Holy Virgin) is so called to distinguish it from an older one of the same name.

CHAPTER FOUR: *On Petrine Fiction*

1 I. I. Golikov, *Deianiia Petra Velikogo*, 12 vols. (1788-1789); *Dopolneniia k deianiiam Petra Velikogo*, 18 vols. (Moskva, 1790-97).

2 Volumes XIII-XVIII (VII-IX of the edition used in this study), covering the years of Peter's reign, appeared between 1863-67.

3 *Russkaia Starina* (Petrograd, 1870-1918); *Russkii Arkhiv* (Moskva, 1863-1917).

4 Prince Pierre Dolgorukov in an afterword to his *Mémoires* (Geneva, 1867), p. 512, released for public use the copyright of all his works published abroad. This, he explained, was done to protect his son and only heir, Prince Vladimir P. Dolgorukov and his descendants from "attracting the wrath of the Russian Government" by eventual authorization of future editions or translations.

5 A tax on beards, for those who insisted on keeping them, was ordered in 1701 and spelled out in detail by a ukase in 1705 (N. G. Ustryalov, *Istoriia tsarstvovaniia Petra Velikogo*, 6 vols. [Sankt-Peterburg, 1858-59], III, 195); in 1700 models of mandatory foreign clothes were nailed to the city gates in Moscow, and in 1701 wearing old-fashioned clothes was formally forbidden by a ukase under severe penalties. (S. M. Soloviev, *Istoriia Rossii s drevneishikh vremen*, 15 vols. [Moskva, 1960-65], VIII, 103).

6 N. V. Kukolnik, "Novyi god," in *Sochineniia*, 10 vols. (Sankt-Peterburg, 1851-53), II, 160-61.

7 [Jacob de] Stählin, *Anecdotes originales de Pierre le Grand* (Strasburg, 1787), no. 41; I. Feoktistov, *Anekdoty i predaniia o Petre Velikom* (Sankt-Peterburg, 1896), no. 25.

8 Fräulein Juliana's fictional diary is an important technical device in Merezhkovsky's *Peter and Alexis*.

9 Stählin, *Anecdotes*, no. 100; Soloviev, *Istoriia*, VIII, 517.

CHAPTER FIVE: *How It Is Done*

1 G. v. Helbig, *Russische Günstlinge* (München, 1917), p. 117; D. L. Mordovtsev, *Russkie zhenshchiny novogo vremeni* (Sankt-Peterburg, 1874), pp. 23-4; M. I. Semevsky, *Tsaritsa Katerina Alekseevna, Anna i Willim Mons* (Sankt-Peterburg, 1884), pp. 59-61; K. Waliszewski, *Petr Velikii*, in *Polnoe sobranie sochinenii* (Moskva, 1911), III, 358-61.

2 Lady Rondeau (Mrs. Ward), *Letters* (London, 1777), pp. 13-16.

3 Mordovtsev, *Tsar' i getman*, in *Polnoe sobranie istoricheskikh romanov*, 18 vols. (Sankt-Peterburg, 1914), II, 23-24. This scene is also repeated almost *verbatim* in his *The Crowned Carpenter*.

4 K. G. Shildkret, *Spas na zhiru* (Moskva, Leningrad, 1931), p. 34. Shildkret also repeated the scene with practically no changes in *The Eagle Cup*, pp. 193-4.

5 In Mordovtsev's *Idealists and Realists*, Zagoskin's *The Brynsk Forest*, Merezhkovsky's *Peter and Alexis*, and A. N. Tolstoy's *Peter the First*, respectively.

6 I. I. Lazhechnikov, *Poslednii novik*, in *Sochineniia*, 2 vols. (Moskva, 1963),

I, 103; M. N. Zagoskin, *Brynskii les*, in *Polnoe sobranie sochinenii*, 2 vols. in 1 (Sankt-Peterburg, Moskva, 1898), II, 4; V. S. Soloviev, *Tsar devitsa*, in *Sobranie sochinenii*, 40 vols. (*Sankt-Peterburg*, 1903-4), I, 46.

7 P. Polezhaev, *Prestol i monastyr'* (Sankt-Peterburg, 1881), p. 253; G. Shild-kret, *Mamura* (Moskva, 1934), p. 265; A. N. Tolstoy, *Petr Pervyi*, in *Polnoe*, IX, 42; L. N. Tolstoy, *"Nachala" romana vremen Petra I*, in *Polnoe*, XVII, 161.

8 Kniaz' B. I. Kurakin, *Gistoriia o Tsare Petre Alekseeviche, Gaga-Parizh, 1723-27*, in *Arkhiv Kn. F. A. Kurakina*, 10 vols. (Sankt-Peterburg, 1890-1902), I, 53; A. A. Matveev, *Zapiski*, in *Zapiski russkikh liudei*, ed. Sakharov, I, 7.

9 I. L. Selvinsky, *Ot Poltavy do Ganguta*, in *Tragedii* (Moskva, 1952), p. 197; M. N. Zagoskin, *Russkie v nachale XVIII-go stoletiia*, in *Polnoe*, II, 332.

10 A. B. Mariengof, *Shut Balakirev* (Moskva, Leningrad, 1940), p. 22; the reigns of Peter I, Catherine I, Peter II, and Anna.

11 Kurakin, *Gistoriia*, p. 11; I. A. Zhelabuzhsky, *Zapiski*, in *Zapiski russkikh liudei*, ed. Sakharov, II, 18.

12 *Pop* is colloquial for priest.

13 A. N. Tolstoy, *Petr Pervyi*, in *Polnoe*, IX, 223; "Martha Rabe", in *Polnoe*, VI, 408.

14 Stählin, *Anecdotes*, no. 27; I. Feoktistov, *Anekdoty*, No. 61. Dolgorukov, *Mémoires*, p. 45; M. Semevsky, *Slovo i delo!* (Sankt-Peterburg, 1885); Mordovtsev, *Russkie zhenschiny*, pp. 55-58.

15 O. Belyaev, *Kabinet Petra Velikogo* (Sankt-Peterburg, 1800), p. 31; F. W. v. Bergholz, *Denvnik 1721-1725*, 4 vols. (Moskva, 1902), I, 147-48.

16 A. G. Eustaphieve, *Alexis the Tsarevich*, in *Reflections . . .* (Boston, 1812), p. 42.

17 Ustryalov, *Istoriia*, IV/1, 275; Bergholz, *Dnevnik*, II, 127.

18 Ustryalov, *Istoriia*, VI, 457; Ivanov, *Noch' Tsar'ia Petra*, in *Imperatritsa Fike* (Moskva, 1968), 126; Polezhaev, *Prestol i monastyr'*, p. 132; Merezh-kovsky, *Petr i Aleksei*, in *Polnoe sobranie sochinenii*, 17 vols. (Sankt-Peterburg, Moskva, 1911-1913), IV-V, 81; Selvinsky, *Ot Poltavy*, p. 261.

19 *Russkii Arkhiv*, 12 (1874), 1579, carries this note:
"*A remark by Peter the Great.*
    Among the notes of the late N. D. Kiselev we find these noteworthy lines: 'Bludov found in Troshchinsky's papers the following words of Peter the Great, reported by Osterman: 'We need Europe for a few decades and then we should turn our backs on her.' (This was written down by the late N. D. Kiselev and made available to us by his nephew, P. S. Kiselev.)"
The remark has been extensively used by historians and novelists as proof of Peter's basic patriotism.

20 *PSZ*, no. 412, VI, 685-89.

21 Mordovtsev, *Tsar' i getman*, p. 111; and *Tsar' Petr i pravitel'nitsa Sof'ia*, in *Polnoe sobranie sochinenii*, 12 vols. (Sankt-Peterburg, 1915), X, 201; Lazhechnikov, *Poslednii novik*, p. 452; Zagoskin, *Brynskii les*, p. 255.

CHAPTER SIX: *The Bronze Statue and the Waxen Effigy*

1 Yu. N. Tynianov, *Voskovaia persona*, in *Zvezda* (nos. 1-2, 1931), no. 2, p. 14.

2 A. L. Kaganovich, *Mednyi vsadnik* (Leningrad, 1965), pp. 41, 54.

3 A. N. Radishchev, *Polnoe sobranie sochinenii*, 2 vols. (Moskva, Leningrad, 1938), I, 149-50.

4 N. P. Antsyferov, *Dusha Peterburga* (Sankt-Peterburg, 1922), p. 27.

5 N. M. Sharaya, *Voskovaia persona* (Leningrad, 1963), p. 5.

6 D. S. Merezhkovsky, *Petr i Aleksei*, IV, 211.

7 In their lifetime, Boureois was Peter's footman, Foma worked as a janitor in the Kunstkamera. There were several other live "monstra" also serving as exhibits in visiting hours.

8 V. B. Shklovsky, *O masterakh starinnykh* (Moskva, 1953), p. 119.

9 *The Effigy*, no. 2, p. 32. Actually, the mannequin has no mechanism to make it rise. Belyaev even quotes an anecdote on Peter's refusing the installation of one because "he preferred the effigy to be left in peace since the model had toiled all his life." (*Kabinet*, p. 23.) Yet the rumor of the mannequin rising persisted long after Peter's death and Tynianov utilized its sensational effect.

CHAPTER SEVEN: *Personality: Appearance and Behavior*

1 E. A. Fedorov, *Demidovy*, in *Kamennyi poias* (Moskva, Leningrad, 1950), p. 150; K. G. Shildkret, *Spas na zhiru*, p. 57.
2 Sharaya, *Voskovaia persona*, p. 30.
3 Selvinsky, *Ot Poltavy do Ganguta*, 199.
4 A. P. Platonov, *Epifanskie Shliuzy* (Moskva, 1927), p. 112; Merezhkovsky, *Petr i Aleksei*, IV, 19; Fedorov, *Demidovy*, p. 17; Yu. P. German, *Rossiia molodaia*, 2 vols. (Leningrad, 1954), I, 182.
5 L. N. Tolstoy, *"Nachala" romana "Sto let,"* p. 208.
6 Stählin, *Anecdotes*, nos. 27 and 32; Ustryalov, *Istoriia*, I, 279-81; L. N. Maikov (ed.), *Rasskazy Nartova o Petre Velikom* (Sankt-Peterburg, 1891), no. 27; I. I. Golikov, *Anekdoty kasaiushchiesia do Gosudaria Imperatora Petra Velikogo* (Moskva, 1798), no. 126; d'Escherny, *Mélanges*, no. 2; Frédérique (margrave de) Bareith, *Mémoires 1706-1742* (Brunswick, 1845), I, 44.
7 Peter's statement on his epilepsy appears in the first version of *Peter the First* (*Petr Pervyi*) published in *Novyi mir* (August-September, 1929), p. 29. It was deleted in the standard edition: A. N. Tolstoy, *Polnoe* (1946-1953), IX, 89.
8 L. N. Tolstoy, *"Nachala" romana vremen Petra I*, p. 177.
9 Jacob Scheltema, *Anecdotes Historiques sur Pierre le Grand* (Lausanne, 1842), p. 88.
10 German, *Rossiia*, II, 410; V. I. Kostylyov, *Pitirim* (Moskva, 1936), p. 331; Soloviev, *Istoriia*, IX, 603.
11 Lord Macaulay, *The History of England*, 2 vols. (London, 1873), II, 668.
12 A. V.Arseniev, *Tsarskii sud*, in *Povesti* (Sankt-Peterburg, 1889), p. 11; F. V. Bulgarin, *Mazepa*, in *Polnoe sobranie sochinenii*, 7 vols. (Sankt-Peterburg, 1839-44), III, 250; Mordovtsev, *Derzhavnyi plotnik*, in *Polnoe*, VI, 148.
13 Nartov, *Zapiski*, no. 22; M. P. Pogodin, *Petr Pervyi*, in *Russkii Arkhiv*, 27 (1879), p. 359; A. O. Kornilovich, "O chastnoi zhizni Imperatora Petra I," in *Sochineniia i pis'ma* (Moskva, Leningrad, 1957), p. 150. D. L. Petrov (Biriuk), *Kondrat Bulavin* (Moskva, 1955), p. 93; V. B. Shklovsky, *Novelly o Petre*, in *Tridtsat' dnei* (1941), no. 6, p. 26.
14 German, *Rossiia*, II, p. 313; Shildkret, *Spas na zhiru*, p. 51; A. N. Tolstoy, *Den' Petra*, in *Polnoe sobranie sochinenii*, 15 vols. (Moskva, 1946-53), IV, 390, respectively.
15 B. A. Pilnyak, *Ego Velichestvo Kneeb Piter Komondor*, in *Povest' Peterburgskaia* (Moskva, Berlin, 1922), p. 108; A. N. Tolstoy, *Den' Petra*, p. 398; German, *Rossiia*, II, 427; Mordovtsev, *Tsar' i getman*, p. 117.
16 A. S. Pushkin, *Arap Petra Velikogo*, in *Polnoe sobranie sochinenii*, 17 vols. in 21 (Moskva, 1937-59), VIII, 10; Fedorov, *Demidovy*, p. 16.
17 Stockings: Stählin, *Anecdotes*, no. 99; Belyaev, *Kabinet*, p. 52; Arseniev, *Arisha Utochka*, in *Povesti* (Sankt-Peterburg, 1889), p. 20; Fedorov, *Demidovy*, p. 148; Merezhkovsky, *Petr i Aleksei*, V, 69. Glasses: Belyaev, *Kabinet*, p. 150; Merezhkovsky, *Petr i Aleksei*, V, 77; Ivanov, *Noch' Tsar'ia Petra*, p. 123; Fedorov, *Demidovy*, p. 262; G. P. Danilevsky, *Na Indiiu pri Petre*, in *Sochineniia*, 24 vols. (Sankt-Peterburg, 1939-44), III, 76, respectively.
18 Krekshin, *Zapiski*, pp. 5-6; Ustrjalov, *Istoriia*, III, 75; S. F. Platonov, *Petr Velikii* (Leningrad, 1926), pp. 103-6; A. Brückner, *Peter der Grosse* (Berlin, 1897), II, 670.
19 Nartov, *Zapiski*, no. 64; Prince A. Galizin, *La Russie au XVIIIe siècle* (Paris, 1863), p. 147; Waliszewski, *Petr Velikii*, p. 204.
20 E.g., Nartov, *Zapiski*, no. 60; Stählin, *Anecdotes*, no. 85.
21 Bergholz, *Dnevnik*, IV, 54; I. Shcherbachev (ed.), "Zapiski datskogo poslannika Juliia Justa." in *Russkii Arkhiv*, 30 (1892), p. 37. The wedding was that of Peter's niece Anna, the future Empress, and the Duke of Kurland.
22 Semevsky, *Slovo i Delo!*, pp. 273-8.
23 D'Escherny, *Mélanges*, no. 31; Nartov, *Zapiski*, no. 27; Galizin, *La Russie*, p. 139.
24 Waliszewski, *Petr*, p. 155; Villebois, p. 149.
25 Belyaev, *Kabinet*, p. 176; Iwan Nestesuranoi (Jean Rousset), *Mémoires du Règne de Pierre le Grand* (Amsterdam, 1730), p. 695; Ustrjalov, *Istoriia*, II, 399; Nartov, *Zapiski*, no. 111.
26 An early outspoken critic of Peter's unbecoming amusements. See Soloviev, *Istoriia*, VII, 543-44.

27 Ibid., VII, 116-17 and 155-57.
28 R. M. Zotov, *Tainstvennyi monakh* (Sankt-Peterburg, 1882), p. 328; Nartov, *Zapiski*, no. 80; Kurakin, *Gistoriia*, p. 66.
29 Pilnyak, *Kneeb*, passim, and *Povest' Peterburgskaia* (Moskva, Berlin, 1922), pp. 11-12; Shildkret, *Mamura*, p. 342; his *Kubok orla* (Moskva, 1935), p. 7; his *Our-Savior*, p. 51; Merezhkovsky, *Petr i Aleksei*, passim; D. L. Mordovtsev, *Tsar' Petr i pravitel'nitsa Sof'ia*, p. 198; A. N. Tolstoy, *Petr Pervyi*, p. 224; German, *Rossiia*, I, 29.
30 Pogodin, *Petr Pervyi*, p. 15; Platonov, *Petr Velikii*, 106.
31 *Pis'ma i bumagi Imperatora Petra Velikogo*, 11 vols. (Sankt-Peterburg, 1887-1964), I, no. 191, 198; and no. 222, pp. 234-35.
32 A. N. Tolstoy, *Petr Pervyi*, pp. 304 and 496, respectively.
33 E.g., J. G. Korb, *Diary of an Austrian Secretary*, 2 vols. (London, 1968), I, 181-83; Zhelabuzhsky, *Zapiski*, pp. 57-8; Ustryalov, *Istoriia*, III, 407 and 626-31; Soloviev, *Istoriia*, VII, 572.
34 P. Polezhaev, *Prestol i monastyr'*, pp. 433-35.
35 I. I. Neplyuev, *Zapiski*, *Russkii Arkhiv*, 9 (1871), p. 642; Golikov, *Anekdoty*, no. 39; Nartov, *Zapiski*, nos. 28 and 88.
36 Galizin, *La Russie*, p. 251.
37 *PSZ*, VII, no. 4345, p. 150; Peter addressing his soldiers before the battle at Poltava, respectively.
38 I. T. Pososhkov, *Kniga o skudosti i bogatstve* (Moskva, 1937), p. 176.
39 N. V. Lazhechnikov, *Poslednii novik*, p. 453.
40 L. N. Tolstoy, *Polnoe*, LXXXV, 114.

CHAPTER EIGHT: *Le Czar s'amuse*

1 Cited in N. N. Gusev, *Lev Nikolaevich Tolstoy*, 4 vols. (Moskva, 1963), III, 131.
2 Korb, *Diary*, I, 199.
3 G. Esipov (ed.), *Sbornik vypisok*, 2 vols. (Moskva, 1872), I, 124.
4 I. I. Golikov, cited in Semevsky, *Slovo*, pp. 321-30; Villebois, *Mémoires*, p. 34; Stählin, *Anecdotes*, no. 97; Eustaphieve, *Reflections* . . ., no. 23.
5 N. V. Kukolnik, *Chasovoi*, in *Sochineniia*, 10 vols. (Sankt-Peterburg, 1851-53), II, 351.
6 Semevsky, *Slovo*, p. 286; I. A. Zhelabuzhsky, *Zapiski*, p. 86.
7 M. P. Pogodin, *Sud nad Tsarevichem Alekseem* (Moskva, 1860), pp. 84-5; Ustryalov, *Istoriia*, VI, 287.
8 L. N. Tolstoy, *Polnoe*, XXVIII, 192.
9 E. A. Salias de Turnemir, *Svadebnyi bunt*, in *Sobranie sochinenii*, 27 vols. (Moskva, 1894), VII, 37.
10 They were ordered to wear yellow patches on their clothes and, so long as they paid double taxes, were left alone as hopeless. Stählin (*Anecdotes*, no. 53) and Feoktistov (*Anecdoty*, no. 18) admire Peter's tolerance.
11 In German's *Youthful Russia*, Pushkin's *The Blackamoor of Peter the Great*, and Kukolnik's *The Tale of the Blue and the Green Cloth*, respectively.
12 Feoktistov, *Anekdoty*, nos. 56 and 39; Golikov, *Anekdoty*, no. 76.
13 Nartov, *Zapiski*, no. 73.

CHAPTER NINE: *Grotesque and Uncanny Features*

1 Bergholz, *Dnevnik*, I, 122. Shildkret, *Savior*, p. 91, and *Mamura*, p. 109.
2 E. Barsov, *Petr Velikii v narodnykh predaniiakh* (Moskva, 1872), p. 5.
3 Soloviev, *Istoriia*, VII, 581.
4 D. L. Mordovtsev, *Idealisty i realisty* in *Polnoe sobranie istoricheskikh romanov*, XI, 138-40.
5 Matveev, *Zapiski*, pp. 66-7.
6 Polezhaev, *Prestol i monastyr'*, p. 398; Merezhkovsky, *Petr i Aleksei*, IV, 252; Shildkret, *Mamura*, p. 235, respectively.
7 Galizin, *La Russie*, pp. 129-30; Ustryalov, *Istoriia*, VI, 44; Dolgorukov, *Mémoires*, p. 14, respectively.
8 Galizin, *La Russie*, p. 156; Nartov, *Zapiski*, no. 82; Stählin, *Anecdotes*, no. 68; M. P. Pogodin, *Anekdoty pro Petra Velikogo*, in *Russkii Arkhiv*, 23 (1885),

426; Eustaphieve, *Reflections*, no. 40; D'Escherny, *Mélanges*, pp. 24-26; Petrov, *Bulavin*, p. 91; Lazhechnikov, *Novik*, pp. 512-13.

9 Voltaire, *Histoire de l'Empire de Russie* (Paris, 1853), p. 316.

10 Pilnyak, *Kneeb*, p. 110; Tynyanov, *Voskovaia persona*, no. 1, p. 5.

11 Pushkin in a letter of April 6, 1834, to M. Pogodin.

12 The full title of Krekshin's *Notes* is: *Short Description of the Blessed Deeds of the Great Lord, Emperor Peter the Great, Autocrat of All the Russias, collected through the unworthy efforts of the meanest of slaves, Peter Krekshin, a nobleman from Nizhnii Novgorod* (1742).

13 A. N. Tolstoy, *Petr Pervyi*, p. 224; Arseniev, *Tsarskii sud*, p. 44; Merezhkovsky, *Petr i Aleksei*, I, 17; Kostylyov, *Pitirim*, p. 437.

14 Mordovtsev, *Idealisty*, p. 232; A. O. Kornilovich, *Tat'iana Boltova*, in *Sochineniia i pis'ma*, p. 51. Lazhechnikov, *Novik*, p. 454, respectively.

15 R. M. Zotov, *Saardamskii korabel'nyi master, ili net imeni emu!* (Sankt-Peterburg, 1841).

16 Rev. 13:18. Peter was accused of hiding his identity as the Antichrist under the letter "M" in the word "Emperor": I(10) + P(80) + E(5) + R(100) + A(1) + T(300) + O(70) + R(100) = 666; I(m)perator.

17 Soloviev, *Istoriia*, VIII, 99-100.

18 Krekshin, pp. 8-11.

19 E.g., Villebois, *Mémoires*, pp. 28-9; Galizin, *La Russie*, p. 127.

CHAPTER TEN: *The Entourage*

1 A. N. Tolstoy, *Petr Pervyi*, pp. 19 and 328; Tynyanov, no. 1, p. 5; Merezhkovsky, *Petr i Aleksei*, V, 204 and 212; P. V. Polezhaev, *Tsarevich Aleksei Petrovich* (Sankt-Peterburg, 1885), p. 175, respectively.

2 Dolgorukov, p. 31; Villebois, p. 149; Tynyanov, no. 1, p. 5; German, *Rossiia*, p. 248.

3 Icons: Eustaphieve, *Reflections*, no. 23; Golikov, *Anekdoty*, no. 14; d'Escherny, nos. 13 and 14; Stählin, no. 36; Kostylyov, *Pitirim*, p. 106; Merezhkovsky, *Petr i Aleksei*, IV, 42; Polezhaev, *Tsarevich*, pp. 116-18; Shklovsky, *Novelly*, p. 27. Asbestos: Nartov, *Zapiski*, no. 103; Golikov, *Anekdoty*, no. 13; Polezhaev, *Prestol*, p. 118; Fedorov, *Demidovy*, pp. 304-5.

4 V. A. Lebedev, *Doomed Freedom*, in *Zvezda* (nos. 9-11, 1975), no. 9, p. 108.

5 Apollon Maykov's (1821-97) poem "Who Is He?" (*Kto on?*); Zagoskin, *The Russians*, p. 451. The axle, so honored, on the village priest's advice was deposited in the church.

6 Helbig, *Russische Günstlinge*, p. 27; Pogodin, *Sud nad Tsarevichem*, pp. 42 and 50; d'Eon, *Les Loisirs*, p. 29; Ustryalov, *Istoriia*, VI, 581.

7 Helbig, *Günstlinge*, pp. 33-4; Villebois, *Les Loisirs*, pp. 156-57; V. Andreev, *Ekaterina Pervaia*, in *Os'mnadtsatyi vek* (Moskva, 1889), 26.

8 Dolgorukov, *Mémoires*, p. 9.

CHAPTER ELEVEN: *Women*

1 Dolgorukov, *Mémoires*, pp. 39-40; Galizin, *La Russie*, p. 242; Semevsky, *Tsaritsa Katerina*, p. 81.

2 Bergholz, *Dnevnik*, IV, 78; Andreev, *Ekaterina*, pp. 22-23; Kornilovich, *Andrei Bezimennyi*, in *Sochineniia i pis'ma*, p. 108; Feoktistov, *Anekdoty*, no. 65; G. F. v. Bassevitz, *Zapiski*, in *Russkii Arkhiv*, 3 (1865), 256.

3 Villebois, *Mémoires*, pp. 28-9; Dolgorukov, *Mémoires*, p. 175; Waliszewski, *Petr*, p. 343.

4 P. Karabanov, "Freiliny russkogo dvora v XVIII-m stoletii," *Russkaia Starina*, 2 (1871), p. 473; Dolgorukov, *Mémoires*, 172.

5 Evdokia's sons: Alexis (1690-1718), Alexander (1691-92), Paul (1693). Catherine's children: Paul (1704-7), Peter (1705-7), Catherine (1707-8), Anne (1708-28), Elizabeth (1709-62), Natalya (1713-15), Margarita (1714-15), Peter (1715-19), Paul (1717), Natalya (1718-25), and Peter (1723). See G. I. Studenkin, *Romanovy* (Sankt-Peterburg, 1878), pp. XIV-XVI.

6 Dolgorukov, *Mémoires*, p. 20; Galizin, *La Russie*, pp. 250-51. Waliszewski, *Petr*, p. 369.

7 N. A. Polevoy, *Istoriia Petra Velikogo*, 4 vols. (Sankt-Peterburg, 1843), IV, 312.

8 Bruce, *Memoirs* (Dublin, 1879), p. 87; d'Eon, *Les Loisirs*, p. 18; Villebois, *Mémoires*, pp. 105-6; Dolgorukov, *Mémoires*, pp. 37-38.
9 Pushkin, *Materialy dlia Istorii*, p. 112.
10 E.g., Shildkret, *Our-Savior*, p. 54; Arseniev, *Arisha*, p. 20; Fedorov, *Demidovy*, p. 55.
11 Mauvillon, *Histoire*, p. 308; Villebois, *Mémoires*, p. 99; Dolgorukov, *Mémoires*, p. 39.
12 Semevsky, *Tsaritsa Katerina*, p. 13.
13 D'Allainval, *Anecdotes du Règne de Pierre I* (n.p., 1745), pp. 2 and 10; d'Eon, *Les Loisirs*, pp. 6 and 9; Lady Rondeau (Mrs. Ward), *Letters*, p. 411.
14 Villebois, *Mémoires*, p. 57; Kurakin, *Gistoriia*, pp. 56 and 69; Ustryalov, *Istoriia*, III, 188.
15 *Pis'ma i bumagi Imperatora Petra Velikogo*, I, no. 21, pp. 18-19.

CHAPTER TWELVE: *The Case of Tsarevich Alexis*

1 Villebois, *Mémoires*, p. 61; D'Allainval, *Anecdotes*, p. 3; Bruce, *Memoirs*, pp. 219-21; Helbig, *Günstlinge*, p. 107; d'Eon, *Les Loisirs*, pp. 31-32; Nestesuranoi, *Mémoires*, p. 232.
2 Pilnyak, *Kneeb*, p. 106; Kostylyov, *Pitirim*, p. 246; Tynyanov, *Voskovaia persona*, no. 1, p. 16, respectively.
3 Ustryalov, *Istoriia*, VI, 525; Polezhaev, *Tsarevich Aleksei*, p. 115; Merezhkovsky, *Petr i Aleksei*, IV, 205; Ivanov, *Noch'*, p. 151.

CHAPTER THIRTEEN: *The Backdrop of Environment*

1 M. Shurgin, *Plyvut alye oblaka*, *Zvezda*, no. 2 (1972), p. 18.
2 *Kikimora* is a creation of Russian folklore fantasy, of uncertain shape but unmistakably evil, whose sighting is always an ill omen. It may have given birth to Sologub's famous surrealistic sprite, "Nedotykomka" in his *The Petty Demon* (1907).
3 Andrey Belyi, *Peterburg* (Petrograd, 1916), p. 349.
4 Shurgin, *Plyvut*, p. 19.
5 A. P. Platonov, *Epifanskie shliuzy* (Moskva, 1927), p. 107.

Plot Summaries

Arseniev, A. V. (1854-96). *Arisha the Ducky.* 1889. Arisha, nicknamed "the Ducky," is Peter's fictional goddaughter, born in 1722, during the Tsar's visit to her father's smithy. She is taken to see Peter on his bier three years later. Orphaned, she is apprenticed to a Dutch seamstress and eventually marries her son. Numerous Petrine anecdotes are woven into the plot.

___. *The Tsar's Verdict.* 1889. The fictional plot illustrates Peter's love of justice, his respect for his own laws, and the the awe he inspires. The hero, Gur, is unfairly deprived by the Senate of his land. In despair he dares to request Peter's intervention, which is forbidden. Luckily, Peter becomes interested in the case, looks into it, and fines the senators, returning the land to Gur. He is also present at Gur's marriage to the heroine, Anna.

Bulgarin, F. V. (1789-1859). *Mazepa.* 1833. A fantastic novel about the Ukrainian Hetman Mazepa (1644-1709), who betrayed Peter by allying himself with Charles XII of Sweden. Bulgarin endows him with a fictional daughter, Natalya, and a son, Ognevik, who, unaware of their relationship, fall in love with each other. Mazepa is justly punished for his treason and for numerous fictional murders and dies poisoned by Ognevik.

Danilevsky, G. P. (1829-1900). *To India in Peter's Time.* 1879. The novel deals with Peter's visit to France in 1717-18 and the ill-fated expedition of Bekovich, who was sent to establish trade relations with India and was killed on the way. The fictional plot about "navigator" Kasatkin and Dunya, Lefort's imaginary daughter and Peter's ward, gives glimpses of Catherine and her court in St. Petersburg and of Peter in Paris.

Eustaphieve, A. (1783-1857). *Tsarevich Alexis.* 1812. A pseudo-historical fantastic play worshipful of Peter.

Fedorov, E. A. (1897-1961). *The Demidovs.* 1941. This novel traces the rise of the Demidov family from humble smiths to owners of foundries and mines all over Siberia. Nikita Demidov, the patriarch, is shrewd, enterprising, talented, and ruthless. He is also very Russian and enhances this characteristic in Peter's image, also resembling him physically. The "Little Father, Tsar" tone of the novel is reminiscent of the works of Lazhechnikov and Arseniev (qq.v.).

Furman, P. R. (1809-56). *Prince Yakov Fedorovich Dolgoruky.* 1897. A patchwork of anecdotes illustrating Peter's fairness and willingness to appreciate the virtues of his faithful servants, such as the prince of the title.

German, Yu. P. (1910-67). *Youthful Russia.* 1953. As early as 1693, during his visit to Arkhangelsk, Peter begins to realize that the centuries-old wisdom and skill of simple Russian sailors, shipbuilders, and even peasants is superior to that of foreign specialists. The involved plot, covering the years of Peter's reign up to 1721, serves to illustrate this maxim, popular in Soviet literature of the period following World War II.

Ivanov, V. N. (1888-). *Tsar Peter's Night.* 1968. A methodically reproduced story of the flight, trial, and death of Tsarevich Alexis. Unlike Merezhkovsky, the author sees nothing metaphysical in Peter's sacrificing his son to the future of his new Russia. Peter is not unfeeling but is first of all a statesman. There are no fictional characters.

Konichev, K. (1904-). *Peter the First in the North.* 1973. A well-researched documentary in fictionalized form, presenting Peter's several visits to northern Russia in 1692, 1694, 1701, and in 1724, a few months before his death.

Kornilovich, A. O. (1800-1834). *Andrey the Nameless.* 1832. Andrey, falsely accused of illegitimate birth and thus deprived of his fiancée, his estate, and his name, finds justice as a result of Peter's personally investigating the case and punishing Andrey's slanderers.

____. "God Remembers a Prayer; the Tsar, Faithful Service." 1825. Another anecdote retold: Peter incognito visits an invalid soldier's home and repays his hospitality with a pension for him and a dowry for his daughter.

____. "Morning's Counsel Is Wiser Than the Night's." 1828. A short story retelling the anecdote about Romodanovsky, after the defeat at Narva, handing over to Peter the secret treasure left by Tsar Alexis for a national emergency.

____. *Tatyana Boltova.* 1828. A novelette illustrating Peter's respect for lawful dispensation of justice and his readiness to forgive repentant criminals—in this case, a former Strelets who had lived as a fugitive for thirteen years.

Kostylyov, V. I. (1884-1950). *Pitirim.* 1936. Pitirim, the Bishop of Novgorod, is a historical personage; but his mistress Lizaveta, her family, and most of the other characters in the novel are fictional. Pitirim's ruthless persecution of his former brothers (Old Believers) and his cynicism and hypocrisy throw their shadow on Peter's image, which seems to reflect the features of this faithful servant of the Tsar.

Kukolnik, N. V. (1809-68). "Avdotya Likhonchikha." 1843. Young Peter, in 1689 offers to forgive one of three rebellious Streltsy brothers, the choice to be made by their mother.

____. "Kapustin." 1842. Peter removes the obstacles to deserving lovers' union by dismissing a neighbor's unjust claims to the hero's property.

____. "The New Year." 1843. Peter's aide Rumyantsev is in love with Marya Matveeva. Her father opposes the marriage, however, because of the low origin of Peter's "fledgeling." Peter makes him promise to give his consent after the New Year, which, according to the old calendar, would be in ten months. But the New Year, January 1, 1700, is proclaimed in a few days, and the boyar thus tricked, the wedding takes place.

____. *The Sentinel.* 1843. A girl in love with Peter's dashing jester Balakirev, being forced by her father to marry another, tries to appeal to Peter but is barred by the sentinel on duty. She tells her woes to him but in vain. On the next morning, the previous night's sentinel proves to be Peter, and the lovers are united.

____. *The Tale of the Blue and the Green Cloth.* 1844. Another example of Peter's sense of justice and of the civic virtues of Prince Yakov Dolgoruky.

____. *Two Ivans, Two Stephanychs, Two Kostylkovs.* 1847. A novel with an involved plot and a happy ending features the conflict between the progressive young followers of Peter's reforms (primarily those concerning foreign clothes and women's participation in social life) and the old generation opposing them. All ends well.

Lazhechnikov, I. I. (1792-1869). *The Last Recruit.* 1833. A novel featuring the fantastic story of the noble and virtuous ward of Pastor Glück, Marta Rabe, later to become Tsar Peter's spouse, Empress Catherine. The protagonist, Valdemar, ward of a mysterious old soothsayer, is discovered to be Tsarevna Sophia's illegitimate son and Peter's enemy. He is forgiven by the magnanimous monarch, and all ends well with the wedding festivities of several secondary characters united by Peter.

Lebedev, V. A. (1934-). *The Doomed Freedom.* 1975. Another novel on Bulavin's mutiny. It is conventional in Peter's characterization, as well as in fictional characters and plot.

Mariengof, A. B. (1897-1962). *Jester Balakirev.* 1940. In this play Peter's jester is wise and noble and serves his master well by opening his eyes to the corruption of Peter's favorite, high-placed bureaucrats. He also arranges a marriage between his friend Vasilyev, an honest bureaucrat, and Liza, daughter of a dishonest one.

Masalsky, K. P. (1802-61). "The Black Casket." 1833. The fictional protagonist, Pavel Nikitin, a talented painter, is discovered by Peter and sent abroad to study (a popular anecdote also used by A. N. Tolstoy in *Peter the First*). The Tsar makes Nikitin rich by arranging an auction of his pictures,

punishes the villain who tries to steal his fiancée Masha, and unites the
lovers.

___. *The Love of Beards*. 1837. A closet drama, according to the author. Stag-
ing would have presented difficulties, as the action consists mostly of
Peter's pageants, masquerades, etc., with the participation of the members
of the "all-crazy, all-drunken council." The play ends with everyone ac-
cepting foreign fashions and shaving off beards and with a wedding of lovers
formerly estranged by old-fashioned parents.

___. *The Streltsy*. 1832. A novel set in the period of Peter's adolescence,
with numerous plots against his life, mostly frustrated by the heroism of
the fictional protagonist, Vasily.

Merezhkovsky, D. S. (1865-1941). *Peter and Alexis*. 1905. This famous novel by
a distinguished Russian Symbolist has strong religious and mystical over-
tones in the characterization of Peter, who is building the new Russia, and
of Alexis, his heir, who wants to reinstate the old order. The period is
1716-18, covering Alexis's flight, trial, and death, with flashbacks to his
childhood. The author introduces a wealth of historic and anecdotic
material and stage settings that create a panorama of the period. Part of
the story is told by Fraülein Juliana, the fictionalized companion of
Alexis's wife, Princess Charlotte. Not only is Peter referred to as the
Antichrist by fictional characters (as he is in other Petrine novels), but
he occasionally looks like one as part of his grotesque characterization.
Alexis is weak, pitiable, and almost saintly.

Mintslov, S. P. (1870-1933). *During the Storm*. 1902. The hero, Vasily, is
drafted into the army with other students of the first school in Russia,
founded by Peter in 1700: after the defeat at Narva (1701) the Tsar needs
officers. After two years of valiant service Vasily rescues Vera from the
Swedes, and they marry in newly founded St. Petersburg. The parallel plot
introduces the Old Believers and the unsuccessful attempt of one of them,
Kirill, to murder the Tsar, an event unknown either to history or to Peter.

Mordovtsev, D. L. (1830-1905). *The Crowned Carpenter*. 1883. The novel consists
of a patchwork of anecdotes and historical events from 1700 to 1703, among
them, the battles at Narva and Noteburg and the founding of St. Petersburg.
There are no fictional characters, but the historical personages, including
Peter, are highly fictionalized.

___. *Idealists and Realists*. 1878. The protagonist is Levin (later Monk
Varlaam), executed for denouncing Peter as the Antichrist. Other historical personages include Tsarevich Alexis and his mistress Afrosinya (both
highly fictionalized) and Peter himself. The plot is contrived; the Idealists are Peter's opponents, the (mostly villainous) Realists, his followers. The novel is unusual in its hostility to Peter, because Mordovtsev,
in his other works, can compete with Kukolnik in his admiration for the
Reformer.

___. *More Enlightenment!*. 1881. The novel overflows with fictional adventures
of two heroines, Fima and Olena, who are kidnapped, rescued, and married by
Peter to their rescuers, his "fledglings." There are traditional "Slavic"
stage sets, including a forest refuge of Old Believers which Peter visits.

___. *Tsar Peter and Regent Sophia*. 1885. A novel set in the years 1682-96,
retelling in traditional terms the Streltsy plots and Peter's adolescence,
marriage, friendship with Lefort, pageants, and new interest in acquiring
access to the sea for Russia. Sophia and her entourage are presented as
villains.

___. *The Tsar and the Hetman*. 1879. The time of the novel is 1703-11, cover-
ing, therefore, the betrayal of Anna Mons, the rise of Catherine, the
founding of St. Petersburg, and the case of Hetman Mazepa's treason.
As mediocre as the rest of Mordovtsev's novels.

Petrov (Biriuk), D. I. (1900-). *Kondrat Bulavin*. 1946. Another novel on the
Bulavin mutiny, freely mixing historic and fictional characters, and actual
events with anecdotes. Peter, in spite of the traditional characterization,
resembles a good Soviet family man, intent on his work (which just happens
to be reforms) and loving justice, his people, and Russia. It could have
been written a hundred years earlier.

Pilnyak, B. A. (1894-1937). *His Majesty Kneeb Piter Komondor*. 1919. Pilnyak's
novella is another telescopic portrayal of Peter and his Russia. Unlike
Tolstoy, he adopts a hostile attitude toward Peter's reforms, which he

denies were built on statesman-like logic, and his personality, which he
endows with grotesque cruelty, coarsenss, and lust. The style is overly
ornamental, imitating that of Peter's court by the end of his reign.
___. *The Petersburg Tale.* 1922. A phantasmagoric picture of the city—Peter's
as ever—during the "snowstorm" of the Revolution.
Platonov, A. P. (1899-1951). *The Locks of Epifan.* 1927. Engineer Bertram
Perry and his death are fictional, but his work at building a waterway for
Peter is a reproduction of the frustrations of Capt. John Perry, who left
Russia after wasting sixteen years at the same task in Peter's service.
Platonov's story is based on John Perry's memoirs, published after his re-
turn to England.
Pogodin, M. P. (1800-1875). *The Trial of Tsarevich Alexis.* 1860. A slightly
fictionalized documentary.
Polezhaev, P. V. *The Throne and the Cloister.* 1881. The struggle for power
during Peter's childhood and adolescence ending in Sophia's defeat. All the
plots against Peter and the executions following them are told in gory detail. The novel is meant as a documentary but is full of misrepresentation
of historical facts.
___. *Tsarevich Alexis Petrovich.* 1885. A thoroughly fictionalized life story
of Tsarevich Alexis. Historical personages are reinterpreted at the
author's will.
Pushkin, A. S. (1799-1837). *The Blackamoor of Peter the Great.* 1828. This
unfinished novel has as the protagonist Pushkin's maternal great-grandfather,
Abraham (Ibrahim) Hannibal; the plot is fictional. The ambivalent attitude
Pushkin displays toward Peter's personality in his poetry is not reflected
here. Thoroughly familiar with Peter's historical background, he also
makes skillful use of some popular Petrine anecdotes, and in these few
chapters adumbrates the first image of Peter the Great in Russian historical fiction, an image lofty and kindly, endearingly simple, awesome, and
wise.
Salias de Turnemir, E. A. (1840-1908). *The Wedding Rebellion.* 1886. A novel
with a fictional plot, illustrating the numerous hasty weddings caused by
Peter's rumored ukase to marry all Astrakhan girls to foreigners. The
bloody rebellion (1705), entirely ascribed to those rumors, was actually
chiefly provoked by Peter's unpopular reforms.
Selvinsky, I. I. (1899-1968). *From Poltava to Gangut.* 1949. This play is Part
II of Selvinsky's trilogy *Russia* (1944-54), which features a symbolic pre-
cursor of the Revolution, Chokhov—a patriotic artisan under Ivan the Terrible, soldier and rebel under Peter, and worker and bolshevik under Nicholas
II. Peter, warrior and reformer, nevertheless owes much of his success to
his Russian helpers, especially those low-born, and to the wisdom of jester
Balakirev.
Shildkret, K. G. (1886-1965). *Our-Savior-on-the-Tallow Church.* 1931. A
tendentious novel meant to show the populace in Petrine Russia oppressed by
greedy, sanctimonious clergy and the Tsar willing to tolerate their behavior
so long as part of their profits was paid to his treasury.
___. *Subjugated Russia.* (1933-35). A trilogy covering Peter's childhood and
adolescence (*The Rebel*), his early reforms and battles, from 1698 to 1708
(*Mamura*), and the case of Tsarevich Alexis, from 1716 to 1718 (*The Eagle
Cup*). The author sees Peter much as Pilnyak does: as a madman on the
throne, a tyrant, and a hypocrite—in short, a Tsar, oppressor of the laboring masses.
Shklovsky, V. B. (1893-). *Novellas About Peter.* 1941. Quaint, short
(sometimes only a few lines) anecdotes about Peter, some popular, others
little known, retold in a manner which makes them appear to be new and significant discoveries.
___. *About the Masters of Old.* 1951. Like Selvinsky's symbolic protagonist,
Shklovsky's lives under different names under the reigns of Peter, Catherine
the Great, and Alexander I. He is a Russian mechanic, inventor of machines
producing outstanding steel artifacts, a patriot unimpressed by anything
foreign, and a link in the historic progress of his Fatherland.
Sokolov, A. I. *Menshikov.* 1947. This is a fictionalized biography of Peter's
favorite from the moment of his first appearance at Lefort's house selling
pies through his fabulous career at Peter's side to his death as an exile
in Siberia.

Soloviev, V. S. (1849-1903). *The Tsar Maiden*. 1878. The rise and fall of the regent Tsarevna Sophia. The plot is purely fictional—Sophia befriends Lyuba, an orphan, who, after the Tsarevna's fall, follows her to the convent—but historical personages play a role in it equal to that of the fictitious characters.

Shurgin, M. A. (1923-). *The Drifting Red Clouds*. 1972. The novel is not a historical one, and the plot concerns contemporary Soviet characters. Yet the Leningrad in which the novel is set is still Peter's creation, his "paradise," and the Bronze Horseman still haunts and towers over his city.

Tolstoy, Alexey Nikolaevich. (1883-1945). *Peter's Day*. 1918. This novella is a telescopic summation of Peter's reign and personality as "One Day in the Life of Peter the Great." The author takes full advantage of the short-lived postrevolutionary abolition of censorship, and Peter's characterization is in startling contrast to that adopted by nineteenth-century authors. Tolstoy notes, however, the grandeur of the statesman side by side with the coarseness and cruelty of the man, as well as the crushing load of responsibility Peter carries alone.

___. "Martha Rabe." 1931. The title is one of the names ascribed to the woman who later became Empress Catherine. The story is a version of her first meeting with Peter, while she is still Menshikov's mistress. The meeting, Catherine, and Peter are materially different from the ones presented by Tolstoy in *Peter the First*.

___. *Peter the First*. 1929-45. Unquestionably, this is the best novel about Peter in Russian literature. It is not a fictionalized biography but simply an ever-changing portrait of him at different stages of his life from 1682 to 1703. It is also a portrayal of changing Russia. The novel, interrupted by Tolstoy's death, was to end with the battle of Poltava in 1709, allegedly because Tolstoy said he "would not know what to do with these people as they grew older." Actually, one may speculate that Tolstoy chose this date because by 1709, Peter and the reforms he had introduced had already matured and could be expected to continue along the same road. By then, that historic process had become irreversible for Russia; Peter's characteristics as man and statesman had become established; and his image had developed its elements of monumentality and the grotesque. A subtle admixture of fictional characters and secondary plots enhances the artistic value of this historically impeccable work of fiction.

Tolstoy, Lev Nikolaevich. (1828-1910). Fragments of the unfinished novel known as "Novel from Peter's Times" and "One Hundred Years." 1872-73.

Tynyanov, Yu. N. (1894-1943). *The Waxen Effigy*. 1931. This novella by a famous Formalist writer concerns Peter's death and postmortem mask and mannequin of Peter—the waxen effigy of the title—made by the sculptor Rastrelli (1670-1744). The novella's quaint, ornamental style contributes to the eerie atmosphere of the Kunstkamera, where the mannequin was sent by Peter's widow, and of Catherine's court, affected by the still lingering power of Peter's ambiance.

Zagoskin, M. N. (1789-1852). *The Brynsk Forest*. 1846. A novel set in 1682 featuring a virtuous young Strelets in love with Sophia, the adopted daughter of a villainous Old Believer who had found her in the forest when she was three. She proves to be the daughter of a rich boyar, and all ends well. Peter's reforms are prophesied by Sophia's godfather.

___. *The Russians at the Beginning of the Eighteenth Century*. 1848. The time is that of the Prut disaster in 1711; the hero, Simsky, accompanies Peter in that campaign. He does well and is rewarded with the hand of Olga, an equally loyal follower of the new way of life established by Peter's reforms.

Zotov, R. (1795-1871). *The Mysterious Monk*. 1834. A novel set mostly in 1682-1701, but with the denouement at Poltava in 1709; it includes plots against Peter by Streltsy and Mazepa's treason. A mysterious foundling, Grisha, is raised by Prince Khovansky and the mysterious monk of the title, Iona, who proves to be Hetman Doroshenko (a historical personage). Doroshenko is in love with Mazepa's (fictional) daughter Elena, wife of Prince Khovansky and mother of Grisha. Grisha saves Peter's life and as a reward marries Masha, the widow of Peter's protegé. A typical "historical" novel of the period.

___. *The Shipbuilder from Zaandam; or, His Name Is Ineffable*. 1841. A play set in 1697, during Peter's stay in Holland as "volunteer Peter Mikhaylov." An extreme example of Peter's deification by early nineteenth-century writers.

Bibliography

FICTION: EDITIONS USED

Arsen'ev, A. V. *Arisha Utochka*, in *Povesti*. Sankt-Peterburg, 1889.
___. *Tsarskii sud*, in *Povesti*. Sankt-Peterburg, 1889.
Belyi, Andrei. *Peterburg*. Chicago, 1967.
Bulgarin, F. V. *Mazepa*, in *Polnoe sobranie sochinenii*. 7 vols. Sankt-Peterburg, 1839-44. III.
Danilevskii, G. P. *Na Indiiu pri Petre*, in *Sochineniia*. 24 vols. Sankt-Peterburg, 1901. X.
Eustaphieve, A. *Reflections, notes and original anecdotes illustrating the character of Peter the Great. To which is added a tragedy in five acts entitled Alexis, the Tsarevitz.* Boston, 1812.
Fedorov, E. A. *Demidovy*, in *Kamennyi poias*. Moskva, Leningrad, 1950.
Furman, P. R. *Kniaz' Iakov Fedorovich Dolgorukii*. Sankt-Peterburg, 1897.
German, Iu. P. *Rossiia molodaia*. 2 vols. Leningrad, 1954.
Ivanov, V. N. *Noch' tsaria Petra*, in *Imperatritsa Fike*. Moskva, 1968.
Konichev, K. *Petr Pervyi na severe*. Leningrad, 1973.
Kornilovich, A. O. *Andrei Bezimennyi*, in *Sochineniia i pis'ma*. Moskva, Leningrad, 1957.
___. "Za Bogom molitva za tsarem sluzhba ne propadaiut," in *Sochineniia i pis'ma*. Moskva, Leningrad, 1957.
___. "Utro vechera mudrenee," in *Sochineniia i pis'ma*. Moskva, Leningrad, 1957.
___. *Tat'iana Boltova*, in *Sochineniia i pis'ma*. Moskva, Leningrad, 1957.
Kostylev, V. I. *Pitirim*, Moskva, 1936.
Kukol'nik, N. V. "Avdot'ia Likhonchikha," in *Sochineniia*. 10 vols. Sankt-Peterburg, 1851-53. I.
___. "Kapustin," in *Sochineniia*. 10 vols. Sankt-Peterburg, 1851-53. II.
___. "Novyi god," in *Sochineniia*. 10 vols. Sankt-Peterburg, 1851-53. II.
___. *Chasovoi*, in *Sochineniia*. 10 vols. Sankt-Peterburg, 1851-53. II.
___. *Skazanie o sinem i zelenom sukne*, in *Sochineniia*. 10 vols. Sankt-Peterburg, 1951-53. II.
___. *Dva Ivana, dva Stepanycha, dva Kostyl'kova*, in *Sochineniia*. 10 vols. Sankt-Peterburg, 1851-53. II-III.
Lazhechnikov, I. I. *Poslednii novik*, in *Sochineniia*. 2 vols. Moskva, 1963. I.
Lebedev, V. *Obrechennaia volia*, Zvezda. nos. 9-10 (1975).
Mariengof, A. B. *Shut Balakirev*. Leningrad, Moskva, 1940.
Masal'skii, K. P. *Borodoliubie*, in *Sochineniia*. 5 vols. Sankt-Peterburg, 1845. II.
___. "Chernyi iashchik," in *Sochineniia*. 5 vols. Sankt-Peterburg, 1845. V.
___. *Strel'tsy*. Sankt-Peterburg, 1885.
Merezhkovskii, D. S. *Petr i Aleksei*, in *Polnoe sobranie sochinenii*. 17 vols. Sankt-Peterburg, Moskva, 1911-13. IV-V.
Mintslov, S. P. *V grozu*. Riga, 1902.
Mordovtsev, D. L. *Derzhavnyi plotnik*, in *Polnoe sobranie istoricheskikh romanov, povestei i rasskazov*. 18 vols. Sankt-Peterburg, 1914. VI.
___. *Idealisty i realisty*, in *Polnoe sobranie istoricheskikh romanov, povestei i rasskazov*. 18 vols. Sankt-Peterburg, 1914. XI.
___. *Svetu bol'she!*, in *Polnoe sobranie istoricheskikh romanov, povestei i rasskazov*. 18 vols. Sankt-Peterburg, 1914. XVIII.

Mordovtsev, D. L. *Tsar' i getman,* in *Polnoe sobranie istoricheskikh romanov, povestei i rasskazov.* 18 vols. Sankt-Peterburg, 1914. II.
___. *Tsar' Petr i pravitel'nitsa Sof'ia,* in *Polnoe sobranie sochinenii.* 12 vols. Sankt-Peterburg, 1915. X.
Petrov (Biriuk), D. L. *Kondrat Bulavin.* Moskva, 1955.
Pil'niak, B. A. *Ego Velichestvo Kneeb Piter Komondor,* in *Povest' Peterburgskaia.* Moskva, Berlin, 1922.
___. *Povest' Peterburgskaia.* Moskva, Berlin, 1922.
Platonov, A. P. *Epifanskie shliuzy,* in *Izbrannoe.* Moskva, 1966.
Pogodin, M. P. *Sud nad Tsarevichem Alekseem.* Moskva, 1860.
Polezhaev, P. *Prestol i monastyr'.* Sankt-Peterburg, 1881.
___. *Tsarevich Aleksei Petrovich.* Sankt-Peterburg, 1885.
Pushkin, A. S. *Arap Petra Velikogo,* in *Polnoe sobranie sochinenii.* 17 vols. in 21. Moskva, 1937-59, VIII.
Salias de Turnemir, E. A. *Svadebnyi bunt,* in *Sobranie sochinenii.* 27 vols. Moskva, 1894. VII.
Sel'vinskii, I. L. *Ot Poltavy do Ganguta,* in *Tragedii.* Moskva, 1952.
Shil'dkret, K. G. *Spas na zhiru.* Moskva, Leningrad, 1931.
___. *Pod'iaremnaia Rus',* a trilogy, Part I: *Buntar'.* Moskva, 1933. Part II: *Mamura.* Moskva, 1934. Part III: *Kubok orla.* Moskva, 1935.
Shklovskii, V. B. *Novelly o Petre,* in *Tridtsat' dnei,* no. 6 (1941).
___. *O masterakh starinnykh.* Moskva, 1953.
Sokolov, A. I. *Menshikov.* Moskva, 1947.
Solov'ev, V. S. *Tsar' devitsa,* in *Sobranie sochinenii.* 40 vols. Sankt-Peterburg, 1903-04. I.
Shurgin, M. *Plyvut alye oblaka.* Zvezda, no. 2 (1972).
Tolstoy, A. N. *Den' Petra,* in *Polnoe sobranie sochinenii.* 15 vols. Moskva, 1946-53. IV.
___. *"Marta Rabe,"* in *Polnoe sobranie sochinenii.* 15 vols. Moskva, 1946-53. VI.
Tolstoy, A. N. *Petr Pervyi,* in *Polnoe sobranie sochinenii.* 15 vols. Moskva, 1946-53. IX.
Tolstoy, L. N. *"Nachala" romana "Sto let,"* and *"Nachala" romana vremen Petra I, Polnoe sobranie sochinenii.* 90 vols. Moskva, 1928-58. XVII.
Tynianov, Iu. N. *Voskovaia persona.* Zvezda, nos. 1-2 (1931).
Zagoskin, M. N. *Brynskii les,* in *Polnoe sobranie sochinenii.* 2 vols. in 1. Sankt-Peterburg, Moskva, 1898. II.
___. *Russkie v nachale os'mnadtsatogo stoletiia,* in *Polnoe sobranie sochinenii.* 2 vols. in 1. Sankt-Peterburg, Moskva, 1898. II.
Zotov, R. M. *Tainstvennyi monakh.* Sankt-Peterburg, 1882.
___. *Saardamskii korabel'nyi master, ili net imeni emu!.* Sankt-Peterburg, 1841.

HISTORICAL MATERIALS: EDITIONS USED

Allainval, Soulab d'. *Anecdotes du Règne de Pierre I, dit Le Grand, Czar de Moscovie.* n.p., 1745.
Andreev, V. *"Ekaterina Pervaia,"* in *Os'mnadtsatyi vek.* Ed. P. T. Bartenev. Moskva, 1889.
Antsyferov, N. P. *Dusha Peterburga.* Peterburg, 1922.
Bareith, Frédérique (Margrave de). *Mémoires, 1706-1742.* Brunswick, 1845.
Barsov, E. *Petr Velikii v narodnykh predaniakh severnogo kraia.* Moskva, 1872.
Bassevitz, G. F. v. *Zapiski. Russkii Arkhiv,* 3 (1865). (Published in French, 1761.)
Bergholz, F. W. v. *Dnevnik 1721-1725.* 4 vols. Moskva, 1902. (Published in German, 1785-88.)
Beliaev, O. *Dukh Petra Velikogo imperatora vserossiiskogo i sopernika ego Karla XII korolia shvedskogo.* Sankt-Peterburg, 1798.
___. *Kabinet Petra Velikogo.* Sankt-Peterburg, 1800.
Bruce, Peter Henry. *Memoirs.* Dublin, 1783.
Brückner, A. *Peter der Grosse.* 3 vols. Berlin, 1897.
Dolgorukov, Pierre, Prince. *Mémoires.* Genève, 1867.
Eon de Beaumont (Chevalier d'). *Les Loisirs du.* 12 vols. in 6. Amsterdam, 1774.
Escherny, François-Louis (Comte d'). *Mélanges de Littérature, d'Histoire, de Morale, de Philosophie.* Paris, 1811.

Esipov, G., ed. *Sbornik vypisok iz arkhivnykh bumag o Petre Velikom.* 2 vols. Moskva, 1872.
Feoktistov, I. *Anekdoty i predaniia o Petre Velikom.* Sankt-Peterburg, 1896.
Galizin, Augustin, Prince. *La Russie au XVIIIe siècle.* Paris, 1863.
Golikov, I. I. *Anekdoty kasaiushchiesia do Gosudariia Imperatora Petra Velikogo.* Moskva, 1798.
Gordon, P. *Tagebuch 1661-1699.* 3 vols. Moskva, 1849-52.
Gusev, N. N. *Lev Nikolaevich Tolstoy.* 4 vols. Moskva, 1954-1970. III.
Helbig, Georg von. *Russische Günstlinge.* München, Berlin, 1917. (Orig. Tübingen, 1809.)
Kaganovich, A. L. *Mednyi vsadnik.* Leningrad, 1965.
Karabanov, P. "Freiliny Russkogo dvora v XVIII-m stoletii," in *Russkaia Starina.* 7 (1871).
Korb, J. G. *Diary of an Austrian Secretary of Legation at the Court of Czar Peter the Great.* 2 vols. in 1. London, 1968. (Published in Latin, 1700.)
Kornilovich, A. B. "O chastnoi zhizni Imperatora Petra I," in *Sochineniia i pis'ma.* Moskva, Leningrad, 1957.
Kurakin, B. I. Kniaz'. *Gistoriia o Tsare Petre Alekseeviche.* Gaga-Parizh, 1723-27. In *Arkhiv Kn. F. A. Kurakina.* 10 vols. Sankt-Peterburg, 1890-1902. I.
Lushev, A., ed. *Petr Pervyi Velikii i ego deiateli.* Sankt-Peterburg, 1872.
Maikov, L. N., ed. *Rasskazy Nartova o Petre Velikom.* Sankt-Peterburg, 1891.
Macaulay, (Lord). *The History of England.* 2 vols. London, 1873.
[Mauvillon, Eléazar.] *Histoire de Pierre surnommé le Grand.* Amsterdam, Leipzig, 1742.
Mueller, Gerhard. *Sammlung Russischer Geschichte.* 4 vols. Sankt-Peterburg, 1732.
Mordovtsev, D. L. *Russkiie zhenshchiny novogo vremeni.* Sankt-Peterburg, 1874.
Nartov, A. K. "Rasskazy i anekdoty pro Petra Velikogo," in *Russkii Arkhiv,* 22 (1884), pp. 354-70; 23 (1885), pp. 425-36.
Nashchokin, V. A. *Zapiski.* Sankt-Peterburg, 1842.
Nepluev, I. I. *Zapiski. Russkii Arkhiv,* 9 (1871).
Nestersuranoi, Iwan (Rousset, Jean). *Mémoires du Règne de Pierre le Grand.* 2nd ed. Amsterdam, 1730.
Perry, Cpt. John. *The State of Russia under the Present Czar.* London, 1716.
Pis'ma i bumagi Imperatora Petra Velikogo. 11 vols. Sankt-Peterburg, 1887-1964.
Platonov, S. F. *Petr Velikii, lichnost' i deiatel'nost'.* Leningrad, 1926.
Pogodin, M. P. *Petr Pervyi: Pervye gody edinoderzhaviia. Russkii Arkhiv,* 17 (1879).
___. *Rasskazy i anekdoty pro Petra Velikogo, Russkii Arkhiv,* 22 (1884) and 23 (1885).
Polevoi, N. A. *Istoriia Petra Velikogo.* 4 vols. Sankt-Peterburg, 1843.
Polnoe sobranie zakonov Rossiiskoi Imperii s 1649 goda. 46 vols. Sankt-Peterburg, 1830-1916.
Pushkin, A. S. *Materialy dlia Istorii Petra Velikogo,* in *Polnoe sobranie sochinenii.* 17 vols. in 21. Moskva, 1937-59. X.
Pososhkov, J. T. *Kniga o skudosti i bogatstve.* Moskva, 1937.
Radishchev, A. *Polnoe sobranie sochinenii,* 2 vols. Moskva, Leningrad, 1938.
Sharaia, N. M. *Voskovaia persona.* Leningrad, 1963.
Sakharov, I. P., ed. *Zapiski russkikh liudei.* Sankt-Peterburg, 1841. (Memoirs of I. A. Zhelabuzhskii, S. Medvedev, A. A. Matveev, P. Krekshin.)
Scheltema, J. *Anecdotes historiques sur Pierre le Grand.* Lausanne, 1842. (Orig. 1814.)
Semevskii, M. I. "Avdot'ia Fedorovna Lopukhina," *Russkii Vestnik,* 21 (1859).
___. *Slovo i delo!.* 3rd ed. Sankt-Peterburg, 1885.
___. *Tsaritsa Katerina Alekseevna, Anna i Villim Mons.* 2nd ed. Sankt-Peterburg, 1884.
Solov'ev, S. M. *Istoriia Rossii s drevneishikh vremen.* 15 vols. Moskva, 1960-65.
Stählin, Jacob de. *Anecdotes originales de Pierre le Grand.* Strasburg, 1787. (Published in German, 1785.)
Studenkin, G. I. *Romanovy, tsarstvuiushchii dom Rossiiskoi Imperii s 1613 g.* Sankt-Peterburg, 1878.
Shcherbachev, I. ed. "Zapiski datskogo poslannika Juliia Justa," *Russkii Arkhiv,* 30 (1892).

Tolstoy, L. N.   *Materialy k romanu vremen Petra I* in *Polnoe sobranie sochinenii.*
    90 vols. Moskva, 1928-58. XVII.
Ustrialov, N. G.   *Istoriia tsarstvovaniia Petra Velikogo.* 6 vols. (vol. 5 not
    published). Sankt-Peterburg, 1858-59.
Villebois, François de (Hallez, Theophile). *Mémoires Secrets.* Paris, 1853.
Voltaire. *Histoire de l'Empire de Russie sous Pierre le Grand.* Paris, 1853.
Waliszewski, K. *Petr Velikii.* Moskva, 1911. (Published in French, 1897.)
Ward, Mrs. (afterwards Lady Rondeau, afterwards Mrs. Vigor). *Letters from a lady
    who resided some years in Russia to her friend in England.* 2nd ed. London,
    1777.
Weber, F. *Das Veränderte Russland.* Frankfurt, 1721.

Index

DESIGNED BY IRA NEWMAN
MANUFACTURED BY CUSHING MALLOY, INC.
ANN ARBOR, MICHIGAN

Library of Congress Cataloging in Publication Data
Gasiorowska, Xenia.
The image of Peter the Great in Russian fiction
Bibliography: p.
Includes index.
1. Historical fiction, Russian--History and criticism.
2. Peter I, the Great, Emperor of Russia, 1672-1725, in
fiction, drama, poetry, etc. I. Title.
PG3098.H5G3   891.7'3'081   78-65021
ISBN 0-299-07690-3